# Making Policy in Europe

# Making Policy in Europe
## The Europeification of National Policy–making

Edited by
*Svein S. Andersen and*
*Kjell A. Eliassen*

Centre for European Studies
Norwegian School of Management

SAGE Publications
London · Thousand Oaks · New Delhi

Editorial material and selection © Svein S. Andersen and
Kjell A. Eliassen 1993

Chapters 1, 2, 3, 14 © Svein S. Andersen and Kjell A.
Eliassen 1993
Chapter 4 © Johan From and Per Stava 1993
Chapter 5 © Frank Dobbin 1993
Chapter 6 © Godefroy Dang-Nguyen, Volker Schneider
and Raymund Werle 1993
Chapter 7 © David Vogel 1993
Chapter 8 © Svein S. Andersen 1993
Chapter 9 © Erik Beukel 1993
Chapter 10 © Yasemin N. Soysal 1993
Chapter 11 © Ellen Ahnfelt and Johan From 1993
Chapter 12 © Finn Laursen 1993
Chapter 13 © Jaroslav Jaks 1993

First published 1993
Reprinted 1994

SAGE Publications Ltd
6 Bonhill Street
London EC2A 4PU

SAGE Publications Inc
2455 Teller Road
Thousand Oaks, California 91320

SAGE Publications India Pvt Ltd
32, M-Block Market
Greater Kailash – I
New Delhi 110 048

ISBN 0-8039-8969 5
ISBN 0-8039-8970 9 pbk

Printed in Great Britain by The Cromwell Press,Melksham,Wilts.

# Editors' Note

This book has been carried out as part of a research project financed under the programme for Research on Organization and Management (LOS), directed by the Norwegian Research Council for Applied Social Sciences. We are grateful for the support and we hope that the book will contribute to the understanding of EC development, focusing specifically on the relationships between EC and national policy–making.

Most studies of policy–making have retained a national bias and this is even true in the case of comparative studies. The national system has been taken as the unit of analysis. The EC has mainly been regarded as external to the national system, almost as a disturbance. Europeification of policy–making implies a need for a new way of delineating the policy context, where the European political system becomes the unit of analysis.

The Europeification of the EC system of policy–making has often been studied from the perspective of international politics, as the extension of foreign policy, or as a formal legal politico–administrative system.

Our approach differs from the foreign policy and formal legal perspectives in emphasizing the totality of the EC institutions and the national political system.

The strengthening of transnational decision–making has not eliminated cross–national competition and conflict. However, the increased importance of the central EC institutions has mobilized a wide variety of interests which are seeking to influence the decision–making process through direct contacts. This, in turn, has further strengthened the role of central EC institutions in relation to member countries, and stimulated the growth of complex game playing centred around the policy–making process.

We would like to thank a number of individuals who helped in the initial editing, layout and translation of the book. These people include Jan E. Lane and Esben Oust Heiberg, Audun Iversen, Gillian Kennedy, Bård Kuvaas, Tom Edwin Manshaus, Tore G. Rokstad, all employed at Centre for European Studies, The Norwegian School of Management, Oslo.

Oslo June 1993

Svein S. Andersen                                          Kjell A. Eliassen

# CONTENTS

# Part I
# EC Policy–Making

# 1
# THE EC AS A NEW POLITICAL SYSTEM

*Svein S. Andersen and*
*Kjell A. Eliassen*

## TOWARDS THE EUROPEAN UNION

Europe is going through rapid and radical changes. In the West, these are most significantly symbolized by the discussions centred around the Maastricht Treaty. The breakdown in Eastern Europe is putting an end to an era that commenced with World War I. Some claim that this upheaval may also be seen as the beginning of the 21st century in European politics. The former empire in the East is disintegrating, while a supranational state is under construction in the West. This process has, however, been met with a certain degree of scepticism which reflects a widespread concern with national sovereignty and democracy.

The latter is both a result of an ongoing process of European integration, designed to maintain peace and stability, and a strategy aimed at meeting the economic challenge from the USA and Japan. Increasingly, integration transcends traditional forms of international cooperation. This is leading to the Europeification of national policy–making, i.e. real integration of policy–making cutting across national boundaries. The result is a substantially more complex context of interest representation, decision–making and implementation.

The process of integration in Western Europe was also originally intended as an attempt to meet the threat from the Soviet Union; a threat which has now disappeared. The breakdown in the East eradicated the external pressure applied of the Cold War and, in this sense, Western Europe has no obvious enemy any more. Nevertheless, the war in Yugoslavia and the potential breakdown of Russia pose new and very difficult challenges for the Western alliance. On the other hand, the end of the Cold War makes it possible for former neutral states to participate in a wider European defence and security cooperation.

All of these changes emphasized the fact that, by the early 1990s, Europe had reached a historical juncture, and it was time to lay down a new structure. The symbolic impact of the reunion of Germany played a vital role. This created new political opportunities that, together with the completion of the Internal Market and the European Economic Area (EEA) process, reinforced the pan–European process of integration.

The federalist vision of European cooperation was aimed at creating a United States of Europe, inspired by the modern North American federation. One important stepping stone in this process was to be the creation of a real common market. The EC treaty of 1957 intended to create such a common market but, by the mid–1980s, considerable non–tariff trade barriers still existed. The Internal Market process was another attempt to realize the ideas of the Treaty of Rome. The successes of the Single European Act stimulated political ambitions pointing towards a higher degree of integration in Europe. The Maastricht Treaty is the first step in that direction.

The concept of a European Union was conceived at a time of economic growth and prosperity in Europe. The EC had successfully launched the Internal Market, the Berlin Wall was still in place and there existed a desire to deepen the cooperation between the EC member states. However, the European Union was destined to be implemented in a totally different situation where the prevalent factors are recession, newly democratic states being established in Central and Eastern Europe and political problems in all the member states.

The formation of the European Union causes a terminological problem for a book like this. The European Community (EC) is an established name, but in the future it will probably be replaced by EU. The main part of the discussion in this book is concerned with topics related to the EC, but sometimes it is necessary to use EU. This is especially the case when we discuss the Maastricht Treaty and its implementation. Generally we have chosen to use EC because of its familiarity, even if we discuss EC after 1993.

The Maastricht Treaty was mainly a product of optimism among politicians and industry leaders. Nevertheless, the concept of a union was, at first, well received by a large majority of the voters. After the Treaty was signed by the Heads of States and Governments in December 1991, political leaders, to their surprise, experienced considerable scepticism among the public. The total lack of parliamentary debate at the national level prior to the negotiations on the plans for European union, caused a great deal of uncertainty in the member countries. The problems were manifested in the narrow Danish rejection of the Maastricht Treaty in the June 1992 referendum.

The slim French majority in favour of the Treaty only served to demonstrate the seriousness of the problem. However, at the summit held in Edinburgh in December 1992, EC leaders proposed a Danish solution to be confirmed in a new Danish referendum. This compromise seems to address more symbolic than substantive aspects, but it has the support of all the Danish political parties and, according to opinion polls, it also has the support of the Danish electorate. UK now seems to be the country where the success of ratification is in the most doubt.

The implementation of the European Union involves two types of changes. Traditional EC cooperation will become wider and deeper. The widening means that the EC will get involved in several new areas of policy–making, and the deepening means increased power in existing areas as well as a strengthening of the competence of the EC institutions in relation to national governments. These changes will also affect the distribution of power and tasks among the central EC institutions. One of the most important elements of supranational authority in the Treaty is the increased importance of majority voting in the Council of Ministers. At the same time, the competence and role of the European Parliament are to be strengthened in the decision–making process, including the introduction of a right of veto in several areas (Bradshaw 1991, Kuvaas 1992).

The European Union includes three new areas:

1. Economic and Monetary Union (EMU)
2. the Common Foreign and Security Policy (CFSP)
3. cooperation in the spheres of justice and home affairs.

The problems in Denmark were mainly related to the EMU, the plans for a common defence policy and a common citizenship. In the United Kingdom, there seems to exist a more general scepticism towards a stronger supranational authority in the EC. The most controversial issue is the EMU. Furthermore, the Treaty incorporates a protocol on "the Social Community", which regulates the cooperation between eleven of the member countries, not including the United Kingdom. Both on the EMU issue and on that of the Social Community, the British opted out during the Maastricht negotiations.

The Economic and Monetary Union is an expansion of the EC Treaty and it establishes a strong element of supranationality and a new EC institution, a common Central European Bank. These factors will reduce the role and influence of both the EC Commission and the member states in these matters.

The two other policy areas are based on more traditional intergovernmental cooperation, with the Council as the most powerful actor. However, the Commission has the right to initiate proposals concerning foreign and security policy matters which is not, at least formally, the case today.

The Social protocol was initially meant as a deepening of the traditional EC cooperation but, due to resistance from the United Kingdom, the Community had to make special arrangements. The protocol incorporating the Social Charter is an intergovernmental agreement, but it will be operational within the Community bodies.

The uncertainty regarding the implementation of the Treaty has three major aspects:

1. Will all countries commit themselves to the Treaty?
2. To what extent and how fast will the Treaty be implemented?
3. What will be the next step on the road towards a United Europe?

The first question will most likely be settled during the summer of 1993. The result will probably be that all the member countries of the EC accept the Treaty.

When it comes to the implementation of the Treaty, one must distinguish between minor changes and significant alterations. Minor changes affecting the balance of power between established EC institutions in existing policy areas will probably be successfully implemented. The introduction of a single currency and a common central bank represents a greater challenge, and these elements might not come to fruition before the end of the decade.

The problem with the EMU is not only the scepticism voiced by some of the member countries. Several of these countries do not, in fact, fulfil the economic demands for membership in the new union. Germany is in a special position because she already plays the main role in European economic and monetary policy and because the risk of unexpected economic costs will increase in the EMU. The lesson to be learned from German unification is that when historical experience is lacking, unexpected problems are likely to arise. The problems in Germany became larger and more costly than anticipated. This has increased German scepticism as to when and how different member countries could be incorporated into the EMU. The continuous problems associated with the Exchange Rate Mechanism (ERM), illustrate how problematic the introduction of a single currency could be.

## FUTURE OPTIONS

What about further development? This will depend on the outcome of the three questions above, but there are only three possible solutions. The three models for development in the 1990s are:

1. A federal Europe, a kind of United States of Europe
2. A Europe of States, where the member countries continue to play the main role
3. A Europe with variable geometry, or a multi–speed solution.

The first model has been well described, even if some of its aspects are still under debate. However, this model would seem to be too utopian to be realized in the near future. National interests are too strong and the cultural differences run too deep. Last, but not least, the economic differences seem to be too great.

The second model would, in practical terms, mean a collapse of the process which is heading towards European union. This seems unrealistic, because the forces of integration are strong. This becomes especially clear where the need for European competitiveness in a global perspective is concerned, and when we look at the challenges related to the economic and democratic development of Eastern Europe. In addition, several countries would hesitate to accept Germany as an uncommitted actor in Europe.

Much of the social science literature and the political debate emphasize the extreme positions of the two first models (Pedersen 1992). We think that the third model is the most realistic. A Europe with variable geometry means that there are several levels of integration, within the existing EC, the EU and the EEA (European Economic Area) as three different organizational expressions.

The third model is the most practical one from a political perspective, even if it cannot be characterized as a coherent alternative from a theoretical and intellectual point of view. It is more representative of a combination of different principles and vague schemes. The idea of a Europe with two or more speeds has been rejected by a majority of EC leaders. However, it seems that there are likely to be some variations as to how fast and to what degree the Treaty will be implemented in member countries. In many ways, this comes close to the EMU solution in the Maastricht Treaty. From a political point of view, the third model would be favourable because it allows for a balance of interests on the Euro-political arena.

A two – or multi–speed Europe stresses the demand for an overall objective and a vision. In several fields, the Maastricht model is likely to be used. Member countries must agree on the overall objectives to be achieved but, at the same time, opportunities will exist for each country to develop according to its own conditions.

Such a development will cause problems for the decision–making structure of the EU. Is it reasonable that fully integrated countries will have greater influence than less integrated countries? What about the common vision? Do all countries have the same understanding of the expressed objectives?

This kind of confusion characterizes attitudes towards the EU. This is due to different opinions in each country and different national models concerning the role of the state and European integration.

The UK represents an extreme example where integration is interpreted as market liberalization, and where a strong scepticism exists towards the central state structure developing in Brussels. France is more positive to the development of strong common bodies, but less in favor of a general liberalization of the markets. Germany is one of the countries which want to go far in both directions.

So far, we have discussed the relationship between the EU and the national states. The problems we have pointed out will be on the agenda at the intergovernmental conference in 1996/97. In addition, the EU has a more pressing problem. As a result of the Danish "no", they have to secure enough support and votes for the Treaty in the member states.

One possible solution to this problem is the idea of subsidiarity. This concept stresses the fact that the EU will be a union of EC citizens, with closer ties between Brussels and the individual citizen. This represents a reintroduction of an old principle in the EC, which never carried much weight. Its reintroduction is a result of pressure from the United Kingdom. The new emphasis on subsidiarity is supposed to gather support for the Maastricht Treaty. The idea is that no political issue shall be decided at a higher level than is absolutely necessary. If an issue can be dealt with at the local level, it should be left to the local authorities, and the same goes for the national level. The EU will only act when there is a strong demand for a supranational European solution.

The problem is that, by itself, the principle of subsidiarity is not enough to satisfy those who are sceptical towards the centralized decision–making carried out in Brussels. The Norwegian slogan "It is further to Brussels than to Oslo" may only be rejected if strong parliamentary democracy is introduced at the EC level. On the other hand, this implies a federal structure but, paradoxically, the countries which are most concerned with the democratic deficit are not interested in a federal solution. As a result, the problematic relationship of the EC with the citizens of the member countries is, from a democratic point of view, almost impossible to solve.

Another possible strategy is to introduce a new regional level and create a regional parliament. This is a part of the Maastricht Treaty which has gained renewed attention after the Danish referendum. The idea behind it was that a greater degree of power could be given to the EU only if more power was shifted from the member states to the regions. The regions are closer to the citizens, and they would be able to wield some influence at the EU level.

The model for this was based on solutions from Germany. The German "Länder" have used Maastricht to advocate their objectives of increased influence at the EC level. The result is that the Länder have developed a new "controlling level" for the whole EU. During the negotiations on the ratification of the Maastricht Treaty, they gained the right to participate in the German work in the Council.

It is not clear what the idea of a "Europe of the regions" will mean in countries without a federal structure, or how a strengthening of this level can better secure the rights and influence of the citizens of the EU. The increased interest in the regionalization of the EC system seems to be a further attempt to create legitimacy for the Maastricht Treaty. This is especially true in Denmark and the United Kingdom. In these countries, local influence is preferred from a traditional point of view, as is demonstrated in the strong belief in "local self–government".

In the debate on the new Europe, some continue to argue for two extremes: on the one hand, federation, and, on the other hand, stagnation or breakdown. We are going to argue for a future which is similar to the history we already know. This is characterized by numerous political compromises which create a Europe where each country cooperates through different levels of integration. In the same way as the EC, the EU will not be a monolithic institution, but a political animal which is constantly changing. In other words, there will be an increasing Europeification of policy–making, but without a federal decision–making structure. Rather than a unified institutional structure, we will have a complex, multi–level, multi–channel policy–making context. We will now develop this notion further.

## APPROACHES TO EUROPEIFICATION

The Europeification of the EC system of policy–making has often been studied from the perspective of international politics, as the extension of foreign policy, or as a formal legal politico–administrative system.

The first viewpoint characterizes the EC as an arena of international cooperation, sometimes in the context of an "integrationist" perspective. Neofunctionalist perspectives are applied (e.g. Nye 1968, Nye and Keohane 1975) to explain the unification of European states (e.g. Lindberg and Sheingold 1971).

Recent years have witnessed an increased interest in neofunctional theories (Keohane and Hoffmann 1990, Laursen 1990, Haar 1991, Moravcsik 1991, Pedersen 1992). This revitalization mainly stems from a hope of using this theory as a relevant explanation for the new momentum experienced in the late 1980s (Tranholm–Mikelsen 1991).

The other viewpoint emphasizes the notion of the EC as a legal entity, focusing on the formal mandates of various institutions and the interpretation and application of law. Institutional and jurisdictional matters have loomed more prominently than substantive law in the legal literature on the European Communities (e.g. Mathijsen 1990). However, there is also a considerable amount of literature relating to substantive EC law (Wyatt and Dashwood 1987).

The predominance of the legal tradition in the study of EC institutions and decision–making has created a bias towards formal aspects. This perspective projects an image of the EC as an orderly system with a common body of law at its core.

Our approach to Europeification differs from the foreign policy and formal legal perspectives in emphasizing the totality of the EC institutions and the national political systems. Up until recently, there has been a tendency to look at national political systems as relatively closed (Olsen 1978:186–187). The transnational dimension has only partly been incorporated into studies involving actors operating across national boundaries. Studies of policy–making have continued to focus on national systems as the unit of analysis, even if national systems are frequently compared.

However, even in a confederal model, the EC is a new form of transnational system, and the link to the EC from each member state is comprised of much more than the mere extension of foreign policy. This creates new challenges and new solutions, in a situation where the logic of economic and social integration continuously demonstrates the need for an increasingly tighter political unity in the EC system. There is a need for an open system approach which also takes into account the complexity embedded in national histories (Andersen and Eliassen 1991, Olsen 1992, van Schendelen 1993).

Formal institutions and legislation provide a framework for policy–making, but there is considerable room for different outcomes. All formal systems have some degree of freedom in this sense. However, the loose structure, combined with complexity and heterogeneity, provides more room for the process in determining outcomes than in national political systems. On the other hand, actors bring with them national styles, strategies and tactics. Consequently, we will emphasize actor strategies, coalitions and dependencies; in short, the complexity of policy–making and lobbying.

We will distinguish between three aspects of complexity.

One aspect of complexity concerns the linking of national traditions through a system of transnational policy–making. This widens the scope of the national policy–making process, as well as the number and types of actors to be taken into consideration. A key dimension is the relation between the national and transnational levels of authority. National traditions may vary a lot in terms of the order and predictability of the policy–making process, but at least they represent familiar settings for the actors.

The second aspect concerns the fact that the EC is not only transnational, but also represents new and changing forms of transnational authority. It experiments with new kinds of political authority and new ways of regulating the economy and society. Harmonization and the principle of subsidiarity, for example, open up a number of possibilities which, to a large extent, have to be clarified through international market and political processes respectively.

The third aspect of complexity stems from the broadening of the EC. For a long time, EC policy was restricted to a few specific areas of economic and social life. The Single European Act and, in particular, the

Maastricht Treaty, broaden the scope and variety of policy issues which will be influenced by the EC. In the future, almost all policy areas will have an EC dimension. This implies wider national differences and more intense conflicts to be dealt with at the EC level.

These developments towards increased complexity of the European policy context require a Europeification of the policy–making process, which extends deep into the national systems. The Europeification of EC policy–making has three aspects: the policy context; the policy–making processes; and the policy outcomes.

Most studies of policy–making have retained a national bias and this is true even in the case of comparative studies. The national system has been taken as the unit of analysis. The EC has mainly been regarded as external to the national system, almost as a disturbance. Europeification of policy–making implies a need for a new way of delineating the policy context, where the European political system becomes the unit of analysis. The scope of national policy–making has to be widened, to include the central EC institutions, the European network of national political institutions and the actors operating at both levels.

Such a definition of a European political system raises the question of how it relates to the wider international context. It is important to see that there are global regimes, principles and institutions, which serve to legitimize and support the general development of the EC. Some of them relate directly to the core areas in the EC, such as the principles of the free market and trade which are supported by international institutions like the General Agreement on Tariffs and Trade (GATT). Other regimes support environmental protection or human rights. They produce both a general ideology and specific institutional decisions which influence European and national policy–making.

A widening of the policy–making context also has implications for the analysis of policy–making processes and their outcomes. A key dimension is the interaction between the national and the EC level. This may be conceptualized as three stages, which are not necessarily separated in time (see Figure 1).

Two aspects of this figure are important. Firstly, it looks like a model describing different phases in a policy–making process where a time dimension is implicit. To us, however, the figure serves more as an illustration of the focus on important actors, processes and policy outcomes.

Furthermore, the model illustrates the fact that, in the book, we do not emphasize a fully fledged "Europeification" of the system. At its most

**Figure 1.** *Europeification of national policy–making in a global context*

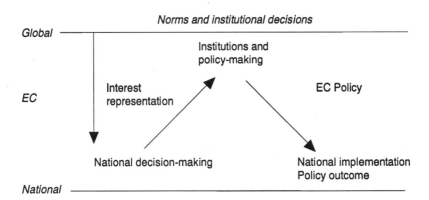

extreme, this would imply a European decision–making system without any national segmentation. As demonstrated in the following chapters, this is not possible in reality.

The concept of Europeification differs, in several ways, from the traditional concept of "integration" employed in EC studies. For instance, we do not assume that a higher degree of Europeification leads to more efficient policy–making. Secondly, the theoretical background for the concept is based more in organizational theory than in neofunctionalism and, as a result, it focuses more on actors and processes than on system properties. Finally, the concept implies a comparative approach across member countries and between states and the European Community.

The concept of Europeification also implies that areas like foreign policy and relations between the EC and Eastern Europe should be addressed from an angle different from than that which we usually find: namely, as a process of integration, incorporating a move from planned to market economies and long–term, sustainable growth.

From our perspective, the key question to be asked is how policy–making is affected; or more specifically, questions of national interests, resources, legitimacy, influence at the EC level and organizational alternatives in the restructuring of the European architecture. This is related to issues like the widening and deepening of the EC. In the case of Eastern Europe, the association agreements may also be viewed as part of the Europeification of the policy context in the associated countries.

The Europeification of EC policy–making leads to increased complexity. A system's complexity is generally thought to be a function of the number of elements, their heterogenity, the number and variations of linkages and the degree to which the system is in transformation. In this sense, the trend towards Europeification is also producing more complexity. The central and national level institutions, interest associations, corporations, regions etc. are being brought together. However, the pattern is not fixed. On the contrary, effective participation in the policy–making process stimulates actors to operate wearing different hats, in different political channels and in changing coalitions (see Figure 2). At the same time, the EC system is undergoing continuous changes regarding the role of the central institutions, the forms of transnational authority and the areas affected by EC policies.

## AREAS OF POLICY–MAKING

When looking at specific policy–making areas, it is important to keep the following questions in mind:

1. What are the factors stimulating or blocking Europeification? What are the implications for complexity?
2. To what degree are policies institutionalized at the EC level and at the national level? In some areas, like energy, there is a high degree of institutionalization at the national level, but policies are weak at the EC level. Immmigration policy is also weak at the EC level.
3. What characterizes the distribution of interests? To what extent can we identify segmented and polarized conflicts between member countries, or member countries and central EC institutions? To what extent are interests overlapping or complementary? What kinds of alliances are possible, and through which channels?
4. At what decision–making level do we find the driving forces? Is it a down–up process driven by initiatives and alliances at the national level or is it a top–down process reflecting central EC initiatives, perhaps supported by fundamental changes at the global level, as we have seen in the case of environmental policies? To what extent is policy development driven by the need to relate to other politic areas?

The result is lobbyfication at the central EC level, while, at the same time, a higher degree of coordination is necessary at the national level,

**Figure 2.** *Complex policy–making*

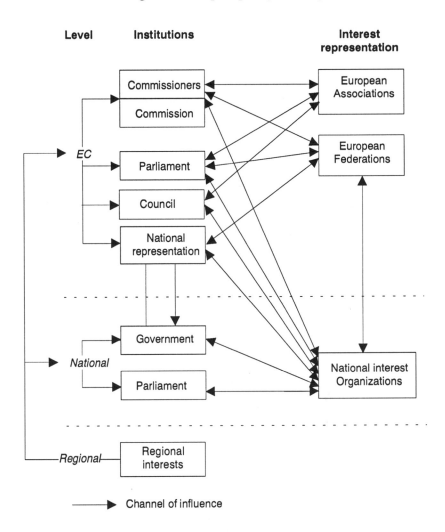

if the national systems are to survive as key actors. The alternative is that various interests in the member countries are articulated independently of, and even in conflict with, that of national authorities. It follows that the nature of the EC policy–making processes may vary considerably, from a relatively high degree of order and rationality, due to control by the member states, to processes that may be somewhat disorderly.

Actors are most likely to pursue rational stategies in areas where there are only a few others with similar attitudes. This normally means that the subject matter limits which decisions can be made, from detailed questions of distribution, to general technical rules. When the number of actors is high and the issue allows for complicated politics, the result may be a lack of oversight and coordination. The latter may be described as organized anarchy – or the garbage–can process (Cohen et al. 1972).

A real implementation of Directives involves not only the incorporation of EC law through national politico–administrative systems and a top–down process. Numerous studies of implementation show that successful implementation also depends, to a large extent, on how the upstream process of legislation has been handled (Siedentopf and Ziller 1988, Philip 1987). As a result, we will emphasize the interplay between legislation and implementation, in order to try and understand why the speed and quality of implementation differs among the member states. Through the treaty of the European Economic Area, some countries are in a special position, being, at the same time, both outsiders and partly insiders. Formally, they are only fully part of the downstream process. With relation to upstream legislation, they are only allowed to air their views at the preparatory stage.

In the next section, we will briefly present the structure of the book, focusing on Europeification and the complexity of EC decision–making in different policy areas.

## THE CONTENTS OF THE BOOK

So far, we have discussed development towards the European Union, and presented some conceptual tools for the analysis of policy–making. Part I of the book develops the conceptual framework for policy analysis in more detail. The focus is on the role and structure of central EC institutions and the rivalry which exists between them and between member countries as part of the tendencies towards Europeification and lobbyfication of EC policy–making.

The development of the EC over the last twenty years has been characterized by continuous rivalry between the key institutions, resulting in a substantial shift of balance in two directions. First, there has been an increase in the importance of transnational authority through majority decisions in the Council of Ministers. Second, there has been a growth in the importance of the only institution which is based on direct popular legitimacy, namely the European Parliament.

The strengthening of transnational decision–making has not eliminated cross–national competition and conflict. However, the increased importance of the central EC institutions has mobilized a wide variety of interests which are seeking to influence the decision–making process through direct contacts. This, in turn, has further strengthened the role of central EC institutions in relation to member countries, and stimulated the growth of complex game–playing centred around the policy–making process.

In Part II, we show how EC policy–making and implementation actually work in selected policy areas. There are considerable differences with respect to the interests and loyalties of member states. Moreover, the nature of the policy area plays an important role in shaping the nature of EC policy–making.

The different studies show how policy development depends upon the ongoing changes in the EC. For example, political integration in the EC has implications for infrastructure which cuts across national boundaries, involving, for instance, railroads, telecommunications and gas transmission lines. Institutional development has also had consequences for harmonization and integration within central policy areas such as labour market policy, immigration, police, etc.

Central questions concerning the relationship between EC institutions and national systems include: When do attempts to structure policy sectors from above actually succeed, creating one dominant institutional form? Under what conditions do certain institutional forms spread through imitation of success – when do national traditions prevail?

In Part III, we explore some of the possibilities for the future of EC and European integration, including the relationship with Central and Eastern Europe. The European Union is not finalized; there is a continuing struggle over the future shape which it should take. The number of countries which should be included, and which ones, are of the greatest strategic importance in this respect. Central and Eastern European countries are more eager to join than European Free Trade Association (EFTA) countries, but the European Union gives preference to the latter group. A central question is how the new European architecture alters the environment for EC development.

The democratic deficit in the EC has, up until recently, received limited attention in the member countries, but it has been of increasing importance for the political agenda of the EC, especially after the signing of the Maastricht Treaty. The main problem is often perceived as a conflict between the federalists who wish an integrated Europe with strong supranational authorities and the confederalists who wish to create a Europe where the national governments have a strong influence. Even if there are minor differences in this picture, it reflects the main dimensions of the political debate.

# 2
# POLICY–MAKING AND INSTITUTIONS IN THE EC

*Svein S. Andersen and*
*Kjell A. Eliassen*

## NATIONAL INFLUENCE AND INSTITUTIONAL COMPETITION

Many studies which focus on the relationship between the EC and member states, begin their analysis from the basis of market systems. They emphasize the idea that the EC is a framework and a set of arenas for the expression of national rivalries. In contrast to this, our point of departure is the central EC institutions and decision–making process.

The main focus is on decision–making. However, in order to understand how decisions are made, it is necessary to grasp some of the key characteristics of EC institutions: their organization, their competence and their interrelations.

The decision–making process in the EC is distinguished by the extraordinary information–gathering which takes place before a proposal even reaches the Council. In addition, the degree of openness which is exhibited is striking, especially when seen in contrast with Southern European and British traditions, although it is not unlike political decision–making processes in the Nordic countries. Impressed by the openness, two British observers noted:

> But there are crucial differences between community and national legislation. Most governments of the world prepare their laws in secrecy and present them as faits accomplis. Until a national chancellor of the exchequer unveils his budget, it is a state secret. The community budget on the other hand, is publicly and endlessly discussed, savaged, restored and usually savaged again before being adopted. So it is with all community decision–making. It involves long and detailed opinion–

gathering, the publication of an ever–changing string of "green papers" for discussion, and above all opportunities for lobbying and for influencing the outcome unknown in national terms. (Budd and Jones 1989:51)

Our analysis of both the formal and informal patterns of interest articulation processes and the national patterns of EC law implementation is based upon an investigation of the formal decision–making process: how it is organized and where and to what extent different EC–level and national interests are allowed to participate. We will focus on the institutions, the actors involved, important sources of variations in the procedures and the relative importance of the actors. This chapter will not give a detailed picture of the institutions and various areas of EC policy as covered in standard text books, e.g. Nugent (1991), but it will instead try to show the role and relative importance of EC institutions and other actors in this process.

This book compares EC policy–making and the pattern of influence, on the one hand, and the organization of national decision–making processes in member countries, on the other hand (George 1991, Greenwood et al.1992, Kirchner 1992). What are the main differences between EC policy–making and national decision–making processes? We compare the roles of individual EC institutions with those of national political institutions and the influence which they have at the EC and national levels respectively.

## THE COMMUNITY INSTITUTIONS

There are several striking facts about the relationship between the EC institutions. After Maastricht, the Commission remains the main European institution in terms of administrative and political capacity. In national terms, the Commission is not only a kind of government and administration but is also, to some extent, a parliamentary committee. The Commission:

- proposes Community policy and legislation and often writes the compromise propositions to the Council of Ministers dealing with the proposals
- supervises the implementation of the decisions taken by the Council of Ministers and supervises the day–to–day running of Community policies
- has its own powers in some areas, notably in those of competition policy and the control of government subsidies.

In looking at the Commission, it is important to distinguish between the 17 Commissioners, their cabinets and the services offered by the 23 Directorates General. As will be seen later, there are differences in the lobbying pattern, according to which "level" in the Commission the interest articulation is directed towards. The more detailed involvement of the different "levels" of the Commission in the decision–making process is discussed in relation to the overall decision–making process.

The main bulk of the Commission's personnel is often referred to as "the services", in order to distinguish them from the Commissioners and their cabinets. This arrangement is modelled on the French Ministers and the role of their cabinets in relation to their Ministers. The services are responsible for the technical preparation of legislation and its implementation. They are mainly staffed by career officials from the twelve member countries. They are the main target for lobbying in Brussels.

The cabinets of the Commissioners are chaired by a "chef de cabinet". The cabinet is her or his personal staff, often recruited on national and/or political grounds and made up of six or more permanent administrators plus secretarial staff. The cabinets have an important part to play in the decision–making process. They are not only involved in the sectors for which "their" Commissioner is responsible but, like the Commissioner, they are involved in all areas of EC policy–making.

The Commission and the Commissioners play a key role, both in their roles as administrators and as government officials. The Commission is involved in EC decision–making at all levels and in relation to nearly all types of issues. However, the Commission has only an indirect and vague representativity through the European Parliament. The Parliament aspires to some kind of general European legitimacy and the Council of Ministers has a national representative base, which is mainly derived from the responsibility of EC governments to national parliaments. It follows that the formal decision–making institutions in the Community do not have the same status vis–a–vis societal interests as national parliaments and governments do.

The very nature of central EC institutions implies that they have different mandates and roles from those of institutions in the national systems (Figure 3). This particular type of system has a greater need, not only for the expertise of interest organizations, but also for contact with and acceptance by affected interests, in order to safeguard its legitimacy in relation to society.

The procedures for decision–making in the Community are based on the Treaty of Rome, taking into account the changes introduced in the Single European Act and the Maastricht Treaty.

There are two major aspects to be noted here. The first concerns the role of EC institutions at different stages. Up until 1987, EC decision–making could mainly be described as a Commission–Council relationship with the European Parliament increasingly trying to become involved, and with the Economic and Social Committee standing on the sideline. The Maastricht reform introduced a new cooperation procedure which goes as far as giving the Parliament a right to veto in certain cases.

The second aspect concerns the quorum: what kind of majority is required when final decisions are made in the Council. Again, the 1987 Single Act introduced a major shift. Before this point, the bulk of decisions required unanimity. However, the Single Act introduced simple majority voting in important areas such as internal market legislation. The Maastricht reform extends this procedure to new areas.

The Maastricht Treaty also increased Commission competence within new areas of EC policy and strengthened the role of the Commission President and European Parliament in the appointment of new Commissioners (Laursen and Vanhoonacher 1992).

From 1995, the Commission's term of office will be extended to five years and will correspond with the election period of the European Parliament. The Commission's exclusive right of initiative is now somewhat restricted by the Treaty Art. 137A which gives the European Parliament the right to ask the Commission to propose new legislation.

The increased competence of the Commission lies within such areas as: education, culture, telecommunications, transport, small and medium sized companies and the environment. Most decisions in these policy areas can be made on the basis of majority voting and this increases the possibility of the Council accepting Commission proposals. In general, the overall balance between the EC institutions is maintained in the first pillar of the new European Union (see Figure 3).

Within the two other pillars shown in Figure 3, there exists more of an intergovernmental type of cooperation, but the Commission will gradually play a more important role in foreign and security policy and eventually, in the areas of justice and home affairs. One could argue, however, that the increased competence in the area of security policy represents only a formal codification of the influence which the Commission has exercised through the EPS cooperation (Petersen and Nedergaard 1992:65).

**Figure 3.** *The European Union*

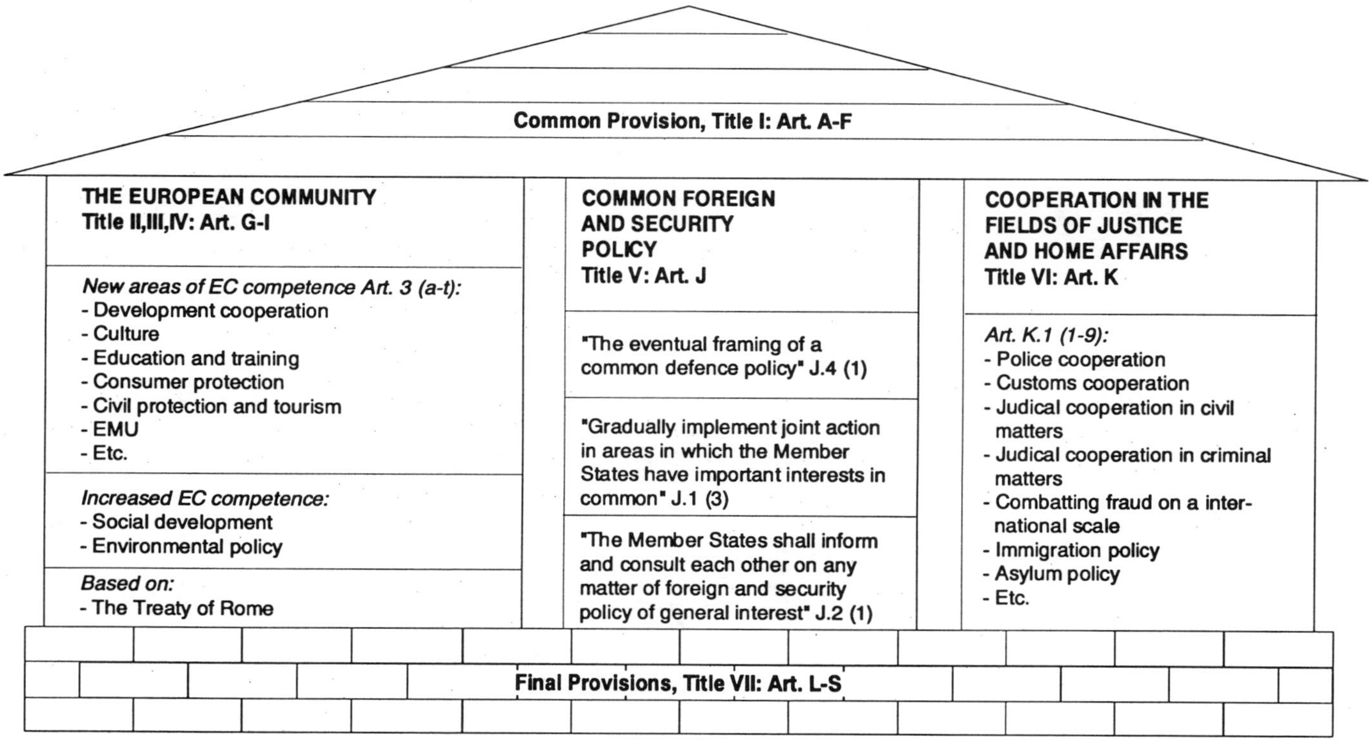

Common Provision, Title I: Art. A-F

**THE EUROPEAN COMMUNITY**
**Title II,III,IV: Art. G-I**

*New areas of EC competence Art. 3 (a-t):*
- Development cooperation
- Culture
- Education and training
- Consumer protection
- Civil protection and tourism
- EMU
- Etc.

*Increased EC competence:*
- Social development
- Environmental policy

*Based on:*
- The Treaty of Rome

**COMMON FOREIGN AND SECURITY POLICY**
**Title V: Art. J**

"The eventual framing of a common defence policy" J.4 (1)

"Gradually implement joint action in areas in which the Member States have important interests in common" J.1 (3)

"The Member States shall inform and consult each other on any matter of foreign and security policy of general interest" J.2 (1)

**COOPERATION IN THE FIELDS OF JUSTICE AND HOME AFFAIRS**
**Title VI: Art. K**

*Art. K.1 (1-9):*
- Police cooperation
- Customs cooperation
- Judical cooperation in civil matters
- Judical cooperation in criminal matters
- Combatting fraud on a inter-national scale
- Immigration policy
- Asylum policy
- Etc.

**Final Provisions, Title VII: Art. L-S**

*Source: Kuvaas:1992:42*

The Council is a major Community decision–making body, particularly when it comes to important policy decisions and legislation. More and more decisions are made on the basis of majority voting and the Maastricht Treaty has increased the importance of this type of decision–making. The Treaty also strengthens the role of the Council in the areas of security, defence, justice and home affairs. To some extent, this could be seen as an attempt to introduce more supranational power (new areas for EC decisions and majority voting), but without increasing the degree of federalism (strengthening the role of the Parliament and the Commission).

After all, the Council has a small staff (2000 people) at the European level. It only meets twice a month (approximately), with different Ministers constituting the make–up of the Council; for example, at one meeting the Finance Minister will be present and, at the next, the Ministers of Culture (Kirchner 1992). The increased work load and their role in security policy will necessitate a more permanent staff and more regular meetings, if not a brand new structure for the Council (Bradshaw 1991).

The Council plays a role in EC decision–making and legislation which can partly be seen as that of a European government and partly as that of a parliament. It wields the final decision–making power over laws and budget issues, at the same time as it is perhaps the most "representative" institution in the EC. The Council is composed of the relevant ministers from the member states, but most of the work is done in Council working groups (COREPER) or in specialist groups. Lobbying of the Council is mainly undertaken through the national interest articulation system in the member countries. Contrary to most other international organizations, the outputs of the EC decision–making processes are binding upon its members and they take precedence over national legislation where the two are in conflict. At the same time, the legitimacy of the decisions rests more on the national governments represented in the Council than on the power of the European Parliament.

The 1987 Act tried to introduce a better "balance" in the policy–making process in the Community by, in two ways, increasing the role of the "European" part of the EC, namely the Parliament, at the expense of both the "administration", the Commission, and the representatives of the twelve "national" political institutions, the Council. The Maastricht Treaty further strengthened the Parliament. The "cooperation" or hearing procedure of the 1987 Act involving the European Parliament was retained and, in addition, a new co–decision procedure was established.

The European Parliament is a directly elected body of 567 members, having been enlarged after the increase in the German representation. The MPs are elected for a period of five years. The Secretariat of the Parliament is located in Luxembourg, although the Parliament's plenary meetings are held in Strasbourg and its committee meetings in Brussels.

There is, however, a fundamental difference in the general democratic representativity of the European Parliament, when compared with any other national parliament in Europe. The main source of democratic legitimacy for EC decisions still lies in the Council's representation of national governments based on national parliaments (Jacobs et al. 1992).

The EC decision–making procedure was changed in 1987, making it possible for the Council to take a majority decision on a proposal, on the condition that the European Parliament has agreed to the proposal at a second hearing. On the other hand, if Parliament has rejected the proposal, the Council has to make a unanimous decision. Most single market proposals are now subject to majority voting by the member states in the Council. However, items relating to taxation, the free movement of persons and the rights and interest of employees, will continue to require unanimity. This procedure has ceded the general legislative process and this is one of the main reasons behind the success of the single market drive in the Community.

The Maastricht Treaty introduces a new co–decision–making procedure which further strengthens the role of the Parliament in EC decision–making. The two procedures are to be used in different types of policy areas. The main problem is, however, that taken all together this "compromise–procedure" is very complex and may result in very lengthy processes which are difficult to use. Only time will show the extent to which these new parliamentary powers will increase the influence of this popularly elected EC institution (Andersen and Eliassen 1992).

The Commission, the Parliament and the Council are the most important institutions in the decision process within the EC. In addition, the European Court of Justice holds a very central position in the total EC system. Anyone can bring a case at the Court: individuals, EC institutions, member states, organizations. The intention of the Court is to safeguard the enforcement of the Directives in the twelve countries.

The Court is not a hierarchical component of the European decision procedure, but its function, including its political function, should not be underestimated. Hence, in some cases, it might be sensible to try to exert influence here. This has been emphasized by the President of the Court, Ole Due (Berlingske Tidende 1989):

"The problems are often due to the fact that the member states formulate their decisions too vaguely in those cases where it's difficult to reach a consensus." Consequently, the interpretation and the final decision are left with the Court of Justice. These problems arise especially when unanimity is required. After the resolution of the Unity Act a lot fewer cases will require unanimity to pass, which will relieve the more political use of the Court, but on the other hand the almost 300 Directives in the Internal Market undoubtedly will lead to an increasing number of differences concerning interpretations.

In the 1970s, the Court of Justice played an important role in the development of EC policies and in defining the relationship between the EC and the member states (decision–making and competence). The revitalization of the role of the Commission and the Council in the 1980s produced a substantial amount of EC legislation which has not yet been tried in court.

The need for Court rulings and precedence will lead to an increase in the role and importance of this institution in the 1990s. At the same time, the increased number of Court cases will create a demand for new reforms of the Court system, in response to the heavy burden of work.

A brief description has been presented of the various institutions in the formal decision–making process. This process is designed to balance the relationship between the national and supranational levels, as well as to balance the roles of the Commission, the Council and the Parliament within the EC.


## EC INSTITUTIONS IN THE LEGISLATIVE PROCESS

There are many different types of EC decision–making. We will focus on the legislative process where the Council plays a key role. Legislation is a core element in EC integration. It is also the most interesting area in which to study the relationship between national and supranational decision–making. At the same time, it presents opportunities to study various sources of external influence (Andersen and Eliassen 1992).

An examination of the different phases in the EC decision–making process is necessary in order to identify the possibilities for influencing this process. We will present the main elements of the Community decision–making process and highlight, in particular, the various patterns of institutional rivalry.

Community legislation is the result of a complex and often lengthy process of consultation and negotiation. Under the treaties, the Commission has the exclusive right to suggest a proposition for new legislation. Where the Council or the Parliament wants action taken, they may request that the Commission undertakes studies and submits appropriate proposals.

The idea of a specific Community initiative may originate from outside the EC or stem from the Council or Parliament. Most initiatives come from inside but citizens, firms, or organizations, can approach the Commission and ask them to undertake a new initiative. The Commissioners and the officials determine which cases should be pursued. Agenda setting is of decisive importance, particularly in a system such as the EC which has limited decision-making capacity.

Once the decision has been made to pursue an initiative, it is then made more specific by the officials of the Directors General. These officials formulate a preliminary proposition, using analysis carried out by independent experts from the member states. Organizations and firms also have the opportunity to be heard at this stage, particularly major European federations or large multinational companies. After discussions in the various offices of the Commission, the case is presented to the Directors General who, on behalf of the Commissioners, attempt to reach an agreement on the substance of a proposition.

National experts are consulted, in an attempt to consider the likely consequences of the Commission proposals. Calculations are made and arguments are considered. The Commissioner responsible for the proposal formulates the proposition and puts it on the agenda for one of the two weekly meetings. If the Directors General have reached a consensus previous to these meetings, the decision is then of a merely formal nature. If this not the case, the subject is discussed before the final vote is taken. If the Commissioners decide to propose a new piece of legislation on the issue in question, the proposal is then sent to Parliament for its first reading.

The work of the Parliament is prepared in different expert committees, each responsible for certain areas (for example, the Committee of Transport). When Parliament receives a proposition from the Commission, it channels this directly to the respective committee, without any preliminary parliamentary process. In each case, the committees choose a chairman who prepares the recommendation.

The recommendation is presented to the different parties and Parliament makes a preliminary comment on the case. Parallel to this, a hearing is run in the Economic and Social Council (ESC). The nine committees of the ESC then prepare the propositions. The three constituent elements of the ESC are employers, employees, and "others", which include consumer councils and national organizations for agriculture. The ESC has only an advisory status and is not regarded as an important part of the EC decision–making process.

After the first hearing in Parliament, the Council makes a temporary statement on the proposition. The daily work of the Council is taken care of by one ambassador and one vice–ambassador from each state, in addition to the national attachés. The twelve ambassadors constitute the group of Permanent Representatives, referred to by the French abbreviation COREPER. It is within this body that the final discussions, coordination and mediation between the different countries take place (Kirchner 1992, Nugent 1991).

The twelve national attachés within the relevant field form a working group. The country which holds the chairmanship decides which of the Commission's proposals should be put on the agenda during the following six months and how they should be dealt with. There are three categories here: (1) the leading issues of the presidency; (2) mere formalities; and (3) "left–overs" from the previous presidency.

After considering the issue, the working group hands over a recommendation to the COREPER. While considering the case, the national attachés stay informally in touch with national interest groups and firms, but at this stage there are no formal hearing procedures.

The vice–ambassadors of the permanent national representations meet in the COREPER II which fulfils a kind of secretarial function with relation to the COREPER I. Here the proposition is discussed and a decision is made as to whether the temporary recommendation from the Council should be passed or rejected. In the next phase, the more controversial propositions are dealt with by the ambassadors in the meetings of the COREPER I, usually after having caused serious disagreement in the COREPER II.

If the ambassadors cannot produce a qualified majority, the proposition is taken to the Council of Ministers. At this stage, it is dealt with by the national ministers who are in charge of the particular area congruent to the issue on the agenda. In order for a final decision to be passed, either unanimity or a qualified majority is required, depending on the case under consideration. In the instance of serious, continued disagreement or a simple majority, the Council advises the Commission to withdraw the proposition or to make sure that necessary alterations are made to get it through. If the COREPER reaches a consensus, the Council merely gives the formal clearance – the proposition is decided upon as an A point.

During the second parliamentary hearing, the preliminary recommendation of the Council is again subjected to a hearing in Parliament and is dealt with according to one of the different procedures laid down in the Treaty, which include the consultation procedure or the co–determination procedure. The outcome, according to the different procedures used, determines the future treatment of the proposal.

The ultimate stage in the decision–making procedure is the final settlement agreed in the Council. After the second hearing in Parliament and possibly also in the Commission, the Council reaches its final decision. If the Parliament has passed the proposition without any objections, it will be sent to the vice–ambassadors of the COREPER II. In the case of conflict with the Council, the proposition is subject to the same procedure as was employed during its first Council hearing.

One thing which should be noted is the power of the Commission. Not only does it have the exclusive right to propose a motion, it is often also able to heavily influence the deliberation stage which takes place in the Parliament and in the Council and also the administration and enforcement of the legislation.

Legislation and decisions are put into effect at the national level. It is most often the case that the national authorities are responsible for the implementation of the legislation, overwatched by the Commission which checks that this is carried out in a satisfactory manner in the various countries (Kuvaas 1992).

We have now identified the major points in the decision–making process where pressure can be exerted. Few examples of systematic data are available as to how the system as a whole works in practice. Below, we will formulate some hypotheses with regards to the overall pattern of decision–making, the rivalry between EC institutions, and the possibilities which exist for external actors to influence the EC.

## HOW AND WHEN TO INFLUENCE LEGISLATION

Community legislation is the result of a complex and often lengthy process of consultation and negotiation. Under the treaties, the Commission has the exclusive right to suggest a proposition for new legislation. Where the Council or the Parliament want action taken, they may ask the Commission to undertake studies and submit appropriate proposals. As a result, the Commission is the most important starting point for attempting to influence the decision–making process. Furthermore, most observers argue that the best time to influence the Community's decision–making is as early in the process as possible (Budd and Jones 1989:61). The Commission is the main European institution in terms of administrative and political capacity and the influence which it can wield on decisions.

It seems to be of importance to make contacts at the correct level in the Commission. Partly in contrast to the findings of national investigations, observers argue that it is not top level contacts, but medium and low level ones which are of the most importance in the EC, particularly those at the lower level who actually draft the legislation. There is a much greater reluctance to contact EC Commissioners directly, than there is to contact permanent secretaries at the national level.

The cabinets of the Commissioners have an important role to play in the decision–making process. They are not only involved in the sectors for which "their" Commissioner is responsible, but like the Commissioner they are involved in all areas of EC policy–making. As a result, most observers argue that the cabinets are extremely important targets for lobbying and interest representation in all sectors of Community policy. This is particularly true when it comes to lobbying which is related to national interests or more politically oriented lobbying on matters close to the political heart of the individual Commissioner.

Several representatives of interest organizations have argued in interviews that the Commission is the most important point at which to direct lobbying efforts. In an organization which is short of both human resources and decision–making capacity, setting the agenda is of crucial importance. Major European associations such as UNICE and ETUC, as well as individual organizations and firms, try to put issues on the Commission agenda. The next important "early" stage for interest articulation is when a new proposal for legislation is being drafted within the Commission and considered by experts and working parties.

As Lodge states: "Commission proposals are not fashioned out of thin air. Rather, they represent the culmination of an extensive process of consultation with leading representatives of Euro–level interest groups, national experts, senior civil servants and politicians (where appropriate)" (1989:38).

There is a fundamental difference in the general democratic representativity of the European Parliament, compared with any other national parliament in Europe. The main source of the democratic legitimacy of EC decisions still lies in the Council representing national governments, based on national parliaments. As a result, the European Parliament has a long way to go before it becomes a truly popular, representative body with its legitimacy derived from the fact that it is elected by all voters in the twelve member states. However, representativity doesn't only rest on electoral representation, but also on institutional influence in the decision–making process.

One reason for the different views as to the role and importance of the European Parliament is that there exist variations across sectors. Within traditional sectors of EC policy and sectors which mainly deal with technical matters, the influence of the Parliament is still weak. In emerging and controversial political sectors such as the environment, social issues, culture and education, the new procedures which have been developed between the Parliament and the Council seem to have strengthened the role of the Parliament.

The European Parliament plays an increasingly important role in EC decision–making today and the necessity to lobby the Parliament has also increased. All actors agree on the fact that it is extremely important to monitor the progression of a proposal and to intervene, soon after it has been submitted to the Parliament. At this stage, the European Economic and Social Committee is involved, as are interest organizations linked to the ESC. However, the importance of the ESC in the policy–making process is questionable and it is not seen as a major source of influence to be used by lobbyists.

Some observers argue that the next Council stage, when the revised draft is being considered by the Commissioners and the COREPER, represents the last chance of influencing the proposal. At this stage, European associations are involved in lobbying or they use national organizations to lobby the relevant ministries in their home countries. It is, however, the Council of Ministers itself which makes the final decision on important matters and on issues where the ambassadors in the COREPER I are unable to agree. At this stage, the involvement of national interest organizations with national governments is thought to be of much greater importance than lobbying at the EC level. As two journalists monitoring the EC state: "Input at the ministerial level must be provided at national capitals. Unlike the United States and Britain, where power is centred only in Washington and London, the EC has many centres of power scattered across its 12 member states" (Wall Street Journal/Europe 13.01.90).

What about the overall picture of the inter–institutional balance and the balance between member states and EC institutions? As argued earlier in this chapter, the Single European Act increased the role of both the Commission and the Parliament. The new cooperation procedure made it possible for the Commission to propose legislation that did not have to take into consideration all the member countries or the need to make compromises in order to finally get the proposition adopted in the Council.

However, the increased legislative influence of the Parliament under the cooperation procedure is still very much dependent on support from the Commission. Changes proposed by the Parliament can only be adopted by qualified majority voting in the Council if the changes have support in the Commission. The codecision procedure which is detailed in the Maastricht treaty,[1] gives the Parliament the right to veto legislation independently of the Commission. This "negative legislative power" has been widely discussed, and it remains to be seen how the Parliament will make use of it.

Based on the fact that the codecision procedure means increased use of majority voting, and that the Commission and the Parliament are the most supra national or European institutions, two hypotheses can be formulated. The first hypothesis is that both institutions will make an effort to maximize the possibilities of both the cooperation and the codecision procedures, in order to drive the Community forward by ensuring that the new propositions will be adopted. This implies that the Parliament will be careful in their right to veto. Second, the Commission, when making initial proposals, will take into consideration the views of important coalitions in the Parliament. This meams that inter–institutional alliances will be more important than before. Experiences gained through use of the cooperation procedure indicate that qualified majority voting encourages the Commission and the Parliament to exploit differences between member states, in order to build coalitions in favour of their propositions.

Increased majority voting means that the Council, on behalf of the member states, delegates power to the supra national institutions. On the other hand, the competence and control of the Council with regard to the new pillars of the EU are increased. However, as mentioned earlier, in spite of the three–pillar structure, one could argue that increasing the Council's power in new areas will also strengthen the powers of the other EC institutions (especially the Commission). It could then be concluded that the Maastricht Treaty strengthens all of the three main EC institutions, in relation to the member countries.

The principle of subsidiarity and the ongoing debate concerning openness might balance out this conclusion. However, it may be the case that the most realistic way to increase member state influence and reduce the "democratic deficit" is to be found at the national level and not in Brussels. This means that the national parliaments must increase their effort to control their governments, and make sure that they become more "national" than European.

Interest organizations, foreign governments, local authorities and private firms try to influence the next stages of the policy–making process too but it would appear that this is less successful, in particular after the final hearing in Parliament. At this stage, it is presumably only lobbying in national capitals which can really result in some influence being wielded on the decisions.

This chapter has provided a general overview of EC institutions and formal decision–making, with particular emphasis on the legislative process. We have also pointed to some of the major opportunities for external influence. In the following chapters, we will develop the decision–making perspective further, taking into account the openness of the system and the many possibilities that exist for informal influence.

## NOTES

1   Along with new powers, e.g. requirements that give the Parliament "assent" to agreements concerning the objectives of the Structural Funds, rights of European citizenship, harmonization of electoral systems for European elections and increased influence concerning international agreements.

# 3

# COMPLEX POLICY–MAKING: LOBBYING THE EC[1]

*Svein S. Andersen and*
*Kjell A. Eliassen*

## LOBBYING IN AN EMERGING EUROPEAN POLITICAL SYSTEM

The focus of this chapter is the increased role of lobbying in decision–making at the European Community level. The most important institution is still the Council which basically acts as an arena for national interest representation. However, direct lobbying of EC institutions constitutes an important part of the decision–making process within the Community, increasing EC autonomy over the interests of member states. Such activities have mushroomed over the last three years. As a result, we can talk about the Europeification and lobbyfication of EC decision–making. However, although it has attracted a lot of attention, there has been surprisingly little systematic research carried out on this topic (Streeck and Schmitter 1991).

Originally, lobbying meant the informal influencing of parliamentarians. However, we define the concept of lobbying by contrasting it with the integrated corporatist participation in public decision–making. Representative associations may engage in lobbying but, in principle, anyone can become involved in lobbying directed at one or more of the EC institutions. Unlike in Washington, where a system of lobbying is well established, the system in Brussels is still in the making. For this reason, EC lobbying includes activities aimed at gathering information and establishing oneself as an actor. These are the preconditions for influencing decision–shaping and decision–making.

Prior to 1987, the European Community decision–making process was mainly a Commission – Council relationship. Lobbying directed towards the main EC institutions did exist. Mostly, it was carried out by representatives of national organizations which were also involved in the representation of special interest groups within a specific country. Relatively few associations and companies were involved in systematic attempts to influence EC institutions directly, independent of the national channels of influence. The situation before lobbying in Brussels really took off is described in a few articles (Philip 1983, Kirchner 1981, Buksti and Martens 1984, Sidjanski 1982), but no comprehensive analysis exists.

The passing of the Single European Act represented a revitalization of the decision–making system in Brussels. The intention was to pass 279 Directives before 1992 and this suddenly made EC common policy–making into an important political arena. In addition to the traditional lobbying through channels which stem from national systems, there has been an enormous growth in the direct lobbying of EC institutions. This is contributing to the development of a European political system which is independent of the member states.

Most of the traditional lobbying was directed at the Council, and this is still important. However, a major part of the new and direct lobbying is directed towards the Commission and the Parliament. This strengthens the legitimacy of EC policy which stretches across national borders. The emerging multi–level and multi–channel system is becoming characterized by the use of elaborate strategies which enable participants to play the whole system. Moreover, actors who come from the national channels of influence, have to take part in lobbying at the EC level.

There has been a surprising lack of systematic research into the questions being raised by the lobbyfication of a more independent EC decision–making process. This is in strong contrast to the large body of literature which exists in relation to interest articulation in national systems, most notably the models of corporate pluralism and societal corporatism (Rokkan 1966, Schmitter 1974 and 1977, Grant 1985, Williamson 1989, Scholten 1987, Damgaard and Eliassen 1978, Buksti and Johansen 1979, Johansen and Kristensen 1982, Heisler 1979). In the US, there are a substantial number of studies on lobbying (Gable 1953; Epstein 1969; Hayes 1981; Birenbaum 1985). The lobbyfication of EC decision–making means that actors representing different national traditions will have to engage in a new form of lobbying.

The aim of this chapter is not to go into detail regarding the exact number and types of lobbyists operating in different policy areas. Instead, a first attempt will be made at describing the overall picture and how the growth of lobbying relates to ongoing changes in the EC decision–making system. The focus will be on three major questions:

1. How does the explosion of lobbying influence the decision–making system in Brussels?
2. Where can influence be exercised in the EC decision–making process?
3. What characterizes lobbying in different policy areas?

The answers to these questions are of great practical and theoretical interest. In the final section, we will briefly discuss how trends in EC decision–making relate to the dynamic relationships which exist between different EC institutions. However, before we enter into these discussions, we will take a closer look at the kind of lobbying-which takes place in Brussels.

## THE GROWTH OF COMMUNITY LOBBYING

The Community institutions have always been the object of lobbying. However, the degree and nature of lobbying have changed dramatically, particularly during the 1980s. The number of lobbyists has increased ten times since the early 1970s, and four times since 1985. While European interest organizations have grown steadily, the explosive growth in lobbyists over the last years is due to the invasion of professional lobbyists, accounting firms, legal advisers and representatives of individual companies, counties and cities (see Figure 4). This means that the relative proportion of European associations among those lobbying in Brussels has dropped.

We will describe the changes in EC lobbying in more detail. However, it is also necessary to look at the phenomenon in the context of the changing relations between EC institutions engaged in decision–making. The EC system may be described as a quasi–parliamentary system. We will distinguish between two major stages in the development of the overall pattern of EC institutions. The first stage is the period of EC stagnation in the 1970s and early 1980s. The second stage is that of the revitalized EC, starting in the mid–1980s.

**Figure 4.** *Lobbying in the EC 1957–1990*

- - - - - - Number of European lobby organizations
———————— Total number of lobbyists

*Growth in EC lobbying*

Lobbying is as old as the EC. In the years after 1957, Europe–wide
pressure groups were established within the various areas of Community
policy. By 1970, it was possible to identify more than 300 Euro–groups
(Philip 1987:75). In 1980, Community officials created a register of all
the formally recognized Euro–groups and these were found to number
439 (Economic and Social Committee 1980). In addition, there were
some unrecognized Euro–groups and other lobbies active in Brussels
(Philip 1987:76). The limited number reflects the fact that the EC was
suffering from a period of stagnation, but also that EC decision–making
was organized around inputs from the national channels of influence.

During the 1970s and early 1980s, the relationship which existed
between the major EC institutions could be described as follows: the
Commission's role was supposed to be the initiation and preparation of

proposals, much in the same way as a government in a parliamentary system. However, it was not able to fulfil this role in the same way as it had done during the preceding years. The Commission's task became mainly one of administering the EC system. EC decision–making was mainly an arena for processing inputs from national governments based on unanimous agreement as there was little room for autonomous EC decision–making.

As a result, the major institution in this period was the Council. It acted not only as a parliament but, in many ways, it also took the role of a government. New proposals had to be sounded out here, before it was worthwhile starting a formal process. The Commission tried to strengthen its position through coalition–building with European associations, in a corporatist fashion (Philip 1987:75). More than 200 "Euroquangos", advisory and consultative bodies with representatives of both interest organizations and Community institutions, have been established (Sargeant 1985:241). Most of these bodies have only an advisory status and the Community has not been very successful in establishing a corporatist structure. One exception to this fact is the Economic and Social Committee of the European Community and its sub–committees. However, the influence of this body but has been limited.

From the mid–1980s it was clear that something was going to happen to the EC. This was reflected in the growth in the number of associations and lobbyists taking an interest in Brussels. A survey from 1985/86 registered 659 federations at the European level which were represented in Brussels, and about 6000 lobbyists and national interest associations in member countries, deemed to be of relevance to the policy–making process in Brussels (Morris et al. 1986).[2]

For 1992, there are no exact figures detailing the total number of lobbyists, but all estimates indicate that lobbying has exploded since 1987. Attempts to count the total number of interest groups or lobbyists results, in general, in a figure of 3–10,000, depending on how lobbyists are defined. The highest number includes everyone trying to get access to and influence key actors at the EC decision–making level. This includes those who come to Brussels in order to pursue particular issues, as well as those who are more permanently positioned in the European capital.[3]

However, because there is no formal registration of lobbyists in Brussels, it is hard to find exact numbers that can illustrate the extent of lobbying which takes place today. Nevertheless, there seems to be a general consensus surrounding the explosive nature of this phenomenon over the last couple of years. Economically, it is a growth business, worth around £ 100 million a year, a figure which has been growing by 100 percent a year in the last three years (Bartholomew and Brooks 1989, Zagorin 1989, Newman 1990). Moreover, even if we do not have exact numbers for different categories of lobbyists, we do have rough estimates.

The actors involved in interest representation and lobbying at the EC level have traditionally been, especially prior to 1987, the same type of actors which we find at the national level. First and foremost there are interest associations, either national organizations or European federations, or in several cases both. Back in 1980, national interest associations and European federations for agriculture, the labour market, industry, business, commerce and finance had by far the strongest representation in Brussels, as they also have on the national scene today. They cover the traditional areas of Community policies.

Of the interest associations recognized by the Community in 1980, 40 percent represented industrial employer interests and one third was from the food and agriculture sectors, totalling 71 percent from these two sectors (Philip 1987: 76). In 1985/86, 55 percent of the European organizations were from industry and agriculture (Morris et al. 1986).[4] Our own interviews indicate that the relative proportion of industry, labour and agriculture has been dramatically reduced during the last couple of years. In 1990, we estimated that only about 30 percent of the interest groups lobbying in Brussels came from industry and agriculture. The new types of actors on the European scene are from associations located in other sectors such as business firms, professional lobbyists (including accounting firms and legal advisers), representatives of companies, counties, cities and diplomats.

Interest organizations from other sectors of society such as trade unions, education, culture, social services and the environment, numbered 126 in 1980, 29 percent of all Euro–groups. They have only recently substantially increased their representation in Brussels. This is due to the growing importance in the EC of areas such as the social dimension and the environment. Today these areas constitute the greatest proportion of organized interests represented in Brussels.

To a larger extent than in the member countries, business firms have established offices with the purpose of influencing Community policies. All major European firms and also several American and Japanese firms are present in Brussels. Some companies are not associated with one specific country. One example of this type of firm is Nestlé. This is formally a Swiss company, but 98.6 percent of its production take place outside Switzerland.

Some major industrial sectors like the car industry have established their own interest organizations. The experience of these businesses is that: "Commissioners prefer to be in contact with manufacturers themselves or their direct representatives. Federations or associations are further away from the "ballgame". The "ballgame" in this field being technical regulations, notably those relating to safety or the environment" (Perrin–Pelletier 1985:85). Today the car industry organization (the CCMC), has some twenty technical groups whose aim it is to influence specific technical aspects of Community and national regulations.

The third type of actor is the individual lobbyist such as lawyer companies and consulting firms. They operate on behalf of associations, firms, regional or local councils in member countries and other institutions. An interesting development is that an increasing number of top civil servants in the Commission take up positions as lobbyists for associations or industry, after leaving their EC position.

The fourth type of lobbying which has expanded rapidly in the last one or two years is that exercised by representatives of various regional and local public councils including county councils, cities and regional development organizations. At the national level, their activities are directed towards the national ministries, parliament and government. On the European scene, we find much the same pattern as in Washington, where local and regional lobby organizations have chosen to establish offices in order to try and influence the legislative process. Important issues are the regional distribution of Community subsidies and the location of certain Community institutions and projects. The number of these associations is rapidly increasing.

Finally, a group which is actively involved in lobbying in Brussels is the representatives of the non–EC nations. In 1990, more than 130 countries were represented by ambassadors to the EC. Both the number of embassies and, in particular, the total number of employees has increased in the last couple of years. Together with groups from the member states, they lobby the appropriate Directorate Generals, the Commissioners, the Parliament, and the European Court.

So far, we have demonstrated the explosive growth and changing composition of lobbyists in Brussels. What is special about this system if we compare it with national systems of interest representation, and how does it relate to theories about interest articulation and mediation versus parliamentary representativity?

## WHAT IS NEW: EUROPEIFICATION AND LOBBYFICATION

The explosive growth in the number of actors with an interest in EC decision–making was paralleled by important changes in the EC decision–making system. After Jacques Delors became chairman of the Commission, it regained its role as initiator of EC policy. The Commission then took on the role of an EC government, while its bureaucracy served as the administration. The Council continued to serve a parliamentary role. The new, directly elected Parliament remained weak, but eager to strengthen its position.

From the mid–1980s, and particularly after 1987, the Commission and to some extent the Parliament became more important as actors within the EC system, gaining some degree of autonomy from the national interests. Suddenly there were two additional channels of influence, in addition to the national. Direct contacts between the Commission and the Parliament serve to provide these institutions with an independent power base vis–a–vis the national interests, much in the same way as intended by the Commission's earlier attempts to forge corporatist linkages with European associations. This has occurred, however, as a result of an unplanned growth in lobbying, involving a much wider set of actors.

What emerges is a three–tier system for influencing EC decision–making. One important implication of this is that the growth of direct contacts between the Commission and the Parliament creates a basis for more autonomous EC decision–making, independent of national interests. Another implication is that EC decision–making becomes a complex system where actors in the national channel also have to engage in EC lobbying, no matter what trait of national decision–making they represent. We call these tendencies the Europeification and lobbyfication of EC politics.

There are some important differences between lobbying and interest representation in Brussels and what we know about similar phenomena on the national level. Normally, studies of lobbying and interest representation take place in a context where: (a) representative political systems are firmly in place, (b) state authority and a set of decision–making arenas are already established (although arenas may change and new ones may develop) and (c) societal actors which have easily identifiable interests are present.

Within such a general framework, studies of lobbying and interest representation have normally focused on the game of politics (liberal tradition), institutional rules governing the articulation of interests with a privileged position in the policy–making process (corporatist tradition) or the interplay between parliamentary and corporatist patterns of involvement (corporate pluralism).

European Community interest representation in the late 1980s and early 1990s differs from national West European systems in two important ways. It is increasingly based on supranational authority; we call this Europeification. Moreover, the EC system is less corporatist and more lobbying–oriented than in national European systems. Whatever their national tradition is, everyone who wants to influence EC decisions has to engage in lobbying. This lobbyfication relates to both special features of interest articulation in the Community and to the Community institutional set–up and decision–making models.

We must keep in mind the special nature of the institutional set–up in the EC decision–making process. The system differs from what we are used to in the representative democracies of both Western Europe and the United States of America:

1. The EC is based on a new form of supranational authority. It is not a state in the traditional European sense. At the same time, the EC is also quite different from the federal state in the United States. The EC is based on strong national systems, with virtually no independent sanctioning power.
2. The Commission plays the key role, with the exclusive right to initiate legislation. It plays the role of government and parliament. The Council is relatively weak because it is not a permanent representation. The Parliament is politically weak.
3. The roles of the civil servants and politicians are almost reversed. The civil servants cultivate relations with special interests.
4. The low importance of democratic representativity and legitimacy. In the EC, functional legitimacy linked to expertise in the Commission has a central role to play.

These features of Community decision–making underline the increased Europeification of the decision–making process, in which national actors have to engage in EC lobbying, no matter what tradition of decision–making they represent. European lobbying has contributed to the Europeification by strengthening the role of both the Commission and that of the European Parliament. Future shifts in the power and legitimacy of Community institutions will, to a large extent, be linked to a continued Europeification of interest representation.

In contrast to national traditions, the EC stands out through a number of unique features of interest articulation related to the following factors:

1. New types of actors can participate. For instance, European consumer interests, individual firms and cities have all established themselves as lobbyists.
2. There are very few procedures regulating participation. Unlike the United States, it is not required that interest associations and lobbyists registrate, and lobbying is not professionalized.
3. Interest articulation takes place on many levels: regional, national and supranational. These levels can operate simultaneously or actors can have another try, if their first attempt fails.
4. The system is still in the formative stage. This means that outcomes of particular decisions are important for the further elaboration of the system. The strategic implications of decisions are great.

The EC is a special form of political system within the liberal Western tradition. However, if we compare it with other political systems it differs, not only in terms of its institutional set–up, but also in terms of the functions it fulfils. Normally, political systems legislate, make decisions, implement, control results and sanction violations. The central EC decision–making process is primarily directed towards only one of these functions, namely legislating.

In only a few cases does the central EC decision–making process lead directly to new legislation. Such decisions, called regulations, are automatically integrated into the body of national law. Most of the time, however, the EC Council decides on Directives. These are not part of Community law, but the member countries are committed to following up their intentions through national legislation.

Moreover, the implementation, control and sanctioning of legislation which is derived from the Directives, are matters for national authorities. The EC Court is an exception. This institution is supposed to supervise and sanction violations of Directives in member countries. However, there is a problem of competence as the Court does not have any supranational sanctioning authority to lean on. In addition, there are problems relating to the politicization of court decisions.

There are a few examples of the actual decision–making power of interest organizations in the EC, primarily in policy implementation processes. Within agriculture, interest organizations participate in some decisions on prices. The Advisory Committee on the European Social Fund was established to provide advice to the Commission on applications submitted to the European Social Fund. In practice, this body has, in fact, influenced the distribution of grants from the Fund (Lodge 1989:53). In the labour market area, some institutions of a more corporatist character have been established, but with rather limited powers, one example being the European Foundation for the Improvement of Living and Working Conditions in the EC.

At this point, it is useful to summarize the developments which have been taking place. There has been a tendency during the 1980s towards a Europeification of interest articulation within the Community. The system is characterized by unclear principles regulating the formation of mandates for stable interest representation, and it is open to lobbying by many different actors, in relation to many issues. There is a multitude of actors in an open–ended access structure. When assessing the opportunities for influencing the decision–making process, it is important to understand the formal structure, and particularly the decision points where pressure can be exerted. The question should then be asked, where do interest groups lobby and why?

## FORMS OF PARTICIPATION

We now turn to the question of how actors are involved in the decision–making and implementation processes. Previously, we defined two main types of participation; interest representation and lobbying. Interest representation is defined as participation in the policy–making process by associations with a high degree of representativeness and regularized contacts with the decision–making institutions. Lobbying, on the other hand, is participation by actors who do not necessarily have a high degree of representativeness and participation is not regularized.

The regular involvement of the European Federation of Shipowners in shipping issues can then be cited as an example of interest representation. However, the involvement of this federation in defining Community competition rules can be described as lobbying, according to our definition. At the same time, the involvement of a lawyer on behalf of the Association of Danish Private Harbors in the drafting of Community shipping Directives is lobbying. Furthermore, the involvement of a consulting firm on behalf of French shipowners in trying to influence a Court decision concerning French shipowners, restricting the activities of Danish ships out of French ports, is lobbying.

Various types of participation can also be described according to the types of activities involved. We will discuss interest representation and lobbying in terms of the following types of activities:

A. Agenda setting
B. Membership on boards and committees
C. Preparing documents and drafting proposals
D. Hearing procedures
E. Formal contacts outside the hearing procedure
F. Informal contacts
G. Interest organizations implementing regulations
H. Influencing court decisions

Nearly all these types of participation could be used at all seven stages in the decision–making and implementation process of Community policy–making, described in Chapter 2. Interest representation could involve all of these eight types of participation. Lobbying could involve all except B and G. Therefore, the question of interest representation or lobbying has to be viewed in relation to the actors and the issue areas involved.

## TYPES OF POLICY DECISIONS

In order to understand differences with respect to participation and how actors operate, we also have to look at the policies they try to influence. In our research, we distinguish between five main types of lobbying, related to:

1. principles for constructing the community
2. making technical rules
3. making rules and systems work
4. getting access to funds and location of projects
5. taking care of externalities.

As we stressed earlier, the whole system is at a formative stage. An important part of lobbying is directed towards the construction of the Community institutions, regulations, Directives and decisions. This is a political task and lobbying is mainly directed towards national governments and the European Parliament. This type of lobbying also includes attempts to strengthen the general awareness of EC institutions concerning certain issues such as the environment and certain industries or geographical areas of the Community.

A large proportion of Community rule–making consists, however, of quite specific technical matters. Questions relating to such issues as harmonization, free competition rules and environmental protection involve not only general principles. They also raise very detailed technical issues.

At the same time, it seems to be easier for lobbyists to influence technicalities as advocates of general principles. With regards to technical questions, the representatives of industry or affected societal interests seem to have more legitimacy. In these issue areas, they lobby the Commission.

Our investigation has confirmed the old problem which the Community has of getting the different rules they make implemented and respected in the member states. We have found a substantial amount of lobbying directed towards that aim. The main reason for the Danish shipowners' association sending a lobbyist to Brussels was to lobby the Commission, the European Court and national courts in the hope of getting EC rules implemented and obeyed by European shipowners.

A special type of policy decision involves the granting of Commission contracts and projects to individual firms, research institutes or national governmental agencies. This category also includes the locating of European institutions or projects in various localities within the member states.

Finally, we have also witnessed increased lobbying directed towards safeguarding against unintended consequences of a free market and economic growth–oriented strategy in relation to such areas as the social dimension and worker participation. These externalities are either related to a specific product or they are more general. The Parliament is the main target of lobbying in relation to general externalities.

The question we put forward is: What variations exist according to policy area when we look at the actors, the way in which they participate and the types of policy decisions taken? In the next section, we will investigate how the characteristics of agriculture and the financial markets influence the pattern of interest articulation. Finally we will briefly discuss how cross–cutting policy areas, like the environment, are dealt with.

## LOBBYING DIFFERENT POLICY AREAS

Policy sectors within the Community can be categorized and grouped according to several criteria. The Community itself has established twenty–three General Directorates which could be used to categorize Community policy. We will distinguish between two types of policy areas: (1) policy areas related to the economic sector and (2) policy areas cutting across policy sectors.

*The industrial sector*
The various industrial sectors differ with respect to the type of activities to be regulated. To what extent can transactions be controlled by external authorities? Do actors have an exit option, an opportunity to move their activities to other systems where regulation is less ambitious? To what extent are market solutions legitimate? We would expect such factors to influence the kind of regulation which we find within sectors. This is conceptualized as degree of embeddedness (Andersen and Midttun 1989).

A high degree of embeddedness means that capital is tied to specific production structures; it is not easily transferred to other sectors and is often closely related to political and societal goals. A typical example is agriculture.

A low degree of embeddedness means that capital is fluid. It is not related to specific production or societal goals. Transactions concern the movement of capital. In such a system, the market is difficult to regulate from the outside. A typical example of this is the finance sector.

Turning to the core business of the Community as detailed within the Treaty of Rome, agriculture is the sector which stands out. This sector is important and it has a well defined set of decisions and a number of legitimate actors. For many years there has existed a well developed and regular pattern of interest representation. Regulation is oriented towards the replacement of the free market, through an extensive administrative system.

Financial services is a sector of major importance in the 1992 programme. In contrast to the agricultural sector, regulatory ambitions are at a minimum. The core idea behind regulation is to ensure that the market functions as effectively as possible. However, this policy sector is quite new and is still at the formative stage. The pattern of interest representation at the European level is not as regularized as in the agricultural sector.

In between these extremes, we find considerable variations of embeddedness. A sector which comes close to the financial sector is shipping. It is one of the few cases where real capital can be easily transformed into financial assets. Moving towards higher degrees of embeddedness, we find different industrial sectors such as the car industry, the chemical industry and mining.

We assume that variations in embeddedness will have a significant impact on patterns of lobbying and interest representation in the specific sectors. To what extent and how do these characteristics influence interest representation and lobbying activities? We focus on those who systematically try to make themselves heard by establishing a permanent presence in Brussels. We will discuss this in relation to actors, types of participation, and types of policy decisions in the sectors of agriculture and financial services (see Figure 5). Note that these are preliminary findings. They serve more as illustrations than as documentation at this point.

*Policy sectors*
If we looked at associations and lobbying interests which are permanently represented in Brussels, we would expect to find a large number related to the agricultural sector. In this sector, with its orientation towards regulation and redistribution, strong Euro–organizations can be expected. There is a strong need for central coordination within specialized sub–sectors, such as in dairy products and feed stock.

At the same time, the comprehensive administrative system in the agricultural sector can be expected to open itself up to different national interests trying to get their share of benefits. This may be done both through the national ministers in the Council and by direct interaction and consultation with the central administration.

In contrast to the agricultural sector, the financial sector is oriented towards general minimum regulations, designed to strengthen the general rules of the market and ensure stability and efficiency. There are no modifications based on special interests in different sub–sectors although they may exist for technical reasons. Rule–making is governed by a strong technical and professional orientation.

**Figure 5.** *Relation between type of capital and lobby–pattern*

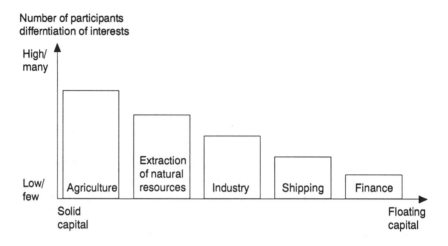

In such a situation, we would expect the general interest to be represented by one or a few Euro–organizations. This would particularly be the case at the rule–making stage. However, even when general rules of the kind we find in this sector are to be implemented, opportunities for lobbying by national interests are much more limited than in the agricultural sector.

Moreover, differences in national interests have to be articulated in technical terms. It is more difficult to use the national ministers as channels of influence. However, it is likely that the importance of a national presence in Brussels will increase when rules are to be implemented. This may be particularly important in relation to the EC Court, as a means of making sure that rules are followed in all countries.

When we look at our data, the actual representation of actors in the two sectors fits our expectations very well. In the agricultural sector there are twenty–two Euro–organizations and the majority of the national interest associations have a permanent representation in Brussels. In the financial sector, on the other hand, we find, that in banking there is only one Euro–association for commercial banks and one for savings banks and no permanent national level representation in Brussels.

There are generally few formal rules regulating participation. However, we would expect to find more rules in the agricultural sector than in others. This sector has a comprehensive body of rules and regulations and an extensive administrative body. The process of bureaucratization has had time to mature, and this will be reflected in the kind of demands made on interest associations and lobbyists wanting to make themselves heard.

In other words, one would expect that parts of lobbying and interest representation in the agricultural sector would take place according to procedures, particularly in relation to regular processes such as pricing. However, one would expect less structured processes around special issues where national interests are at stake. In such cases, interest articulation follows a dual path, in relation to the Commission, the administration, and through the Council of Ministers. This reflects the fact that issues are not always about agriculture as such.

In the financial sector, there is likely to be less need for formal procedures. The strong emphasis put on professional arguments has a disciplinary effect. The kind of interest that can be articulated has to be argued from a general perspective. Moreover, at the present time, the number of actors is small, and the sector is new. No regulation has yet reached the implementation stage. This stage may open up for more specific interests related to the operationalization of specific rules, and the way it is practised in specific cases.

Once again, our findings come very close to what we were led to expect on the basis of our analytical scheme. However, a major impression is that participation in both sectors is largely informal. Formal procedures do exist in the agricultural sector, but most are of an informal nature and are implicit. In the financial sector, there is no formal procedure governing participation. The orderliness stems from the small number of actors involved.

What we have said already indicates that in the agricultural sector, the types of decisions which interest groups are lobbying for, are likely to be oriented towards the operating of the system, rather than the making of it. However, as the system is presently under reform, there is likely to be a new interest in general policy principles. In addition, the new system may have to put more emphasis on technical matters, rather than on politics. An important aspect of the reform process is decentralization aimed at giving more of the responsibility to national authorities. However, there will be funds available from the EC level.

In the financial sector, the focus is presently on the making of the system. Attention is likely to be directed towards technical matters in relation to general policy principles. Promotion of different interests prior to decision–making, dressed up in professional language, is likely to be an important part of this.

In this section, our findings are less conclusive. Our preliminary findings are consistent with our expectations. Some differences stem from the indigenous characteristics of the sectors. We do find that the political aspect plays a more important role in the agricultural sector than in the financial sector. However, due to the uneven distribution of professional resources among member countries –Britain versus Greece, for instance – politics come in through the back door, since the most advanced banking countries take a leading role. On the other hand, the stage of development that the sectors are at – reform versus system formation – seems to account for important similarities as well.

## LOBBYING CROSS–CUTTING POLICY AREAS

The economic policy sectors may be viewed as part of a strategy for growth through market liberalization. Agriculture is in a special position, since it has proved to be a very difficult area for that liberalization. Some important policy areas cut across sectors, such as consumer, environmental and work and safety issues. These areas emerge around a certain kind of unintended consequences produced by a successful economic growth strategy.

Some consequences are specific, in the sense that they may be related to special products. In such cases, producers may be held responsible as part of sector regulation. Sometimes they are taken care of by actors in a sector who see it as their responsibility. One example of this is when the use of chemicals in agricultural production leads, over time, to high concentrations in food products.

In both of the examples above, unintended consequences may be handled as a part of sectoral policy. Initiatives may be taken by actors involved in the sector or by external pressure groups. The lobbying associated with this is part of the sectoral pattern directed mostly towards the Commission.

The European associations of consumers (the BEUC), employees (the ETUC), and for the environment (the EEB), may direct their lobbying towards the Commission. However, a prominent characteristic of these issues areas is that they are genuinely political. They involve values and priorities that cannot be decided on the basis of technical expertise. For this reason, these organizations direct a major part of their energy towards the European Parliament.

The association of consumers has a reputation for being very effective. Interestingly, it does not limit its activities to traditional consumer affairs. It has also played a very active role in relation to environmental issues. The weakness of the environmental lobby is that it is very heterogeneous and many of the political views which they hold lie outside the bounds of traditional party politics. The position of the ETUC is also characterized by many different traditions and ideological orientations.

Environmental policy may have been the fastest growing area of EC policy over the last decades. From 1965 to 1975, the number of items of EC environmental legislation totalled about five per year. In the 1980s, the number had grown to more than twenty items per year. Environmental policy is likely to be one of the key areas of EC policy–making in the 1990s.

An interesting element in this cross–sector lobbying is that the various groups have common interests with the European Parliament in strengthening the representative political authority in the Community. The Parliament thrives on political issues that cannot be reduced to technical issues. Because of the way the EC system is constructed, the cross–sector policy area related to the social dimension may carry more weight than it would otherwise have done. However, it is worth noting that the influence of both the Parliament and the interests of consumers and environmentalists are presently weaker at the EC level than they are in the member states.

To summarize, it can be said that our expectations seem to fit the actual pattern of interest representation and lobbying in Brussels quite well. However, we must keep in mind the fact that finance is a new sector still in formation. The picture of policy areas cutting across sectors stresses the relationship between lobbying as such and inter–institutional rivalry. What we have presented here is a glimpse of a system in transition. We will briefly discuss some possible future developments.

## NOTES

1   *An earlier version of this chapter has been published in European Journal of Political Research, 1991, Vol. 20, No. 2.*
2   Our own calculations.
3   This definition is not very far from the one used to registrate lobbyists in Washington. Registration is based on contact made in relation to particular issues.
4   Our own calculations.

# 4
# IMPLEMENTATION OF COMMUNITY LAW: THE LAST STRONGHOLD OF NATIONAL CONTROL?

*Johan From and*
*Per Stava*

## EUROPEIFICATION OF IMPLEMENTATION?

Decision–making is becoming increasingly Europeified in the sense that what happens at the EC level, now penetrates more and more areas of national policy–making. The member states are not, however, inclined to give up their central position. They have taken care of their own interests by use of the "committology" system. National representatives sit on the committees which control the formation of EC policy.

It is easier to pool member states' authorities at the decision–making phase than at the implementation phase. Implementation either has to be the responsibility of the member states or the responsibility of EC bodies which possess the necessary authority to enforce it. To give implementation powers to the Commission and to the Parliament, commensurate to the scope of EC policy, would be to transfer authority to the EC level without the national gate–keeping functions provided by "committology". Faced with such a dilemma, the Council and the member states have so far opted for clearly sub–optimal implementation regimes.

The implementation deficiency created by this is growing wider as the Community becomes active in ever new areas of policy. The evolution of the Community has so far not been a linear development. Rather, major changes have occurred as a consequence of deeply felt crises. It may well be that the implementation deficit builds up to a crisis which has to be solved. The solution to that problem would tell us much about the direction which future developments in the Community are likely to take. This stems from the fact that the causes of the implementation deficit go directly to the heart of many EC paradoxes and problems; the quest for member state control over EC activities being the greatest. It would be a good litmus test because the "both–and" approach possible in the decision–making phase would not be possible here. The answer would have to be "either – or".

Sub–national governments (SNGs) are important in this context. If SNGs were allowed to play a more active and more integrated part in EC decision–making and feedback, implementation could be significantly improved. This is also the only viable strategy for implementation improvement which does not directly challenge the controlling role of national governments. By incorporating SNGs into networks designed for feedback on how EC policies work and are applied at the operational level, implementation considerations could be incorporated into the decision–making process.

The importance of having implementers participate in decision–making was one of the major conclusions drawn by the most comprehensive study of Community implementation so far:

> One of the most significant results of this study was the establishment of a link between the preparation of Community law and its application: the more intensive the preparation and the more those who have to apply it are included in the creation of the Community rule, the less problems there will be during its application. (Ciavarini Azzi 1988: 191).

It remains to be seen whether this insight will be transposed into action. To an increasing degree, though, the direction which Community implementation takes tells us as much about its development trajectory as does a scrutiny of new policy developments.

In this chapter, we will elaborate on these conclusions. In particular, we will give a brief account of some of the aspects of implementation theory which are relevant in the EC context and present the "implementation regime" of Community institutions, focusing on that of the Commission.

## COMMUNITY IMPLEMENTATION: RELEVANCE OF THEORY

The descriptions of the Community's implementation record are diverse and sometimes contradictory. As an illustration of this, one can compare the following statements:

> Compared to other species of international cooperation, implementation in the EC is sophisticated and precise, characterized by a "particularly well developed legal system". (Rhodes 1986, building on Wallace 1984). At the most general level, there has been a crisis of control of the whole Community budget. (Levy 1990: 75). To read these reports and the complementary documentation by the Commission of failures to implement Community legislation is to become aware of one of the principal challenges facing the Commission and the Community in the 1990s. (Ludlow 1991: 108)

These statements are not as contradictory as one might think. In our opinion, each of them is basically true. The consequence of this is that even the best standard of international organization implementation is not good enough, given that the Community is not a standard intergovernmental organization. Implementation theory may be of some help in trying to give a "bird's eye" view of Community implementation.

Pressman and Wildawsky (1984) put implementation firmly on the research agenda. According to their studies, what should surprise us is that correct implementation takes place at all. Problems in this area are, according to them, to be expected. One major reason for this is that correct implementation usually involves several semi–independent organizations or agencies, each of which can, to a large extent, block or change the direction of implementation. The probability of implementation being carried out is equal to the product of the individual probablities. Even if each of these is high, the product probability soon becomes very small.

It is, of course, strange to have a theory which makes whatever implementation takes place look like a wonder. Alexander (1989) has looked into why the Pressman and Wildawsky approach produces such results. He concludes that the conclusions are all in "the eyes of the beholder". The conclusions are built into the assumptions of the Pressman and Wildawsky theory, especially into their assumption that each "clearance point" is independent. If this assumption is relaxed, probability of implementation may increase drastically.

These theoretical developments are highly relevant when discussing implementation in a Community context. It can be argued that the EC implementation structure is a close approximation to the situation described by Pressman and Wildawsky; implementation of EC law is the responsibility of the member states acting as implementers in a quite independent capacity. According to the theory, serious implementation problems are to be expected in the Community. The root of these problems lies in the absence of institutionalized interdependencies between the decision–making level (the EC) and the implementing level (the member states).

This argument may be taken one step further. In member states with a federal or a decentralized structure, most implementation is taken care of at sub–national levels. If these levels are not incorporated into networks or implementation structures, implementation problems will probably be further aggravated.

How serious these problems are considered to be, depends on the frame of reference. Compared to traditional intergovernmental cooperation, implementation structures in the Community are fairly interdependent. Article 5 of the Treaty is, in this context, a key article:

> Member states shall take all appropriate measures, whether general or particular, to ensure fulfilment of the obligations arising out of this Treaty or resulting from action taken by institutions of the Community. They shall facilitate the achievement of the Community's tasks. They shall abstain from any measure which could jeopardise the attainment of the objectives of this Treaty.

The duty to cooperate extends also to the administrative and judicial bodies of the member states (Vervaele 1992: 7). The Court has gradually extended the obligations so that they also cover enforcement. From a position where the member states had the competence to enforce and punish violations, they now have an obligation to do so. Moreover, the "instrument chosen by the Member State for enforcement and punishment, must be effective and proportionate" (Vervaele 1992: 9).

The members of the Community have much stronger and more extensive contact than is usually the case in the field of intergovernmental cooperation. The interdependencies created by this and the stronger legal base of the Community, make for a very favourable implementation situation when compared with traditional intergovernmental cooperation.

However, the Community is much more than an arena for traditional intergovernmental cooperation. Expectations and ambitions are clearly higher than what are common in such organizations. Talking about the Community as a union, clearly conveys the fact that ambitions are pitched at a higher level. If these ambitions are applied to the implementation of EC law, high standards of implementation are a necessity. In this context, EC implementation may be considered as a major challenge and an important area for improvement. The more deeply the Community penetrates member state policy–making, the more important implementation becomes:

> Uneven implementation of EC rules could distort competition across the market quite as much as having no rules at all. The setting of penalties for breaking EC Directives is left to the member states. If some states enforce EC law punctually, while others either fail to get EC decisions onto their statute books or pay scant attention to them, there could be a backlash from virtuous states, leading to a bureaucratic tit–for–tat, and a "single market" sliding back into an anarchy of covert protectionism rather as the Common Market did in the 1970s. (Colchester and Buchan 1990: 132)

Information is an important element for improving implementation. If the Commission gets precise and coherent feedback on how EC law and programmes are practised in the member states, it has something to work on. If feedback is lacking or poor, other measures and improvements will be difficult to achieve.

How effective is the system of feedback? Does the Commission get the information it needs to monitor implementation and take the necessary steps to correct problematic situations? We do not have systematic data to help us answer this. As far as we know, there have been no systematic studies of the extent of information fed back to the Commission. What we present here are some preliminary sketches in this direction.

## THE IMPLEMENTATION REGIME OF THE EC

*How is implementation understood?*
The EC has given the term implementation a new meaning. In the literature it has basically meant: Are decisions put into effect at "street level"? Implementation has to do with actions which are relevant to a target population. What antecedes these actions is part of the decision process. In EC parlance, implementation usually means: Has Community legislation been correctly transposed into the national legislation of the member states? As a result, a Community Directive which has been

implemented in the Community sense, may not have been implemented in the usual sense of the term.

It may be useful to distinguish between the two notions of implementation. We will call actual application, administrative implementation or simply implementation. The incorporation of legislation into national law, we will call legal implementation. Administrative implementation connotes the idea that some administrative unit is actually applying the decision or Directive.

The reasons for this change of meaning may be relevant for the understanding of implementation challenges for the Community. In our view, there are two main reasons for this new meaning:

1. The novel nature of the Community, especially its unique mix of intergovernmentalism and supranationality.
2. The predominance of the legal framework in Community life.

A strong tension between intergovernmental cooperation and supranational sovereignty lies at the heart of Community development. In our context, this tension means that the Community has a strong supranational element, manifesting itself in extensive lawmaking. For the most part, though, these laws are not directly applicable – they have first to be transposed into national law. The intergovernmental aspect has so far precluded abolition of national law where Community law is passed.

Transposition into national laws are, in this situation, a necessary prerequisite for actual implementation. Transposition is by no means a simple and straightforward task. There may be both legal and political difficulties to be overcome. In such a situation, it should not be a surprise to see so much attention being paid to legal implementation.

What is more surprising is that to many EC bureaucrats, and certainly also politicians, this is where Community interest should stop. The Community, according to this view, has no mandate to ask the next logical question: Are the transposed laws actually implemented in the member states? The follow–up on this question is the responsibility of the member states. Others see the need for a much more active role for the Commission and other EC institutions. We see the tensions between these different views as an important point of departure in studying Community implementation.

The other reason for the change of meaning in the term implementation, is the strong legal basis of Community politics. This may, in part, be a consequence of the lack of a common European identity. Most nation states can build on a strong national loyalty among their citizens, using lawmaking as a supplementary instrument. The EC is almost solely dependent on the latter. This is also consistent with the view of Louis (1990) that it is difficult to find any comparable unit so dependent on law to perform its functions.

This legal bias also spills over onto the frame for understanding implementation. The focus is mainly constrained within a legal framework. According to this framework, the Community represents a relationship between the EC institutions and the governments of the member states. As a result, it is the responsibility of the member states to follow up on implementation. The Community institutions have no mandate to by-pass national governments. This is illustrated in the monitoring of environmental law implementation. The Commission is not allowed even to gather data that can be used as a basis for evaluating actual implementation (e.g. Financial Times 1992).

This legal approach to implementation seems to be the dominant one, judging from interviews which have been carried out in the Commission. In so far as this approach is dominant, the Community is completely dependent on member state cooperation in order to carry out administrative implementation.

This picture is not complete, however. The Community does reach beyond and below the national level in certain areas and under certain conditions. Firstly, individuals and corporations can complain to the Commission or European Court of Justice over non–compliance with EC law. These institutions can then deal directly with all parties involved. The initiative in these cases must lie with the plaintiffs. Usually neither the Commission nor the ECJ can take the initiative.

The Commission can, in certain areas, take the initiative to monitor implementation and take action if need be. This is especially true in areas where the Commission has a mandate to act on its own, for example with regards to questions concerning the implementation of the Internal Market. This more active role of Community institutions in administrative implementation is not, however, reflected to the same extent in the thinking about implementation. It has not been systematized into an alternative implementation "model" among EC bureaucrats.

Given a legalistic understanding of implementation, a situation with rapidly expanding EC policies, one would expect the frequency of non–implementation or problematic implementation to increase – as is indeed the case. Is it possible to establish an adequate implementation scheme within the confines of a legalistic approach? We will return to this question below.

## How is implementation monitored?

EC monitoring of implementation reflects the legal understanding of it. There is much attention paid to implementation at the Community level. What is "visible" to an outside observer, is predominantly legal implementation. For example, in connection with the introduction of the Internal Market, the Commission prepares an annual report on the (legal) implementation of EC law. Statistical data are presented on how well the different member countries are doing in transposing EC Directives into national law.

There is also close contact between the Commission and national administrations concerning the issue of legal implementation. The questions and challenges arising from this transposition are not trivial. Legal structures are different, so there is no standard way in which to carry out legal implementation.

It is difficult to get a picture of how and to what extent administrative implementation is monitored. As far as we know, there has been no comprehensive research into these questions. Neither are there reports addressing this question in any detail in the Community system. Our picture is based on interviews conducted in the Commission and examples from case studies.

The most comprehensive study of Community law implementation, that produced by Siedentopf and Ziller (1988), primarily looks at the member state level. There is a brief chapter on the role of Community institutions in monitoring compliance and control. The role of the Commission is important, but again it is exclusively restricted to questions concerning legal implementation.

Without information on how well EC law is practised by member states' administrations and to what effect, it is of course impossible to learn from past experience and improve lawmaking. The Commission has different means of gaining such information, amongst them the following:

- Notification of member state actions. This is the case for state aid. Every member state – or county or local authority – is obliged to notify the Commission. Action is not legally binding if notification has not taken place.

- Complaints and contacts from citizens and enterprises. The Commission is contacted by citizens or enterprises who may complain that their rights according to EC law have not been upheld. This may be an important source of information and means of supervision; however we have no data to determine how important it really is.
- Networks. Employees of the Commission are part of many working parties and committees. These committees are important elements of the networks of which the Commission is an important part. Experts from the member countries are frequent members of the committees. They are important sources of information, both in the policy formation process and in relation to implementation. The role of these networks in policy formation has been described in various studies (e.g. Rhodes 1986, Rhodes and Marsh 1992). Their role in implementation monitoring has not been analysed.
- Transparency is a keyword in recent EC legislation. The Directives, regulations and financial arrangements are to be framed in such a way that they can be easily monitored. Tenders Electronic Daily (TED) may serve as an example. It is open to everyone to look into what projects are up for tendering and on what terms. Monitoring implementation is of course easier in a transparent system than in an opaque one.
- Delegating monitoring to interested parties. When creating an internal market with transparency, monitoring can be "delegated" to interested parties. Those who lose in a competitive tender can check whether the rules have been followed or not. They may take the case to court.
- Newspapers as sources of information. Commission employees scan newspapers and other news media in order to pick up information relevant to implementation of EC law.

Ludlow sums up and evalutes the monitoring approach of the Commission:

> The official line in the Commission is that the latter has deliberately adopted a "private sector" philosophy with regard to its surveillance functions. Instead, in other words, of mobilizing large resources to keep a constant check on the performance of those implementing policy in the member states, the Commission uses spot checks, exhortation, and more general political pressure through the Council and Parliament. In the

light of successive auditors' reports, this argument seems rather thin. (Ludlow 1991: 107–108)

## How is implementation organized?

In general, implementation is an integral part of the work in the different DGs. Relatively few resources are devoted to implementation–related functions. This situation is exacerbated by the fact that the administrative resources available at EC level are very limited relative to the tasks at hand. Given scarce resources, implementation has not been given top priority. Ludlow (1991) summarizes this situation:

> There has always been a bias within the Commission in favor of policy formulation as opposed to policy execution. Senior Commission staff are, for the most part, better at drafting Directives then they are at implementing them, stronger at planning programmes than they are at administering them. (p. 107)

There are, though, some organizational units specifically devoted to implementation work.

Fraud is a special case of faulty implementation. Fraud against the Community has attracted quite some attention. In this area, special organizational units have been created. In 1985, a working group was established (Group Inter–Services de Coordination des Contrôles sur Place). This was a fairly weak coordinating group. In 1987, the Commission stated that only two groups were to be specifically responsible for combatting fraud: the Fraud and Irregularities agency of DG VI (agriculture) with fourteen officials, and a group of five officials in DG XXI (Customs Union).

In 1988, a special fraud unit – UCLAF – was created. It replaced the working group established in 1985. The new group is located within the Secretariat–General of the Commission. Officials of member states' administrations are seconded to this unit for several years.

Apart from in the area of fraud, it is difficult to get a clear picture of the implementing organizations of the Commission because they are so integrated into other types of work. This integration may well be fruitful if there is a conscious strategy behind it. With the – until now – scant attention paid to implementation, chances are it is more reflective of a deficient implementation set–up. Dehousse (1992) has the same diagnosis: The EC is not well–endowed institutionally to go beyond legal implementation. There are "huge bottlenecks at the implementation level" (p. 391).

In certain areas, though, the Commission has acquired more extensive implementation powers. That is the case in relation to competition law and sectors like agriculture and fisheries. The Commission has its own inspectors for fisheries and export butcheries. However, the fisheries inspectors cannot directly inspect fishing vessels. They can only inspect the national inspectors and work in conjunction with them.

### Role of sub–central governments

Sub–central government (SCG) is responsible for implementing major parts of EC policy. The exact extent of this is, of course, dependent upon the division of responsibilities between the different tiers of government in each member state. It is one of the most consistent findings of implementation research that good implementation presupposes participation of implementing organizaations in the decision–making processes. To what degree do SCGs participate in EC decision–making? If participation is inadequate, why is that so? Are there realistic ways to improve participation? These are central questions in efforts to improve EC implementation.

Rhodes (1986) lists three ways in which such participation can take place:

1.  Direct contact between the Community and the SCGs. In this case, the SCGs become an integral part of the Community.
2.  Contact with national governments concerning EC policies. One important aim of the SCGs in such discussions and negotiations will be to influence the national governments to take into account the needs of the SCGs as implementing authorities.
3.  Participation in Community–wide associations. These associations have fairly easy access to the Commission.

From an implementation point of view, the first method should obviously be the prime form of contact. In this case, the points of view and the needs of the most important implementing bodies will get access directly into the decision–making processes. Many of the Directives and decisions which are almost impossible to implement could then be stopped or improved. Rasmussen (1988) refers to this problem:

> ....application agencies are often associated with the preparatory phase...Yet that method could not be used in a number of Directives. Indeed, in 11 out of the 17 Directives, a large number of locally or regionally placed officials were seen to handle the day–to–day application

without any possibility existing of integrating them and their insight into the process of adoption and implementation. (pp. 113–114)

Participation in Community–wide associations is a weaker approach because of the diversity of responsibilities, status and points–of–view between SNGs in the member states. Contact with national government is of course a necessary approach but, in itself, it will not be sufficient. National governments and SNGs sometimes have different needs. In these cases, the needs of the SNGs may not be adequately represented in the decision–making process by central government.

This problem is probably aggravated by the "negotiating style" of national participation in EC decision–making (Scharpf 1988). In negotiations, some issues become salient, others recede into the background. When the SCGs as prime implementers are not present, the chances are that considerations concerning implementation will recede into the background. EC lawmaking to date is a strong corroboration of this point.

SCG participation in EC decision–making has been difficult to achieve. The reason for this is national government resistance. Rhodes (1986) describes this problem: "Whichever means is preferred, they all encounter a recurrent problem: the tension between the need for imformation and expertise, especially on the implementation of policy, and the determination of national governments to reserve supranational negotiations unto themselves" (p.29).

The consequence of national resistance to direct SCG participation has been to keep important information away from EC decision–makers and probably also to keep implementation low on the Community agenda. It is now, however, becoming increasingly difficult to ignore it. Media attention to fraud is but the most visible and obvious case – it may not be the most important one.

There are signs that SNG participation is now forcing its way into the formal EC system. The Maastricht Treaty establishes a Regional Committee. This committee may not be in the strongest formal position, but it will be part of the central EC system. In the area of Community structural policies, SNGs have now acquired a formal position, independent of national governments. Gary Marks is one of the first scholars to have pointed to the significance of this:

....there have been fundamental innovations in the administration of the structural Funds. The Fund administrations are coming to play a pivotal role in allocationg resources and in developing and monitoring programmes. For the first time the administrations are creating policy networks that encompass subnational governments and private interests in individual regions. (Marks 1992: 192).

These trends are so far tendencies more than tidal waves. However, "once policy networks linking subnational governments to the EC have been created, there is no certainty that they can be dominated by national government" (Marks 1992: 217).

One possible development is that the "implementation deficit" has become so large that something has to be done. The emerging tier–spanning networks will provide one important means to bring the deficit into balance.

## CONCLUSION

Implementation may be one of the areas where Europeification clashes head–on with the need for national control of the important Community processes. As the "breadth and depth" of EC policies increase, the gap between the ability to formulate policy and the ability to apply and enforce it becomes ever more evident.

The tensions created by these widening gaps have to be resolved at one point. The only viable solution to this dilemma is to further incorporate sub–national governments into the networks and formal decision procedures of the Community. However, even this approach may be unacceptable to national governments. The Regional Committee of the Maastricht Treaty is one step in this direction, but the committee has a fairly weak link to the major decision processes of the Community.

As we have documented in this chapter, the importance of implementation has been pointed out by several observers and academic writers. One important step would be for the Commission to broaden its view on implementation and develop coherent implementation strategies beyond legal implementation. Incorporating sub–national governments into the decision–making process would be one way of achieving this.

# Part II
# Sectoral Studies

# 5

# WHAT DO MARKETS HAVE IN COMMON? TOWARD A FAST TRAIN POLICY FOR THE EC

*Frank Dobbin*

## INTRODUCTION

One of the original hopes for European unity was that a huge frontierless economic region could replicate the economic dynamism of America's post–war economy. In the past decade the common "market" took on another meaning as Europe became disillusioned with interventionist public policies and explicitly turned to privatization and markets to promote growth. Europeification has come to mean not only efforts to break down trade barriers, but a shift away from national–level interventionism toward the sort of the market organization of economic life associated with Adam Smith. The European Community is increasingly seen as a structure for imposing discipline on governments that might otherwise meddle with industry – as a referee in an enormous free market.

Neoclassical theory poses the market as the economic state of nature –what exists in the absence of meddling states. This idealized market is driven by transcendental economic laws of exchange that determine what is efficient and what is not, and that thereby help to shape social institutions. The particular set of laws that neoclassical theory has identified suggest that economic efficiency operates best in the absence of disequilibrating political intervention. The modern social institution that has done most to promote modernization and progress (the state) plays no role in the constitution of markets or efficiency. On the contrary it can only act to disrupt primordial or natural markets. Great expectations for the economic future of a Europe can, in essence, negotiate modern states out of the economic picture.

One paradox of this way of thinking is that while economic theory treats the market as a universal that is understood to mean the same thing everywhere, in fact people mean very different things by "the market". When states appeal to markets to produce efficiencies of various sorts, they appeal to widely different kinds of social processes. Moreover, states themselves take very different institutional roles in markets – some behave as if their actions may disturb natural markets, others are charged with reinforcing market mechanisms, and still others behave as if they must actively constitute markets. I will argue that economic integration under a single European market will not be as simple as eliminating industrial interventions that interfere with natural markets, but will involve integrating conceptions of (1) how and where markets produce efficiencies, and (2) the role of the state in the constitution of various markets. This will demand not a withering away of European states but the imposition of some new pseudo–state structure that will effect some particular, as yet undefined, vision of the market.

*The integration of institutionalized economic worldviews*
Students of the European Community see the problems it faces as largely political (e.g. Sbragia 1992, Haas 1958). How will the EC resolve sectoral and national interests (Fligstein and Brantley 1992)? How will nations with divergent interests reach consensus (Lange forthcoming)? Will cross–national sectoral interest groups emerge (Andersen and Eliassen 1991)? These very questions lead analysts to bracket the issue of how divergent economic worldviews will be reconciled in the European Community. Market mechanisms are institutionalized very differently in Italy, Spain, Germany, the UK, and France, and as a result Europeans have widely different ideas about what markets are.

Neoclassical economics and modern common sense alike treat "the market" as a singular ideal–type, which actual economic behaviour patterns can only approximate. But the idea of a "perfect" market implies transcendental economic laws that drive economic behaviour patterns to converge everywhere. The origin of modern economic practices is, then, thought to be a sort of overarching economic geist that takes the form of a set of mathematical models. A more sociological approach makes weaker assumptions about the universality of economic laws by treating ostensibly "objective" laws as things that are distilled from social experience. We know, for instance, that neoclassical theory was distilled from the early experiences of the UK and the United States. If all economic laws are simply glosses on experience, then understanding the diversity of economic experience – and the sorts of indigenous economic laws that result – becomes important to understanding economic behaviour patterns. The main source of cross–national diversity in economic experience is certainly the nation state, as institutional economists contend (North 1981, 1990). With these insights, economic sociologists have explored market mechanisms with a social constructionist lens. They find that even within a single industry, capital markets, consumer markets, sourcing markets, and other kinds of markets may operate on entirely different principles (White 1988). They find that over time more and more realms of social life are subjected to "market" processes (Zelizer 1988, Reddy 1984). They find that particular economic behaviour patterns are sustained as actors collectively construct them as rational, and enact them with reciprocal expectations about the behaviour of others (Granovetter 1985). If the meaning of the market differs by social context, how can widely different varieties of markets be reconciled in an integrated Europe?

To illustrate the diverse conceptions of the market that will have to be reconciled if Europeification is to be successful I explore the different varieties of markets to be found in French and British high speed train policy. British and French policies constitute disparate technology markets, consumer markets, capital markets, producer markets, secondary markets, and international markets. Taken together, policies in these market realms point to incompatible conceptions of the market, and of the role of the state in the market. Policies in both countries appeal to market forces. But in the UK public policy is driven by the notion that markets and economic activity are exogenous to, and prior to, the state; in France policy is driven by the notion that markets and economic activity are produced, stimulated, and guided toward national goals by the state. What will the European Community's high speed train market look like, given that European nations have such divergent institutionalized conceptions of markets?

I argue that nations' conceptions of the role of government in the market are glosses on institutional experience, and that the key supranational governing institutions that will shape emergent Community–wide conceptions are already in place. Those institutions carry implications for the relationship between the European Community–qua–government and economic behaviour patterns, or markets. I argue that the institutional logic of the EC will favour certain conceptions of markets and disfavour others. Of the three principal high speed train policies now under consideration – system integration, bilateral service agreements, and the "airline model" – only one is compatible with the conception of government–market relations embedded in the current structure of the Community. In short, Europeification implies the imposition of a particular kind of market model, and that model is already implicit in the very institutional structure of the EC.

## FAST TRAIN POLICIES IN THE UK AND FRANCE

France operates state–of–the–art 300 km/h trains on a new network of rail lines dedicated to fast passenger service. The UK operates 1960s– technology 200 km/h "High Speed Trains" on the nation's nineteenth- century freight/passenger network. The kneejerk reaction of political scientists has been to call French policy statist and British policy market– oriented, and to use this typology to explain all such differences. Yet on close scrutiny, as we will see below, the typology breaks down. In fact, France subjects elements of the railway industry to private competition or market forces that the UK dominates with state control. More generally, in both countries rail policy is state–oriented, in that railways are nationalized, and in both countries rail policy is market–oriented, in that policies are explicitly designed to employ markets to achieve economic goals. Hence the British think they are using public policy to create efficiency through market processes, but then so do the French. These outcomes are better explained as the result of very different ideas about market efficiency and the role of the state in the market.

The UK's industrial culture (Dyson 1983) makes entrepreneurial drive the source of economic dynamism, and makes positive state action a threat to entrepreneurialism, markets, and growth. France's industrial culture generates a different vision of the roles of state, market, and entrepreneur in the pursuit of economic efficiency and growth. In France, state technocrats play a key role in transforming entrepreneurial drive into progress, and the state must stimulate, guide, and contain both entrepreneurs and markets to achieve efficiency and growth. Whereas in the UK policy has been organized on the premise that markets spring up naturally from civil society, in France it has been organized on the premise that markets are created by the state. Whereas in the UK policy has constituted civil society as the generator of supply and demand, in France policy has constituted the state as the generator of supply and demand. Whereas in the UK the state is exogenous to the market, in France it is endogenous.

These different institutionalized conceptions of the relationship between state and market produced remarkably different high speed train policies. Space limitations prevent me from discussing the origins of national industrial strategies and conceptions of markets in detail, but recent studies suggest that national "industrial cultures" (Dyson 1983) and "industrial policy paradigms" (Hall forthcoming, Andersen 1993) are found to be consistent across industrial sectors, emerging in the nineteenth century (Dobbin forthcoming). Thus the conceptions of markets behind high speed train policies adopted between the 1960s and the early 1990s are rooted in British and French industrial traditions. The experiences of this sector are by no means unique, and they will no doubt ring familiar. Next I review the effects these institutionalized relationships between state and economy had on policy in various sub–markets of the high speed train industry.

*Technology markets*

The success of Japan's high speed Shinkansen line, opened in 1964, stimulated both the UK and France to adopt fast train programmes by the end of the 1960s. But where would the technology for trains come from? Both countries operated nationalized railroads with internal development departments, but they approached the issue of technological supply differently. France treated the state as the optimal supplier of the technology, but used private sector capital to finance rolling stock. Politicians and state technocrats assumed that the state's designers were best suited to design rolling stock and infrastructure. France's Société Nationale des Chemins de Fer (SNCF), the state–owned railway, established a Research Department in the mid–1960s and set to work developing a train that could run at unprecedented speeds. The official commitment to a high speed train linking Paris and Lyon was made in 1972, and over the next four years SNCF perfected the technology that would first go into service as the TGV (train à grande vitesse) in 1981. The trains were built by a public–private joint venture under the Compagnie Générale d'Electricité. French policy engaged the private sector to build the TGV, but never opened up technology design or construction to market competition.

Across the Channel, British Rail (BR) took the initiative for technological supply in the late 1960s by establishing two in–house high speed projects. The "High Speed Train" project produced the 125–mph

InterCity 125 by making minor modifications to existing train technology. The more ambitious Advanced Passenger Transport (APT) project aimed to build an entirely new, and much faster, train. In 1982, after three trial runs that brought technological problems to light, BR dubbed the APT project a failure and abandoned research (Potter 1989). While the engineering community saw the train's deficiencies as remediable, the Government doubted the state's capacity to manage the development of such a complex technology (Potter 1989). In the belief that private entrepreneurs could better design high speed trains, BR spun off its rolling stock division (BREL) with the explicit aim of locating technology supply in the more efficient private sector. British Rail has since moved to a strategy of competitive tendering for high speed train technology which makes now–privatized BREL one among private equals (Potter forthcoming). In short, the French have employed private–sector agents to build the TGV but have presumed that the state was best equipped to design the technology. By contrast, the British were easily discouraged with the state's efforts to develop a new technology and after a minor failure chose to externalize technology development in an effort to engender a competitive market for technology supply.

### Consumer markets

Where does demand come from? French and British fast train policies were predicated on estimates of market demand, but they carried very different ideas of the origins of demand. French policy treated demand as a result of public policy. In the 1960s SNCF had substantial autonomy to act as they saw fit when it came to planning new railroads (Faujas 1991). First, they embraced France's then–popular "free market" approach to public monopolies, which suggested that they behave entrepreneurially to stimulate sectoral demand. This entrepreneurial strategy was outlined in a widely read government report inspired by the experiences of the Electricité de France (Beltran forthcoming: 4). SNCF underwent an "intellectual makeover" which "resulted in their no longer reasoning as a monopoly but as one element in a highly competitive sector" (p. 1). One principle of this strategy was that SNCF could create demand by competing with road and air transport.

In accord with this entrepreneurial approach to nationalized enterprises, SNCF staffed its new Research Department with economists trained in projecting highway demand whose techniques were based on three ideas that were revolutionary in the rail industry. First, in their models increases in demand were not a linear function in increases in speed;

dramatic increases in speed could produce geometric increases in ridership by drawing travellers from road and air transport. Second, their models assumed that an aggressive public fast train policy could increase ridership sufficiently to achieve economies of scale, which would decrease travel costs, and to increase the frequency of service, which would increase convenience. Low rates and frequent service would make railroads even more competitive and spur demand even further. Third, an aggressive public transport policy could do more than draw traffic from other forms of transport, it could generate new demand. Pierre–Louis Rochet, the Chief Executive Officer of the firm that builds the TGV, argues that the SNCF had the foresight to see what fast trains could do: "France's high–speed trains generated a new market for rail travel, nearly doubling the number of passengers using trains. Nearly half were new passengers who never took the train before or opted for rail over air and road transportation" and many of the former would not otherwise have travelled (May 1992: d13). This assumption that travel demand was not a zero–sum game was quite revolutionary, and it proved sound.

The underlying assumption of these new models was that an aggressive public fast train policy could generate substantial demand in the industry. With these rosy projections for demand in hand, SNCF economists could make compelling arguments for the viability of new rail lines (Polino forthcoming). The Paris–Lyon line's success proved them right, and the Government soon gave the go–ahead for high speed rail lines connecting Paris with Lille, Calais (and the Channel Tunnel), and Brussels to the north; with Le Mans, Tours, and eventually Bordeaux to the south–west; with Nancy and Strasbourg to the east; and with Marseilles and Cannes to the south (Neher 1989).

By contrast, British policy–makers have operated on the assumption that demand was a result of forces in the private economy that were exogenous to the state, and thus was fixed and impervious to state manipulation. For one thing, British Rail has consistently used conservative estimation techniques for demand that are premised on the notions that public policy cannot draw riders from other forms of transport, create economies of scale that would reduce costs, or influence aggregate demand. British Rail's initial projections were based on the effects of incremental increases in speed on the West Coast line after its electrification in 1966. The Ministry of Transport's economists assumed that the 0.8 percent to 1.3 percent increase in ridership for each 1 mph increase in speed was a constant and as late as 1985 refused to accept the French evidence that at very high speeds, the increase in ridership could be much more dramatic than this (May 1992). As The Economist wrote in 1985, "The ministry of transport denies that a better service would attract many new passengers, basing its argument on the assumption that each 1 mph increase in speed brings in only 0.8% in increased passengers." (1985d: 26). The Ministry sustained this position despite subsequent evidence from their own experience with the HST125, as The Economist wrote:

> Trains can benefit from the gloss provided by novelty: the introduction in the UK of the HST125, the world's fastest diesel train, resulted in traffic increases far greater than could be accounted for by traditional forms of measurement. [However] the ministry of transport [still] refuses to allow the word "image" into their financial equations. (1985b: 30).

The consequence of the UK's doubts about the ability of the state to create demand for a dramatically improved rail service was a series of conservative ridership projections showing that French–style high speed trains would be a tremendous drain on the Treasury. This undermined the political viability of an all–new high speed rail network.

*Capital markets*

Both SNCF and BR rely on private capital to finance railway development, but they approach private capital markets very differently. In France SNCF is charged to behave entrepreneurially to attract capital to its projects. For all intents and purposes, the national railway can use whatever means it deems necessary to raise funds. For its first two lines SNCF went to international capital markets just as a private entrepreneur might have. The government did not guarantee private capital; thus investors used the same criteria they would have to back a private project. For the Paris–Lyon line fully a third of the capital came from New York banks alone and for the Paris–Atlantic line fully 70 percent of the 13 billion francs needed came from international capital markets (U.S. House 1984: 26, The Economist 1984, Macdonald 1991). The debt for these first two lines has already been paid off, and to attract capital for its new projects, SNCF invited 200 financiers to travel on the latest record–breaking train between Paris and Angers to hear a financial pitch. SNCF finance director Pierre Lubek argues: "SNCF's main priority is to build up large, liquid lines of stock in the French market that will attract investors from abroad as well as locally" (Macdonald 1991).

France's newest financing strategy makes the private sector not merely a source of capital, but a co–owner. SNCF will build the TGV–Est, from Paris through Strasbourg, in a consortium with private developers that will lease the line to SNCF for a period of 30 years, whereupon it will become the property of the state (International Railway Journal 1990). Similarly, to pay for new rolling stock, SNCF has arranged to sell new trainsets to a banking consortium and lease them back from the consortium (Black 1991). When it comes to capitalization, the SNCF utilizes markets just as an entrepreneur might, and behind its strategy is an assumption that acting as prime mover, the state can generate legitimate demand in private capital markets. Moreover they have convinced the banking community of this. As one British banker put it: "In the TGV, SNCF has a good product that makes money. If they want to borrow to build more of them, I don't see there being a problem finding investors" (Macdonald 1991). An underlying assumption is that the state can be a successful capitalist.

British policy, by contrast, presumes that the state cannot generate legitimate demand in private capital markets because it cannot produce economically successful enterprises. One result is that the British state insists on guaranteeing all private investments in state–owned railroads, with the argument that public projects are inherently uncertain and that private investors should not be exposed to this kind of risk. This approach severely delimits the capital British Rail can collect, because guaranteed bonds come under Parliamentary limits on the national debt (Black 1990). One British Rail executive has argued that since SNCF does not guarantee loans, neither should BR: "Why should they? ... If banks are prepared to lend to Poland or Brazil, why not to SNCF, or us? Is SNCF likely to collapse? France is likely to collapse first. These loans would be "gilt". And if you give us access to the capital markets, the whole argument for privatisation collapses" (Black 1991). British Rail has also been restricted in its efforts to pursue innovative financing techniques. To get around public borrowing limits British Rail proposed to sell trainsets to a banking consortium and lease them back as the French now do, but government economists blocked the deal by arguing that such arrangements should be counted against the debt limit (The Financial Times 1992). This caution is peculiar to British rail policy, for as the Labour Party's John Prescott has pointed out, private investment is common "in European railway systems, and it is only ideological nonsense and Treasury daftness that prevents us doing it in this country" (Freeman 1991). The British inclination to think that any rail expansion will be the financial responsibility of the state, despite evidence of willing private investors, is not limited to Conservatives. The last Labour government cancelled an earlier Channel Tunnel proposal because cost–

benefit analyses, which used the conservative estimation techniques that doomed other fast train projects, showed that a new Tunnel–London fast train link could not pay off private bondholders (The Economist 1988).

*Producer markets*

Who will provide railway service? The question persists despite the fact that both countries have operated nationalized railroads for roughly half a century. In France the state holds an unchallenged monopoly, and no calls for privatization have been heard because most French policy-makers see no advantages in a private producer market. Neither policy-makers nor capitalists have advocated the introduction of private railway services in France. Transport minister Paul Quiles summed up the French position: "Our analysis shows there is no advantage to the community – privatisation is not on the agenda. Our aim is to have a railway in a sound financial state, meeting the demands of the community. Good management is in no way at odds with the concept of a public company" (Black 1991). It is generally believed that the nation's rail network demands coordination and orchestration of a sort that the state can best provide, and there is a presumption that public management is perfectly efficient. Even when a downturn prompted Mitterand to delay for fiscal reasons the construction of the Paris–Atlantique line, which was projected to turn a healthy profit, fast train advocates never suggested privatization to solve the problem (The Economist 1984). In France, the introduction of private, marketized, production of rail service is simply not seen as a route to efficiency.

By contrast in the UK there has been a sense, for several decades, that the railways were really run better when they were private entities. In the UK, plans to allow private parties to provide rail services, or to somehow make BR operate more like a private company, have been heard again and again. The argument most often made is that public managers are simply incapable of running enterprises efficiently because they are not driven by the profit motive. Privatization makes anything more efficient. There is a peculiarly non–market logic in some of these proposals, which would create private monopolies in the place of public monopolies. Competition among producers is not the key to the efficiency of these proposals; the profit motive is.

First, after privatizing BR's rolling stock division, British Rail put out tenders for bids for the new HST250 in 1991 in an effort to stimulate private production. The tender offer expired without producing bids, but BR has been pursuing this strategy and is expected to purchase Swedish or Italian tilt–train technology in the future (Potter forthcoming, Flink

1991, 1992). Second, the UK has tried to reorganize BR internally according to private managerial principles. In the 1980s British Rail was reorganized into "profit centres" on the M–form model of cost accounting, with separate divisions that keep independent books. The aim was to produce distinct, competitive, divisions handling freight, commuters, passengers, etc. that would operate on an entrepreneurial, rather than bureaucratic, model (Black 1991). The success of the regional operating divisions established by BR was heralded in these terms in The Economist in 1985: "it is noticeable that the lines in Cornwall and Scotland have shown a good deal more enterprise since they were granted a degree of independence" (1985a: 60). Third, BR has tried to spin off as many divisions as possible as private enterprises. As early as 1982 British Rail began selling off the profitable divisions that had a chance of attracting private buyers, including the National Freight Company, British Rail Hotels, and the rolling stock company BREL. Transport Secretary Rifkind sees privatization as a panacea for inefficiencies in the system: "Many of the criticisms against BR are justified. I would like to see as much of BR as possible privatised in the next Parliament" (Black 1991). Fourth, a proposal now under consideration would create private regional operating monopolies (Roche 1991). As Tory MP Robert Adley argued in a debate over how to privatize:

> All that we have to do in order to do what the Japanese are doing is the following: we build 2,000 kilometres of mainline railway for high–speed trains at public expense. Then we transfer British Rail, free of charge, to six non–competing regional monopolies, financed by the public sector. Having done that, we write off all BR's debts and financial commitments. (Black 1990)

This is not, incidentally, what the Japanese have done. Here the logic is to turn the rail system over to private companies that will have a greater incentive to turn a profit than public managers have had. Finally, in May of 1992 the Government announced an alternative strategy to private, regional, monopolies. The new plan would allow private firms to run trains on British Rail track, in direct competition with BR service. The "airline" model of rail organization would make BR only one among competing producers of rail service. The state would maintain the network in return for user fees, and the government's InterCity trains would be ineligible for further government funding (Potter forthcoming, The Financial Times 1992).

In sum, the French show no inclination to believe that private parties would be more efficient operators of rail service than would public managers, while the British have, all along, devised strategies for reintroducing private efficiencies into the rail system.

*Secondary markets*

Approaches to the secondary effects of railroads on national markets differ markedly. In France, it is the role of the state to stimulate economic development – to create and foster markets for all sorts of goods and services. As a result, the secondary economic effects of public investments are part of the calculus of infrastructural development. Policy–makers presume that it is the duty of the state to underwrite infrastructural projects that will stimulate growth in dependent parts of the economy. As in the UK, French rail projects are expected to produce a net return of 8 percent, but in France, projects that are not anticipated to meet this target are subsidized by central and regional governments when their secondary economic benefits are substantial. A case in point is the new TGV Est, which was projected to return 4.5 percent. Rather than scrap the project SNCF organized public capital infusions that would be forgiven, on the principle that regional growth would more than compensate for public outlays (International Railway Journal 1990). Moreover France has continued to subsidize TGV research and development in the belief that improved trains will increase internal demand, and generate international buyers for its trainsets (Neher 1989). Broadly speaking, French policy has been oriented to the notion that transport policy can, and should, generate secondary growth in non–rail markets.

The British have followed a very different logic about secondary economic effects. Long before the Conservative Party's recent pro–privatization decade in the 1980s, British policy–makers contended that railways should be self–supporting, and that it was not the province of the state to second–guess the side–effects of transport subsidization. With the exception of a few areas of service that have been subsidized for reasons of tradition, the state has sought to streamline British Rail so that only profitable portions would survive. Thus, even at the beginning of the 1980s British Rail was permitted public subsidies that amounted to only 0.29 percent of GNP, whereas national railroads in her Continental neighbors (Germany, France, Holland, Spain) average 0.7 percent of GNP. By 1990 British Rail subsidies amounted to only .12 percent of GNP (Black 1991). "The British philosophy is that people who use the railways should pay the lion's share of the costs "up front" in fares"

(Black 1991). This logic is linked to the test of "commercial viability" that is applied to new rail projects: they must be self–financing and profitable. That logic has undermined a series of proposals to build a high speed link between the Channel Tunnel and London, despite the fact that a bottleneck at the British entrance to the tunnel is expected to effectively exclude the UK from full participation in the EC (Black 1990). Margaret Thatcher responded to proposals for public subsidization by arguing that private parties would finance the line if it were worth building: "We don't believe we should subsidise international rail services" (Black 1990). More generally, the prospects of new investment in high speed rail within the UK "are heavily conditioned by the continued insistence of the British Government that any investment in improved InterCity rail infrastructure must be wholly commercially viable" (Nash forthcoming: 7). In these policies, and in the rhetoric surrounding them, there is the very clear idea that it is not the government's duty to involve itself in decisions about how the nation's capital will be invested. The market should make such decisions, and if private investors do not see the merit in a project, the state should certainly not second–guess them. Public capitalization of projects that would lose money constitutes a misallocation of the nation's capital, and threatens to create externalities that are ultimately inefficient.

*International markets*
Since the very beginning of the TGV project, SNCF and their rolling stock partner have been attuned to the international market potential of the new fast train technology. Despite the rapid proliferation of national projects to design high speed trains – virtually every European government initiated a project – the SNCF was determined that its technology should become the industry standard. The national railroad built the Paris–Lyon line as one big advertisement for French high speed train technology, and even before the Lyon line opened in 1981, SNCF and GEC actively promoted the technology in international markets. Since 1981 they have engaged in unabashed boosterism: inviting foreign dignitaries to ride on the TGV, nurturing fast train proposals from infancy in a wide range of countries, and developing comprehensive TGV proposals for markets around the world. In 1989 they convinced Spain to buy the technology. They succeeded in promoting modified TGV trains for the Channel Tunnel, which will also operate on connecting tracks in the UK and Belgium. In the US they have promoted TGV technology for systems in Florida, the Midwest, California/Nevada, and Texas, where Texas TGV

won a major contract in 1991. They are now wooing Australia, Canada, Korea, and Taiwan (Menanteau 1991, Schmeltzer 1992, May 1992, Agence France Presse 1991). The costs associated with competing internationally have been large, because as Hubert Autruffe, undersecretary of the Ministry of Transport, argues

> a TGV cannot be exported in the same way an Airbus can, which requires only an airport: TGVs require a particularly costly, heavy infrastructure that demands two to three years of preliminary studies that only the most advanced countries are capable of conducting. The required experience – to design in Texas one of the most important infrastructural projects ever realized in the United States – our clients simply do not possess. (Menanteau 1991)

Moreover in their determination to remain internationally competitive, the state and GEC have committed to ongoing research investments to ensure that the TGV remains at the cutting edge of technology (Neher 1989). In short, the public–private venture that builds the TGV has been aggressively entrepreneurial on the international scene, and much of the initiative has come from public policy–makers who believe that a state–dominated company can compete successfully in world markets against private firms.

While British Rail's tilting train technology potentially enjoyed a much larger market than the TGV, because tilting trains can operate at high speeds on virtually every existing rail system in the world, British policy–makers never discussed the Advanced Passenger Transport project as a possible source of international income. Sweden and Italy embarked on similar tilt–train projects at about the same time the UK did, and both are now marketing trains aggressively to other countries. Swedish fast trains are expected to be operating on Amtrak's Northeast Corridor in the not–too–distant future, and both Sweden and Italy have sought British contracts (Flink 1991, 1992). Of course the decision to abandon the APT in 1982 effectively killed off the project, but the decision was predicated on the belief that the state would not be able to market the technology abroad to recoup initial research and development costs. For British Rail engineers there is no small irony in the situation, because they developed the initial bogie innovations that made France's TGV possible, and eventually did little to exploit the new bogie technology save for installing them on conventional trains to create the HST125 (Potter 1989: 103). In short, British Rail's thinking about international markets has presumed that the state cannot act as an effective international entrepreneur –France, Italy, and Sweden have behaved otherwise.

*The state and the market in French and British fast train policy*
In France and the UK state policies constitute very different sorts of
markets, and very different conceptions of the relationships between
state, market, and individual economic actor. The results are distinct
approaches to the sub–markets in the fast train industry. First, French
policy is motivated by the belief that the state can and should generate
market activity in society; British policy is motivated by the belief that
the state neither can nor should generate market activity. Second, French
policy is motivated by a belief that the state is a competent economic actor
that can play the role of efficient, self–interested, entrepreneur when need
be; British policy is motivated by a belief that the state is an incompetent
economic actor that had best eschew direct economic action whenever
possible. Between French and British policies we do not simply see a
continuum of intervention, but very different conceptions of how markets
work and of the role of the state. These conceptions shape how nations
perceive economic problems, and they shape the sorts of public solutions
nations conceive to those problems.

These remarkable differences in state orientations will make it
difficult for the European Community to use a single, market–oriented,
policy regime to structure the high speed train industry of the future. How
can these differences possibly be reconciled in an industry, like the
railway industry, that is transnational in nature and that, with the
completion of the Channel Tunnel, will bring the UK and France into one
integrated network? Coordination of rail policies across these two
countries alone would necessitate a major restructuring of the industry,
but coordination of high speed train policies across a dozen or more
European countries implies massive changes everywhere. What will
Europe's fast train policy look like?

## EC FAST TRAIN POLICIES

My aim thus far has been to provide evidence to bolster two claims. First,
that the creation of an integrated European market in the rail sector will
involve more than simply setting market mechanisms loose, because
markets in the rail sector are actively constituted in very different ways
by state policies. Second, that the EC will have to make positive choices
about how to constitute sub–markets and that these choices will in turn
generate particular types of markets. What might an integrated policy
regime look like?

I have been arguing that institutions create conceptions of markets and of economic efficiency – that the national differences I have outlined result from highly institutionalized, traditional, relationships between markets, entrepreneurs, and states in the UK and France. In essence, the high speed rail policies that have emerged since the 1960s were not created de novo, rather they were organized along the lines of existing policies to take advantage of existing conceptions of efficiency – of how economies work. By extension, I argue that the European Community has developed a discernable institutional structure that implies a certain collective policy orientation. I contend that this policy structure favors certain outcomes, because it contains an institutionalized conception of economic behaviour. The process of Europeification, then, will involve the subordination of these national conceptions of economic behaviour to an overarching conception that is institutionalized at the supranational level. My contention is that consensus was reached on this new conception of markets when decisions were made about the broad institutional structure of the European Community, even if the participants in the process did not realize it at the time.

My argument is distinct from two prevailing arguments. One group of scholars contends that the European Community will be constrained by its institutional capacities to the role of regulation. I have been trying to show that the participating countries will have entirely different ideas about what regulation means, because they have entirely different ideas of what markets are and of whether, for instance, the state is endogenous to or exogenous to the market. Another group of scholars argues that consensus on important policies will be impossible in the European Community because the decision–making structure contains many veto points that will allow dissenters to quash controversial policies. One implication of this argument is that there will be great diversity of opinion among national groups over key issues. But if some consensus can be reached about the roles of governing institutions and markets in economic life, then consensus about EC industrial strategies may be possible. Today, French parties of very different stripes are able to agree on broad rail strategies because they share a conception of state and market, and Conservative and Labour parties in the UK are able to agree on rail strategies because they share another conception of state and market. By extension, if EC institutions produce a coherent conception of state and market, different national interests may be able to agree on broad policy strategies.

In this section I review three proposals now being considered for a fast train network in the European Community. I argue that the conception of markets embedded in European Community institutions favors one of these three solutions. What does this institutionalized conception look like? While America's federal system may be a poor political analogy for the European Community (Sbragia 1992), it is a good institutional analogy. The European Community was designed to break down trade barriers between nations and to put firms on an equal footing in competing for European markets. The result is an administrative structure in which regulation and lawmaking are central, and in which the possibilities for large taxing and spending programmes are nil (Peters 1992: 77). On the one hand, the European Community is set up to act as a referee in a free market by ensuring that producers do not have unfair advantages, such as state subsidies. Administrative mechanisms are organized around such regulatory oversight, which aims to end the practices associated with what has come to be called "industrial policy", or public instruments that offer advantages to particular industries and sectors. On the other hand, to level the playing field, the EC is designed to break down both barriers and subsidies. As a result, the Court of Justice has come to play a central role as arbiter of what constitutes unfair public intervention (Shapiro 1992). This administrative structure almost perfectly parallels the federal administrative structure in the United States. It is conceptually compatible with only one of the existing proposals.

The European Community, the UIC (Union Internationale des Chemins de fer), and the European Conference of Ministers of Transport have all acknowledged the need for some sort of master plan for an European fast train network, and have actively debated the advantages of alternative strategies among themselves (ECMT 1986). Each group has discussed three different proposals in some detail. The Community has organized a workgroup that produced a proposal for a network of international high–speed routes, and the UIC has called for a European investment of £ 60 billion in railways over the next three decades (Black 1990, Hoop 1991). Thus there is some consensus on which routes should be served, and how much new construction will cost. But how will the network be organized?

*System integration*
The proposal that comes closest to the French strategy is for an integrated international high speed rail network, with one operator, one technology, and presumably one international trainset supplier (Conférence Européene

des Ministres de Transports 1992: 37). The integrated strategy would follow the model of the Channel Tunnel, which is in essence a joint venture between the British, French, and Belgian national railroads. The Tunnel is run by a single operator using one train technology. One advantage of such a system is that it could transcend the problems faced by the TEE, the current international rail system, which stem from incompatible technologies. The TEE was originally envisioned as an effort to standardize technology, but in the end participating railroads simply agreed on broad performance guidelines (ECMT 1986). For fast trains the problems of technical incompatibility are more complex. Choices of train and track technologies are not independent, because non–tilting trains like the TGV can only run at high speeds on tracks designed especially for them. The choice between tilting and non–tilting trains, then, is linked to the choice between using existing freight/ passenger lines and building new, dedicated, fast train tracks. Signalling systems standardization is also demanded by high speed trains, which are computer–guided (CEMT 1992). A single, unified, system operated by the European Community would resolve all of these problems.

The conception of markets embedded in this proposal is essentially the same as that embedded in French train policy, but it is not compatible with the structure of the European Community. On the one hand, the EC is not designed to undertake the sort of proactive role that would be implied, of imposing substantial taxes on member states, orchestrating public and private financing, selecting train technology, etc. But equally important is the fact that the members of the EC have already consented to an economic model in which proactive government has no role. Ironically, then, it appears that the EC is neither institutionally nor conceptually suited for developing a fast train policy modelled on the most successful case in Europe: the French case.

*Bilateral service agreements*
A second proposal is for a system of bilateral joint ventures for particular cross–border routes. This proposal is based on the belief that integrating the operations of diverse national railroads with different technical systems, operating regulations, and policy environments may be impossible. Instead, some suggest that national railroads of different countries make agreements to provide jointly operated services between major cities. The arrangements would allow for a diversity of technologies to exist within Europe, and would call for standardization only on particular routes. In the past efforts at technological standardization

between national rail networks have been only moderately successful. For instance, trains running between Italy and France are required to change locomotives at the frontier due to technical incompatibility. The Channel Tunnel train designers had to overcome the problem of three different electrical currents between the continent, the UK, and the tunnel itself (Harrison 1991). However, the use of such adaptive technologies could solve problems of technological integration on a pairwise basis between countries, without interfering with internal standards and procedures (Hoop 1991).

A prima facie case can be made that it is the most likely outcome because it most closely resembles the existing system for international rail transport. But this solution appears to be conceptually incompatible with the EC's governing mechanisms because it involves public monopolies. Bilateral service agreements would involve exclusive contracts between national railroads that would preclude the entrance of private providers of service. Such a system would conflict with the EC's consensual institutional mission to open markets to private entry and to eliminate public subsidies. The system would both close markets, and sustain public subsidies. It seems likely that potential private providers of rail service would object to such a system, and would use the Court of Justice to try to overrule a decision to create such exclusive bilateral agreements.

*The airline model*
The third proposal for a fast train network draws on what is sometimes called the airline model. It would allow independent operating companies, including national railroads and probably private concerns as well, to compete for international customers on the existing rail network, or ideally on a rebuilt system financed by user fees. The airline analogy comes from the independent and competitive character of operators, and the state's role in providing infrastructure financed by user fees – as is the case with airports. Predictably, Tory Transport Secretary Malcolm Rifkind has been one of the central advocates of such a system: "I would look forward to the day when any railway operator within a single internal market in Europe ... was free to provide services that the travelling public, or which industry, might find it useful to use" (Freeman 1991). Already the EC has issued a Directive which aims to eliminate all barriers to international freight carriers, so that any freight operator can compete for business between Manchester and Milan or Madrid and Berlin (Freeman 1991). And the European Community Task force, Group Transport 2000

Plus, has backed such an arrangement for fast passenger transport, which would charge national governments, or perhaps a special authority with responsibility for international lines, with building and maintaining infrastructure that would permit operators to compete freely (Hoop 1991). Under such a system, broad technological standards would be decided upon by the EC, and companies would be permitted to choose their own trainset suppliers.

This system would be conceptually compatible with the institutions of the European Community because it would put an end to public subsidies, eliminate national barriers to competition from extra–national firms, and end such barriers to market entry by private firms as now exist. Under this system, private operators would not necessarily become major players, because national railroads would certainly be the initial entrants. However, under such a system the traditional national subsidies for rail transport would probably be outlawed. National railroads that could not break even would quite possibly be forced out of the business of providing services, although they might continue to build and service the network of tracks in return for user fees. While it may seem unlikely that states would allow their national railroads to be bankrupted and closed down by international competition, this is exactly the arrangement the EC transport ministers have agreed to in the airline industry, where public subsidies for national carriers will be eliminated.

## CONCLUSION

If this airline model of organization were to prevail, what would the implications for high speed rail sub–markets be? The technology market would be subjected to anti–subsidization and pro–competition rules that would allow publicly–held firms to compete as equals with private firms. Consumer markets might remain under the control of national governments, because national–level agencies would presumably build and maintain lines. This could permit France, for instance, to continue its policy of generating demand by building lines in anticipation of demand, while the UK could continue to follow demand. For capital markets, as in the current British scheme governments would not be able to subsidize the capitalization of operating companies, but as in the current French scheme, national railroads would probably operate freely in private capital markets. Producer markets would inevitably be opened up to competing companies. Thus, for instance, France would no longer be able to limit access to TGV trains, and it is likely that Swedish or Italian fast trains, that can operate on nineteenth–century routes, would serve French destinations that the new TGV system does not now serve. Secondary markets would not be taken into consideration in most service decisions, again because states would not be permitted to subsidize operators. Finally, international markets would look very different. States would not be able to favour domestic producers of trainsets, for instance, as the UK, France, Italy, and Sweden have done in the past. Most important, in the provision of services this system would effectively eliminate national borders and would encourage national railroads to compete with one another for service on all routes in the international network.

What are the likely long–term effects on the industry? European experience offers few examples; however, American experience in the early railway industry and in the contemporary airline industry are suggestive. Both have the same essential characteristics as Europe's fast train industry would under the "airline" model. The EC Directives that prevent subsidization of competitive industries could well speed consolidation of such a system. In America's nineteenth–century rail industry, the Act to Regulate Interstate Commerce of 1887 put into effect a similar "market" model, and it led to an industry shakeout that produced rapid consolidation. Similarly, the recent deregulation of the American airline industry has led to a shakeout in that industry. Likewise a "competitive access" system of international rail operators would stimulate competition that would inevitably leave some national railroads bankrupt. The most likely outcome is the emergence of a single national operating company as the last standing competitor. Conventional wisdom suggests that the SNCF could be that operator.

# 6
# NETWORKS IN EUROPEAN POLICY–MAKING: EUROPEIFICATION OF TELECOMMUNICATIONS POLICY

*Godefroy Dang–Nguyen,*
*Volker Schneider and Raymund Werle*

## INTRODUCTION

The field of telecommunications policy exemplifies the transformation of the European Community (EC) from a state–centric bargaining system to a transnational policy network. The main thesis of this paper is that the creation of this transnational network was mainly driven by European institutions primarily concerned with promoting their institutional self–interest as corporate actors. In telecommunications, this policy initiative was remarkably successful and led, within a relatively short time span, to the convergence of very different national administrative systems and industry structures.

However, this Europeification of sectoral policies by means of a policy network implies some political costs. The definition and, more important, the implementation of a European policy requires time–consuming and often burdensome negotiations with a mushrooming set of policy actors from different political arenas, including those within the member states. Government agencies, business associations, large firms and trade unions with a national or a European constituency number among the actors. Policy making in a transnational policy network is responding to increasing interdependencies and coordination problems. For the time being, this may be the only effective way to handle complex political problems. However, the lack of transparency, democratic legitimation and control of "networked policy making" suggests that the development of these new political institutional forms represents only a transitory stage on the way to an emergent European state.

Before describing the emergence of this sectoral policy network and the dynamics unfolding in this institutional transformation process, and then analysing the historical process of the Europeification of telecommunications policy, we will briefly outline the conceptual framework which has guided our interpretations.

## THE EC AS A CORPORATE ACTOR AND THE GROWTH OF TRANSNATIONAL POLICY NETWORKS

The EC as an institutional entity has always been difficult to define. It has been conceptualized as a federation in the making (Hallstein), a supranational organization (Haas), an intergovernmental bargaining system (Scharpf), an international regime (Hoffmann) and a concordance system (Puchala).[1]

Each of these concepts focuses on specific combinations of organizational facets, but all of them fit into a rank order with respect to the stronger or weaker autonomous action capacities of the EC. The federation approach, attributing the largest amount of power resources to the EC, clearly indicates the upper end of this scale, viewing the EC as a supranational authority incorporating significant control capacities and sovereignty over its members. In contrast, pure intergovernmental approaches rank at the lower end of the scale, treating the EC as a pure bargaining system. Finally, the regime approach[2] and the concordance concept[3] locate the major integrative forces on the intergovernmental level, but they add important cognitive (common knowledge) and normative elements (norms, rules, procedures) facilitating cooperation. They also address the supposed paradox of a relatively powerful and integrated complex of European institutions on the one hand and an intergovernmental decision structure on the other (Hoffmann 1982).

The crucial problems of the different approaches may be summarized by outlining two points. First, even when European institutions are explicitly included in the analysis, they tend to be seen as a passive social environment (norms, rules, frameworks) rather than as active components with autonomous action capacities. Second, European policy making is primarily analysed in terms of state–centric interaction with governments aggregating and representing national political and economic interests, thus widely neglecting the existence of both genuine European interests, which have to be enforced in national political arenas, and a wide variety of national and European actors which need to be coordinated and concerted in European policy–making.

As a result, European institutions may not be seen as the mere rule systems which regime theory suggests, but must be treated as autonomous "corporate actors" with autonomous action capacities and autonomous institutional self–interests (Kenis and Schneider 1987, Schneider and Werle 1990). The Commission, the Court of Justice and the European Parliament are more than passive institutional frameworks for intergovernmental policy coordination. The European Commission, in particular, is more than an agency passively registering and executing orders issued by the member states via the Council. The Commission plays an active role in the identification and formulation of Community interests, emphasizing interests that strengthen the Community as a whole and its position in the "Eurocracy". More than the other two genuine European institutions, the Parliament and the Court of Justice, the Commission has shown its ability to act as an autonomous actor with a tendency to enlarge its areas of competence, to mobilize new action resources (including legitimacy) and to enter new policy fields; on occasion, the Commission has even got involved in open legal or political conflicts with one or several member states.

This autonomy can be exemplified in several ways. The now famous achievement of the Single Market, which grew out of the revision of the Treaty of Rome through the Unique Act, is rightly considered to be one of the Commission's greatest achievements. However, this initiative resulted from a failed attempt of the European Parliament to improve European integration. The now forgotten "Spinelli proposal" was rebuffed by the European Council, and this essentially triggered the Commission's initiative. Another example of the Commission's autonomy comes from sectoral policy. The Traty of Rome does not encompass all relevant issues for economic integration. As a result, the Commission has been able, at several points in time, to put new issues on the political agenda. Meeting with only limited success in the 1960s and 1970s, the Commission's initiatives have been more frequently adopted by the Council since the early 1980s. The Framework Programmes for Research and Development, the completion of the Single Market, and the liberalization of the markets for telecommunications, air transportation and banking, traditionally strongly controlled at the member state level, had not been addressed in the Treaty, but they are now part of the institutional fabric of the European Community.

The EC complex should therefore be seen as a corporate actor with its own action resources and institutional self–interests geared toward greater integration. A corporate actor, however, is <u>not necessarily a powerful hierarchy</u> controlled and steered by a single centre. Corporate actors can be highly decentralized, with network–like organizational forms (Teubner 1992). Although the EC member states have transferred a number of competencies to the Community level, they have not, as yet, set up a supranational hierarchy in which the constituent units lose all autonomous decision–making capacities. Indeed, most Directives are issued by the Council under the unanimity rule. There are few texts that a member state must apply without first having approved them. For dissenting member states, exceptions are often explicitly built in, albeit for a transitory period.

The division of power between the national and the European level is thus fairly complex. EC law is formally superior to national law. However, until now, Community legislation has not been automatically effective in the different member states, but must be adopted by national parliaments. Such national implementation processes do not merely constitute formal ratification systems for EC regulations or Directives; national legislators (especially in the case of EC Directives) have some degree of discretion and, to some extent, have the final say. Even when a member state is formally obliged by the European Court of Justice to adopt a piece of legislation, national legislators have considerable power to delay, hinder or even obstruct legislative harmonization (Scherer 1990).[4]

The EC is thus in a position similar to national governments regarding difficulties with policy implementation. Notwithstanding their formal power to execute a policy, national governments may be unable to mobilize the necessary resources to put legislation into force. In many policy domains these resources are dispersed to such a degree that, without the cooperation of relevant target actors, a policy programme would remain ineffective (Mayntz 1983). In order to mobilize cooperation and support, national governments often incorporate the relevant social and political interests into the process of policy formulation. Potential conflicts in the implementation phase are thus prevented through early bargaining and interest accommodation.

The success of an EC policy programme depends, not only on the harmonized adoption of it by twelve national parliaments, but also on its effective implementation in twelve different national arenas. In order to achieve maximum synchronization of EC legislation and its adoption by member states, European policy formulation is preceded and accompanied by processes of consultation, information exchange, accommodation of interests and alliance formation. These processes lead to socio–political configurations which are currently conceptualized as "policy networks" (Marin and Mayntz 1991). These networks of policy interaction at the EC level are therefore far more complex than the "two–level bargaining" model of EC reality. Formally there exists a two–stage sequential process in which the member state governments first negotiate in the Council and then ratify the agreements separately in the member states (Putnam 1988). However, a complex array of informal relations has evolved around this formal structure, between sub–national actors in different countries on the one hand, and national and supranational players, such as the CEC or European Interest Groups, on the other. Through these relationships, the actors within the EC policy system enjoy access to much more information about one another than is common in traditional diplomacy (Puchala 1972: 282).

Studies of Community lobbying (Andersen and Eliassen 1991) show that the Commission and the Parliament are approached by a wide range of very heterogenous actors including individual firms, regional associations, cities, professional lobbyists and national as well as European interest associations. The participation of heterogeneous interests in mushrooming committees also illustrates the network characteristics of EC policy–making. Between 1983 and 1988, the number of committees and expert groups almost doubled to 1400; most are affiliated with the Commission or the General Directorates (Grote 1990, Wessels 1990, Sidjanski 1989). EC policy networks are not usually restricted to supranational and international actors, but tend to incorporate the key actors from national policy arenas as well. EC policy networks are thus hybrid mixtures of national, supranational, intergovernmental, transgovernmental and transnational actors and interrelationships (Nye and Keohane 1973, Keohane and Nye 1974).

In many cases, actors' "membership" in the networks is based on formal cooptation into advisory committees or expert groups, but in a number of domains the incorporation also works on a very informal basis. However, increasingly formalized structures are evolving. In recent years, the Commission has encouraged the growth and differentiation of formally organized interest groups at the EC level (EIOs) to represent their constituent interests collectively rather than individually toward EC institutions (Greenwood et al. 1992). The Commission is pursuing a policy of "recognizing" EIOs to which it gives preferential treatment during EC policy–making processes (Sargent 1985).

However, despite their growing number, these interest organizations are still weak in comparison with their national constituencies. They are still far away from being in a position to make binding decisions for their members. Most member organizations command far greater resources than their nominally superior peak units. As a result, corporatist arrangements, which often work at the level of national policy processes, seem difficult to achieve at the European level (Schmitter and Streeck 1991). Large firms tend to be directly represented by their own offices in Brussels (for the automobile industry see Jordan and McLaughlin 1991).

EC policy networks exhibit a highly pluralist pattern. This is not only a consequence of numerous actors' efforts to influence the European political process at an early stage of policy formulation; it is also a result of a deliberate networking strategy implemented by the European institutions, especially the Commission. To ensure national adoption of EC policy programmes and legislation, participation in programme formulation cannot be restricted to actors at the EC level alone. The relevant national interest groups, government officials and administrative experts have to be incorporated as well (Wessels 1990). In some cases, the Commission even forges alliances with national interest groups in order to pressurize governments and legislators into channelling policy development towards Community goals. For instance, multinational corporations sometimes act as "reverse lobbies", supporting the EC institutions through their pressure on governments and business associations in their host countries (van Tulder and Junne 1988). A pluralist structure also means that the policy network is not under the control of EC actors, although the EC Commission certainly does exert a large degree of influence.

## THE EC IN TELECOMMUNICATIONS POLICY[5]

The following case study of EC policy making in telecommunications is aimed at giving some insight into the structure, operation and development dynamics of EC policy networks in the telecommunications area which has only recently been "Europeified". This policy sector offers an interesting case of EC domain expansion driven by external pressure and active engagement on the part of the Commission. Complex alliances on the national and European levels have led to the synchronization and harmonization of policies in areas that would have been unthinkable only ten years ago.

## The first trials of European telecommunications policy

Although the field of telecommunications has a long history of international cooperation, significant EC policy activities did not evolve in that area until the early 1980s. During the preceding decades, the exclusive forum for cooperation was the European Conference for Post and Telecommunication (CEPT). Created as an inter–administrative body by a diplomatic Conference in 1959, the CEPT was the exclusive domain of the traditional Post, Telephone and Telegraph (PTT) administrations. It dealt primarily with tariff principles and other relevant issues to be settled among the PTTs (long–range planning, common position in international fora, etc.). From the mid–1970s on, the CEPT also had the function of implementing (on a consensual basis) technical standards necessary for the interconnection of telecommunications networks.[6]

The EC's entry into this area and the Europeification of telecommunications policy which, as a side–effect, reduced the relevance of the CEPT considerably, must be seen in an industrial policy context in the information technology sector. Telecommunications was understood by the European Commission as a part of the information technology industry, which encompassed microelectronics, computers, consumer electronics, professional electronics and telecommunications. The Commission was concerned because European firms were losing ground in this area. The leadership of American firms in both microelectronics and computers and the bold attempt of the Japanese to catch up with the US firms in microelectronics through the VLSI programme had very much impressed the Commissioner responsible for Industrial Affairs, Viscount E. Davignon. The initial conditions, however, were particularly unfavourable to EC action, especially in the telecommunications sector. They can be described as follows:

1. There was a complete absence of a European dimension in the semiconductor, computer and related industries, due to the refusal of the French government in December 1974 to support the merger of Siemens, Philips and CII (French computer manufacturer) interests in the computer industry, in a joint venture called Unidata. To some extent, Unidata had been built on the pattern of Airbus and Ariane as a European, government–supported answer to the American leadership in a high technology sector. However, unlike Ariane and Airbus, Unidata was not able to achieve a

political consensus between the French, the Dutch and the German governments. The failure of Unidata created much mistrust among member states concerning the possibility of cooperation in information technology industries.[7]

2. The telecommunications sector, like other public utilities (such as electricity), was exempted from the public procurement Directive which stated that governments should open their tenders to European manufacturers: The purchase of equipment still remained a national affair, and telecommunications remained a sector for which the Treaty of Rome did not apply.

Within this context, the EC has, since the late 1970s, successfully entered the telecommunications field, and, in doing so, has opened up a further area of economic and political integration. The first interventions in this sector occurred in 1979 when communication policy was discovered as being a relevant factor determining the industrial competitiveness of Europe vis a vis the USA and Japan.[8] This led to the launch of ESPRIT (European Strategic Programme for Research in Information Technology), and to a proposal by the Commission, suggesting the introduction of new, Europe–wide telematic services.

At least three stratagems in the Commission's intervention can be distinguished. First, an <u>incremental approach</u> was developed with the aim of harmonizing and standardizing the introduction of new, mainly telematic, services and equipment at the European level. The EC thought that it would be easier to harmonize new equipment markets. This approach failed, for one thing, because the French, the British and the Germans were not ready to harmonize their telematic equipment (in particular videotex), and, for another, because, even if standards had been harmonized, the subsequent failure of telematic services, except in France, would have prevented the European industry gaining a competitive advantage. No market had been opened for videotex services around the world.

The only success in harmonization was achieved in the definition of services with a long–term perspective. In 1982, the Groupe Spécial Mobile (GSM) of the CEPT agreed to introduce a Pan–European cellular telephone service within ten years (by 1992!), and to reserve a bandwidth for that purpose. In addition, the coordinated introduction of ISDN was also foreseen. This means that, at that time, PTTs were prepared to commit themselves to harmonizing their services, only in areas which would demonstrate growth in the longer run. As a result, the incremental approach did not produce especially spectacular results.

Second, a <u>federative approach</u> was attempted. The goal here was to go beyond a mere standard setting and mobilize resources for a Europe–wide telecommunication infrastructure. The first step was the creation of the Euronet/Diane network in 1979,[9] as well as the CADDIA and INSIS programmes in 1982. Euronet was an X.25 (packet switched) data network designed to convey on–line information between European databases all across Europe. The purpose of this network was to permit interconnection with the national X.25 networks as they became available. In addition, the dissemination of information about Europe across the EC was expected to contribute to the achievement of the European Market.

INSIS was a project which was designed to create an office automation network between Luxembourg, Strasbourg and Brussels, thereby interlinking all the offices of the European institutions. Beyond the rationalization expected from the common use of electronic office documents within the European institutions, a more subtle aim was to stimulate the adoption of office automation products on telematic networks. Finally, CADDIA was a project designed to rationalize the customs procedures between member states by means of electronic networking, thereby facilitating the free flow of goods and services inside the Community.

It is interesting to note that the policy networks involved in the two general approaches were largely different. The harmonization of markets for telematic equipment was tackled by DG III (Internal Market) and relied mainly on relationships with professional associations, manufacturers and the Departments of Industry in each member state. This harmonization programme had the support of Commissioner Davignon, who dreamt of the Commission as a European MITI, boosting the competitiveness of the European industry.

The people involved in Euronet, CADDIA and INSIS came from a different background. The projects were supported inside the Commission by DG XIII, which was in charge of Information Services, which, in turn, were responsible for the diffusion and dissemination of technical and scientific information in the EC. Their main partners were libraries, information agencies, public laboratories (with a strong interest in keeping in touch as efficiently as possible), and public administrations (customs, finance ministers etc.). The policy network around DG XIII was clearly less powerful than the one around DG III.

At the same time, while the incremental and federative approaches were taking shape, a third approach was being used by EC institutions: the <u>legal approach</u>. A series of legal actions in telecommunications had been undertaken in the past. In particular, in reaction to a complaint by SWIFT (Society for the Worldwide Information and Fund Transfer), which manages the international data networks of banks, DG IV (Competition) instituted an inquiry in 1978 on the restrictions imposed by the PTTs upon the use of international leased lines as well as on the PTTs' prohibitive tariffs. After a compromise had been reached between the CEPT and SWIFT, the inquiry was abandoned.[10]

Other legal actions were taken during the late 1970s and early 1980s. In 1979 the European Court of Justice ordered the British Post Office to discontinue its restrictive practice on the use of international telex circuits. On the basis of an appeal by the Italian government, the Court confirmed that PTT business was mainly commercial activity, and that, in this capacity, the PTTs were subject to the conventions of the Treaty of Rome. With this ruling, the Court established the principle that telecommunications as public utilities were not immune from Community action.

Unlike the incremental and the federative approaches, the legal approach was not contingent on the mobilization of a large policy network. However, as the SWIFT case has shown, players strong and knowledgeable enough to lobby DG IV, could succeed in challenging the immense power of PTTs at that time. On the whole, European institutions and, in particular, the Commission were very active in trying to influence the development of telecommunications in Europe. However, the actions lacked coordination, there was no clear vision of what the European telecommunications policy should be and the instruments of these actions were limited in scope. As a result, the Commission's initiatives had only limited success.

Another inhibiting factor was the lack of vested interest in the promotion of a Europe–wide telecommunications policy. The PTTs were satisfied with the CEPT arrangement, and the equipment manufacturers were looking outside the Community for their exports, in particular to the third world. Only the users, often multinational corporations, sometimes complained about the inflexibility of PTTs, high tariffs, poor quality of services, and obstacles to strategic planning because some PTTs revised their budgets every year. However, the users' complaints were not yet voiced in an organized fashion. Most of the traffic was still concentrated in telephony, which was considered to be part of (and concealed in!) the overhead costs of a company. IBM, just discovering telecommunications as a key area for diversification, was entangled in an antitrust case with the European Commission and had to adopt a low profile. Other service providers such as Telenet, Tymnet and GEIS were hardly investing in Europe at that time.

To summarize the situation up to 1983, the model of policy concentration in telecommunications policy at this time looked very similar to a "state–centric" model, with governments and PTTs acting, very reluctantly, as the only interface with the European institutions. Transnational policy networks, if existing at all, were still weak and rather unstable.

*The Europeification of telecommunications policy*
In the early 1980s the situation changed. A conjunction of, sometimes only weakly correlated, events created the context for a "quantum leap". Within a few years the political weight of the EC in the national telecommunications sectors increased considerably. A key event was certainly the deregulation and liberalization of telecommunications markets in the US. After the divestiture of AT&T and the liberalization of the remaining core in US telecommunications, AT&T entered European markets through joint ventures with Philips and Olivetti. At the same time, IBM diversified into telecommunications by purchasing stock in MCI. In the eyes of EC industrial policy makers, this was an alarming development. They feared that US multinationals, in addition to their hegemony in information technology, would also conquer Europe's communication market. If Europe was to have any chance of remaining internationally competitive, the Community would have to act.

Additional impetus for Community action came when the US government began putting the Europeans under pressure to open their telecom markets as well. Combined with the threat posed by American firms, this created a situation in which the Commission was able to wrest new competencies from the EC member states. Thus, a Special Task Force was created in 1983 within DG III (Internal Market), in order to implement the actions that Commissioner Davignon had in mind. To increase the competitiveness of the European telecommunications industry, the Commission proposed the opening up of the internal telecommunications market by means of national liberalization and deregulation measures.

In the period that followed (1983–1986), the Commission, and more precisely the newly created Special Task Force under the responsibility of Carpentier, achieved its goal of creating awareness of this new sectoral policy domain. This awareness strategy was basically oriented toward three goals: legitimating EC action in telecommunications vis a vis the hostile national PTTs; creating a coalition of supporters for this action by mobilizing those who were positively affected by community action; and stimulating and coordinating the various initiatives taken so far within the Commission by DG XIII, DG III and DG IV, not to mention DG XII, within a single and supposedly more efficient political context.

The pace at which the Commission entered into telecommunications policy is indicated by the short intervals at which recommendations, Council decisions, Directives and regulations were issued. Between November 1984 and January 1989, the Commission passed seventeen major decisions (see Cordaro 1990, Delcourt 1991). In the same period, consulting committees answerable to the Commission's DG XIII and responsible for information and communications technology, increased considerably, from two during the period 1980–1984 to fourteen in 1985 (Grote 1990: 242).

Concerning the major goal of liberalization, two phases can be distinguished, each creating a different actor configuration and varying power relations in telecommunications policy. The first phase extends from the creation of the Task Force (1983) up to the publication of a Green Paper (1987), during which the EC was still struggling for legitimacy. The second phase starts after the Green Paper, when the EC began to implement the principles expressed in the Green Paper's policy guidelines.

The period from 1983 to 1986 may be termed the support seeking or awareness phase. In this period, the Special Task Force launched a series of studies by consulting firms, mostly American, to show that Europe was losing ground in telecommunications and that coordinated action was necessary. These studies were presented in open fora to which major representatives of industries were invited. Growing awareness helped to formulate "Six Action Lines" for the promotion of a European telecommunications policy.[11]

Essential at this time was the creation of committees which were to lay the foundation for the Commission's policy network. The SOGT (Senior Official Group for Telecommunications) was established as an advisory body to the Commission in November 1983, along the same lines as the COREPER (Comité des Représentants Permanents). The GAP (Groupe d' Analyse et de Prévision) was created in 1983 with the task of helping the Commission forecast the long–term development of telecommunications networks and discussing the issues related to this. However, both SOGT and the GAP were dominated by PTTs, due to the balance of power which existed at that time.

In the area of standardization, the Commission revived the CEN/ CENELEC as the consequence of the so–called "New Approach" to standardization.[12] The aim was to reduce the power of the CEPT and to eliminate the PTTs from the standard–setting procedure. In response to this, the PTTs created the European Telecommunications Standardization Institute (ETSI) in 1988. However, as a political compromise with the Commission, they also opened this institution to non–PTT organizations such as telecom equipment manufacturers and users.

In addition, the Commission tried to stimulate the awareness of user groups. Since the national associations of telecommunications users[13] were relatively weak and mainly affiliated to the PTTs, the Commission tried to find representatives of large users at the international level. As a result, INTUG as well as UNICE became involved in the process of advising the Commission on policy issues in telecommunications.

*The Green Paper on Telecommunications*
Parallel to the expansion of EC activities in telecommunications, the 1992 (Internal Market) process began to unfold – a further supportive element in EC telecommunications policy. In order to establish guidelines for European telecommunications policy in the context of the 1992 programme and to forge intra– and trans–European alliances for deregulation and liberalization, the Commission issued a <u>Green Paper on telecommunications</u> in the summer of 1987. Unlike the Action Lines, the Green Paper received wide recognition and support from most of the parties involved.[14] This has to be seen as a direct consequence of the awareness building policy of the Commission and some significant changes in the international policy environment. A year after the divestiture of AT&T in 1983, the British privatized British Telecom and licensed a competitor, Mercury, which entered into business in 1986. The Japanese privatized NTT and opened up competition in 1985. The Dutch, the French and the Germans were preparing reforms at this time. The conditions for success were thus very different from past initiatives.

The key provisions of the Green Paper were aimed at achieving deregulation and increased competition. However, the provisions of the network infrastructures and basic services were to remain unchallenged, under the exclusive control of the national PTTs. Concerning enhanced services and terminal equipment, however, the Green Paper called for radical liberalization. It also called for a separation of the regulatory and operational activities of the PTTs (Ungerer 1989).

After publication in June 1987, the paper was sent to the Council, the European Parliament and the Economic and Social Committee. In a broad consultation process, the national PTTs, the telecommunications industry, the computer industry, a number of user representatives, some trade unions and other organizations representing social interests were invited to make comments. By January 1988, more than 45 organizations had responded.

Among the non–public operators in Europe, it was British Telecom and Swedish Televerket who responded to the Green Paper – the public operators had been consulted via intergovernmental linkages. The manufacturers were represented by three individual multinational firms, four national peak and sector organizations, but only two European Associations, the peak organization of employers (UNICE) and the organization of the European Telecommunications Producers (ECTEL). A further representative body of manufacturers was the Roundtable of European Industrialists. User interests were represented through several large firms and a large number of national, European and international user organizations covering all usage and application aspects. In addition, the national Chambers of Commerce reacted primarily as representatives of business users. At least three organizations were committed to the labour or personnel interests of the telecommunications operators but no organization is listed as representing the interests of labour in the manufacturing sector. Other organizations commenting on the Green Paper were standardization bodies, special European organizations like CERN and RARE, the US government and EFTA.

The Commission published the conclusions of the consultation process and formulated an implementation plan including a list of measures and a strict timetable. A subsequent Council resolution (30 June 1988), strongly supported the Commission's major policy objectives. The policy lines were then commented on by the European Parliament on 14 December 1988. In the following year, several Directives were passed in line with the Green Paper programme.

A volume published by Ungerer et al. (1989: 463–472) provides an analytical summary of the reactions expressed by these organizations toward the Green Paper. On the basis of this "interest matrix", it is possible to group the different actors into three major cliques: the status–quo oriented (trade unions, consumer federation, the European Space Agency, BT, the CEN, the European Service Industry Forum); the strong supporters (INTUG, the information service providers, IBM, the Belgian Telecommunications Users Group, the telecommunications manufacturers); and a third clique (including the American Chamber of Commerce, the Dutch Business Telecommunications Users Association and Digital Equipment) also broadly supports the Green Paper but still believes that voice monopoly is not sustainable.

The significance of the Green Paper has to be seen in a broader perspective. Basically, this document owes most of its success to its "marketing" by the Commission. In the same way that the "White Paper for the Completion of the European Market by 1992" has become the reference text of what is now called "Europe 1992", the Green Paper is the cornerstone of the achievement of a European telecommunications policy. In its content, the Green Paper does not differ very much from the "Six Action Lines" adopted by the Council in 1984. The two major differences are the Open Network Provision (ONP) concept and the separation of regulation and operation. The latter was implemented by the most influential European countries at that time (the UK, France, Germany). At least in the case of Germany, as we will show in the next section, liberalization was initiated, discussed and legislated during the same period of time in which the Green Paper was finalized, with the EC participating in the German segment of the emerging European telecommunications policy network. ONP was directly derived from the US Open Network Architecture and adapted to the European context. Unlike ONA, ONP was not intended to break down the public networks into basic elements, but was instead intended to offer clear and well defined interfaces for the access by users' and service providers' equipment.

We assume that the pace and density of measures employed in the shaping of a new EC action domain could only be realized in a constellation where telecommunications was still a minor policy matter not receiving much attention from the broader public and the actors of "high politics". As the far–ranging implications of the new policy became clear, the status of telecommunications policy rose on the agenda, the major achievement of the Green Paper. From then on, the functioning of the policy–making process in telecommunications followed very much the same lines as a "transnational network model".

In the subsequent period, EC telecommunications policy became something of a victim of its own success. Shortly after the Council approved the Green Paper guidelines, the greater significance of the policy agenda created more intensive conflicts between more liberal and rather protectionist countries. Inside the Commission as well, some opposition emerged. DG IV, under the guidance of <u>Sutherland</u>, issued a Directive on the liberalization of the terminal equipment market. Although this was part of the Green Paper recommendations, and thus approved by the Council, the "1988 Directive", for instance, was the subject of an appeal in the European Court of Justice by the French government, which was subsequently joined by Belgium, Germany, and Italy.

What was contested by the member states was the fact that the Commission had applied a too broad interpretation of Art. 90 §3 of the Treaty. Based on these provisions, the Commission can take measures to ensure that the special rights which some of the national companies or administrations received from their governments, do not obstruct the full completion of the European Common Market. According to the plaintiffs, by issuing their own Directives (and not a Directive approved by the Council), the Commissioners established a regulatory power which went far beyond their normal supervisory competencies. Art. 90 § 3 was seen by the Member States as a legal trick aimed at undermining the position of the Council in the definition of a European telecommunications policy. A very significant fact in this matter is that the contested Directive was formulated outside the new transnational policy network, carefully set up by the Commission around the Green Paper. The Directive was issued by DG IV without consulting DG XIII, and the other stakeholders.

In general, the far–reaching consequences of this Directive show that the Commission has acquired a much stronger position in European telecommunications than it had a decade ago. The decision of the European Court of Justice, issued in March 1991, generally strengthened the position of the Commission vis a vis the member states and the Council and formally broadened the corridor in which the Commission can bypass other relevant actors in telecommunications.

When developing its more general strategic plans, the Commission continues to rely on the transnational policy network, within which the specific goals are formulated and adjusted to a broad common denominator of a moderate Europe–wide liberalization. Examples of this are the conflicts which unfolded during the formation of the ONP and the service Directives, which were, this time, Council Directives; the member states could not compromise on the definition of value added services to be completely opened to free competition. While the Northern European member states, led by the UK and Germany, were advocating full liberalization of data networks, the Southern European countries (including France and Belgium) were still in favour of monopoly. It was only possible to reach compromises after a long and painstaking negotiation process in December 1989.

In Section 3 we have emphasized that the EC is often in a similar position to national governments regarding difficulties in policy implementation. To ensure effective policy implementation, it has to organize cooperation and support through incorporation of the most relevant social and political interests in the European and national policy arenas. Since the success of EC telecommunications policy integration finally relies on the harmonized adoption of the Directive by the member states, the Commission often backs up this synchronization of EC Directives and national legislation by transnational alliance building – a form of diagonal interaction which is inconceivable within two–level game models. In this case, the Commission directly intervenes in national policy arenas and forms alliances with national policy actors, in order to exert pressure on national governments and legislators. The parallel formulation of the EC Green Paper and the legislation of the German telecommunications reform, is a good example of such diagonal interaction linkages.

## THE EC COMMISSION IN A NATIONAL POLICY ARENA: THE GERMAN TELECOMMUNICATIONS REFORM

The Commission of the EC was not only involved in the executive tasks of formulating proposals and collecting and aggregating national opinions toward a common European telecommunications policy, but it also directly participated in the national German policy process. We mentioned above that, parallel to the formulation process of the Green Paper, Germany also passed a telecommunications reform law.[15] In 1986, the German government established an expert group made up of representatives from the most relevant socio–political groups (the so–called "Witte Commission"). This commission was charged with developing reform proposals, and only a few months after the publication of the Green Paper, it recommended the "Restructuring of German Telecommunications", in a manner quite similar to the guidelines made in the Green Paper (cf. Witte 1988). The major proposals aimed at the organizational separation of telecommunications from the other branches of the PTT, the separation of regulatory functions from operational tasks, and some significant liberalization in the service and equipment domain. The new TELEKOM was to keep its network (transmission) monopoly and also its monopoly on telephone services, but all other services were to be offered in competition with other providers. The market for terminal equipment was to be completely liberalized. One of the experts reporting to the Witte Commission was <u>Herbert Ungerer</u> from DG XIII of the CEC.[16]

The draft on the reform act was largely based on the Witte Commission's proposals. In September 1988, the draft was presented to the Parliament, which passed it on to its committee on post and telecommunications. This committee then organized two hearings. The first hearing was related to the Green Paper and took place in February 1988, a few months before the "Witte report" was published and the reform act was drafted. Once again, Herbert Ungerer participated as the representative for CEC. This hearing was seen by many participants, as an anticipatory hearing on the eve of the German reform. Ungerer was also present at the second hearing in November 1988 which dealt exclusively with the German reform act. Both hearings were attended by more than 50 individuals and organizational representatives.

After the enactment of the reform law in mid–1989, two of the authors of this chapter carried out a survey among the most relevant policy actors, in order to find out what the structures of influence reputation and communication were. While the general results of this analysis have been published in Schneider and Werle (1991), these data are, in this case, used to identify network linkages between the national policy arena in Germany and the European Community context.

It is interesting that, in the telecommunications policy network, 22 of 38 organizations (responding to a questionnaire) reported intensive information exchange with the European Community during the formulation of the German reform law. All 22 of these were national organizations; only 2 of them had governmental status, the other 20 organizations were parties (4), national interest groups (9) and firms (7). On the basis of these network data, we computed indicators relating to the structural position of the CEC in the formulation of the German reform law and found that the CEC had a rather prominent position: it was well integrated in the political communication process, and its influence in the reform process was rated well above the average by the other actors in the network (influence reputation).[17]

# CONCLUSION

The description of the policy formation and implementation processes which exist at the European level demonstrates the important role played by transnational policy networks. They are frameworks for concertation and synchronization of European and national policy processes. From such a perspective, the EC Commission should not be seen as a mere executive agent controlled by the member states but also as an actively participating corporate actor with its own institutional self–interests. The Commission, however, is structurally bound. The Commission and the other EC institutions enjoy autonomous action capacities but they are structurally "biased" towards policies strengthening the EC as a whole.

The Europeification of national policy making in transnational policy networks has been an explicit goal of the Commission. These networks have emerged as a means of coping with increasing interdependency and power dispersion in contemporary national and international politics, as much as a way to bypass PTT incumbency in this field. Just as many nation states are only semi–sovereign with regard to their own society, the European Community has even less power over its member states. Since the dispersion of power resources renders hierarchical governance infeasible, the only way of achieving concertation seems to be through horizontal coordination in policy networks.

The growing Europeification of policy sectors within transnational policy networks also involves some negative aspects. The first point, not explicitly addressed in this paper, refers to the question of inclusiveness or comprehensiveness of the networks. Although the networks often seem to attract most relevant actors, not every actor succeeds in getting access. European policy networks are selective. Interests not represented by resourceful and powerful corporate actors seem to be excluded: the trade unions, for example, and also smaller equipment installers, have had little influence in the debate on deregulation. They could only articulate their opposition after the Green Paper was drafted. However, these actors were influential enough to block, at the national level, any drastic reform of the PTTs in France and in Germany. Moreover, those special and parochial interests which cannot be aggregated within a European dimension are inclined to be neglected or bypassed: the space and satellite segments of the telecommunications market are a case in point. Since economic interests are usually better organized and better informed on the European or transnational level, it seems quite plausible that these developments will create further structural asymmetries in the organization of social interests groups (Kohler–Koch 1991: 63).

The second point to be made is that European policy networks aggravate the difficulty inherent in the classical forms of democratic control already existing at the national level. Bureaucracy in general gains influence at the expense of both the European and the national parliaments. Community legislation normally develops within the framework of closed–door negotiations. Power is increasingly concentrated in the hands of small bureaucratic groups representing key ministries, often successfully insulated from parliamentary control and public scrutiny. Control over EC policy processes may even be used by national governments to widen their existing advantages over parliamentary control, when negotiators in Brussels advance their particular (national) interest positions on the one hand and cite the need for harmonization to quell dissenting opinion at home on the other (Brickman et al. 1985: 67). Warnings about such negative effects of transnational politics were formulated rather early (Kaiser 1972). With respect to European telecommunications, similar reproaches were made by Fangmann (1990), who frankly questioned the democratic legitimation of the EC in this sector.

Finally, we must assess the ability of the European Commission to influence the restructuring of the national telecommunications sectors' operation and to break up the traditional postal–industrial complexes in most of the European countries. The Commission succeeded in transforming this primarily national issue into a European one, pushing the member states towards harmonization of their policies and setting the pace for the constant and convergent development of the legislation in the direction defined by the Commission itself. Therefore, in less than a decade, the telecommunications operators lost their status as public administrations, forming a part of the sovereign core of nation states. To achieve such results, the European Commission had to succeed in mobilizing a network of supporters at the European and the national levels (large users, information technology firms eager to enter the telecommunications area, standardization bodies, "friendly" governments), as well as neutralizing the traditional telecommunications complex. The implementation of the recommendations in the Green Paper is now completely out of the hands of the telecommunications administrations and it has become the almost exclusive domain of the European Commission.

# NOTES

1 Cf. Hallstein et al. (1969), Haas (1964), Scharpf (1988), Hoffmann (1982) and Puchala (1972).
2 Ruggie (1975: 570) defined the regime as a "set of mutual expectations, rules and regulations, plans, organizational energies and financial commitments which have been accepted by a group of states". A more focused definition treats the regime as "institutional and normative arrangements to facilitate cooperation and concerted action" (Stein 1982: 301).
3 In Puchala's (1972: 277) concordance system "actors harmonize their interests, compromise their differences and reap mutual rewards from their interactions". This is facilitated by institutionalized procedures which all actors commit themselves to use and respect. The predominant style of interaction is bargaining; coercion or confrontation is alien to this system.
4 This does not mean that the remarkable integrative power of European judicial review should be underestimated (see e.g. Dehousse and Weiler 1990, Weiler 1991).
5 This sections covers the same topic as an earlier paper by two of the authors (Schneider and Werle 1990) but with a greater emphasis on internal relationships within the EC and the evolution of the actor network in this policy domain.
6 It was not restricted to the EEC countries but included EFTA countries as well. Delegates used to work in subcommittees which met every six months, while a plenipotentiary session was held every two years which defined the working plan of each subcommittee (Labarrère 1985). The PTTs were pleased with the institutional arrangement of the CEPT since it gave them great freedom and was established as a "gentlemen's club". Any difficult decision on which a consensus could not be found had to be delayed to the next meeting six months later.
7 The best account on Unidata can be found in Jublin and Quatrepoint (1976). According to these authors, Unidata failed because the Compagnie Générale d'Electricité (CGE), which was one of the two shareholders of CII with Thompson, successfully lobbied the then President Giscard d'Estaing to turn down the initiative.
8 Basic points of the "definition of the situation" had been outlined by Nora and Minc (1978) in a report to the French president.
9 The European Commission poured $ 3.5 million into the Euronet project (Dang-Nguyen 1986: 276-277).
10 The ability of SWIFT to reach its objectives in negotiations with the PTTs says a great deal about the position of pressure groups in the European context. First, SWIFT is based in Brussels and is quite familiar with the intricacies of the EC bureaucracy. Second, SWIFT is an international consortium of influential banks. Given these conditions, as early as in 1977 SWIFT was able to recognize the importance of legal instruments and to lobby DG IV to get from the PTTs what the Commission is now trying to obtain (fifteen years later!) with the Leased Lines Open Network Provision (ONP) directive: tariffs related to costs.
11 The official document is referred as Com(83) 573 final. It was discussed and criticized by the Senior Official Group for Telecommunications, a group of highranking civil servants from the member states, created by the Council in

November 1983 to advise the Commission on telecommunications issues. The revised version of the Action Lines was issued by the Commission to the Council under the reference Com(84) 277 final.

12 The New Approach applied to any sector, and was designed to accelerate the process of harmonizing the technical conditions of operation of industrial and agricultural goods within the Community. On the "New Approach" see Pelkmans (1987).

13 Such as AFFUTT in France or Deutsche Telecom e.V. in Germany.

14 Some comments by the main stakeholders, including trade unions, on the Green Paper were published in the winter issue of Le Communicateur, December 1987.

15 For a more detailed account of this process see Werle (1990).

16 See Annex 1 in Witte (1988).

17 The value 0.56 compared to the maximum influence of 0.87 and the mean of 0.42. When the highest empirical value is set on a theoretical maximum of 1.0, the Commission displays an influence reputation of 0.64.

# 7

# THE MAKING OF EC ENVIRONMENTAL POLICY

*David Vogel*

## ENVIRONMENTAL REGULATION UNDER THE TREATY OF ROME

While the word "environment" does not appear in the 1957 Treaty of Rome which established the European Community, during the mid–1960s the Community began to recognize that the establishment of a common market also required the enactment of common environmental regulations. The EC adopted its first environmental Directive in 1967: it established standards for classifying, packaging and labeling dangerous substances. Three years later the Council approved a Directive on automotive emissions. In October 1972, at the Paris Summit, the EC Heads of State issued a communique stating that economic expansion was "not an end in itself", and that economic growth should be linked to the "improvement in living and working conditions of life of the citizens of the EC" – a phrase that was taken from the Preamble to the Treaty of Rome (Freestone 1991: 135). The summit called upon the Commission to draw up a Community environmental policy and authorized the European Commission to establish a separate administrative body or directorate whose responsibilities included environmental protection.

The following year, the Council of Ministers adopted the EC's first official environmental programme. Based on Article 2 of the Treaty of Rome, which defined one of the Community's objectives as the promotion of "a harmonious development of economic activities", the EC's "action plan" stated that "major aspects of environmental policy in individual countries must no longer be planned or implemented in isolation... and national policies should be harmonized within the community" (O'Riordan 1979: 249).

The plan stated that the EC's environmental policy would be guided by three objectives or principles (Briggs 1986: 110–111). The first was to reduce and prevent pollution both by "developing protective measures" and by requiring that the "polluter pay". The second principle was that both national and Community regulations should seek to protect the environment as well as improve the quality of life. Thirdly, the Community pledged its support for international initiatives to address environmental problems that could not be adequately addressed on either a regional or national basis.

The Community's Second Environmental Action Programme, adopted in 1977, restated and extended these aims. It also stressed the need for additional research and data collection, and expressed the EC's intention to develop a system of environmental impact assessment. The Community's Third Programme, which was approved in 1983, reflected the growth of concern about unemployment and resource depletion: it emphasized the role of environmental regulation in both preserving scarce resources for future use and "creating employment by developing environmentally compatible industries and technologies" (Briggs 1986: 110–111). It also shifted the Community's priorities from pollution reduction to pollution prevention.

Each of these three action plans was accompanied by a steady expansion in the scope of Community environmental regulations. Between the early 1970s and the mid–1980s, the Community issued 120 Regulations and Directives. A Regulation is directly applicable to all member states and thus automatically becomes part of national law. A Directive establishes a framework for national policies; it only becomes effective after member states have enacted legislation implementing it. Directives generally specify the result to be achieved, leaving it up to national authorities to determine the means and mechanisms of implementation. Most EC environmental rules take the form of Directives.

The EC's environmental policies enacted during this fifteen–year period covered a wide range of areas: the regulation of air, water, noise pollution and waste disposal, the prevention of accidents, safety requirements for chemicals, environmental impact assessment as well as wildlife and habitat protection. The EC's efforts to improve water quality were particularly important: the so–called "bathing water Directive" established uniform standards for bathing water, drinking water and shellfish waters, while another group of Directives limited the discharge of various toxins and chemicals into Community waters. The Sixth Amendment to the Framework Directive on Dangerous Substances, adopted in 1979, established a Community–wide system for the screening of new chemicals.

In addition, the EC addressed a number of global environmental problems. It ratified the Washington Convention on Trade in Endangered Species (CITIS), and the Bonn Convention on the conservation of migratory species; it also banned all imports of seals and seal–pups. Thus by the mid–1980s, most important aspects of both national and international environmental policy had been addressed, in one form or other, at the Community level (Haigh 1989). And in many critical areas of environmental policy–making Brussels had come to play as important a role as the nationstate.

The growth of EC environmental regulation during the 1970s was due to a number of factors. An important role was played by political developments in Europe. EC environmental policy was in part a response to the increase in public concern about environmental issues that took place throughout the entire industrialized world during the late 1960s and early 1970s. A survey taken in the (then) nine EC member states in 1973 reported that "pollution was cited as the most important problem, ahead of inflation, poverty and unemployment" (Liberatore 1991: 289). At the same time, environmental organizations became more politically active in a number of European countries, and most national governments significantly expanded and strengthened the scope of their own regulatory controls over industry.

In order to preserve their legitimacy, EC institutions attempted to respond to these new political forces and public pressures by enacting environmental regulations as well. EC environmental policy represented a way for Community officials to address the "democratic deficit": the gap between the Community's power and its lack of accountability to the electorate of its member states. At the same time, environmental policy–making provided a way for officials in Brussels to preserve the momentum of European integration, which in many other respects had stagnated during the 1970s. Indeed, the steady pace of environmental regulations, Directives and decisions enacted during this period stands in sharp contrast to the "political vicissitudes, budgetary crises, and recurrent waves of Europessimism of the 1970s and early 1980s" (Majone 1991: 95).

Economic considerations also contributed to the expansion of EC environmental regulation. The steady expansion of national environmental regulations posed a potentially serious threat to both the creation and maintenance of a common market. If nations were allowed to adopt their own product standards, such as for chemical safety or automobile emissions, nations with stricter environmental standards would be likely to attempt to "protect" both their citizens and their industries by excluding goods produced in member states with weaker regulatory requirements. Consequently, the free flow of goods within the EC would be impaired.

In the case of production standards, nations that had adopted more stringent pollution controls than other member states would find the goods produced by their industries at a competitive disadvantage. They would therefore be forced to choose between excluding goods produced by member states with weaker regulatory requirements or lowering their own standards to those of other EC member states. The former threatened economic integration; the latter made national regulatory policies hostage to those of the least strict member state.

A third motivation for EC environmental policy was geographic. The twelve Member States of the EC comprise a large land–area – roughly 1.6 million square kilometers – and encompass a considerable diversity of climate and topography. Certainly, the environmental problems of nations on the periphery of the Community, such as Greece and the Netherlands, have little in common and their national environmental policies do not affect the citizens of the other. However, a number of member states are physically close to one another and the quality of their physical environment, as well as the health of their population, is significantly affected by the environmental policies of their neighbours. For example, the Rhine flows west through three EC member states, namely Germany, France and the Netherlands; accordingly the quality of Dutch water is largely determined by the severity of German and French pollution controls. On the other hand, because winds in Europe travel from west to east, the air quality in northern Europe is affected by industrial emissions from Britain. As one journalist observed, "Environmental regulations are among the world's toughest in ... West Germany and the Netherlands. But that does little good when winds waft Britain's loosely regulated power–plant fumes and their product, acid rain, eastward" (Diehl 1988: 1). Equally important, industrial accidents do not respect national boundaries.

A number of important EC environmental initiatives reflect the high degree of physical interdependence of the Community. For example, the "Seveso Directive" was adopted in 1982 following a major industrial accident in Italy that unleashed large quantities of the chemical dioxin into the atmosphere. It addressed the issue of accident prevention and required industries to prepare safety reports and emergency response plans. The EC's Directive on the Conservation of Wild Birds, adopted in 1979, required member states "to preserve, maintain or reestablish a sufficient diversity and area of habitats for birds", many of which migrated across national boundaries (Haigh 1989: 288). And following the disclosure that 41 drums of waste from Seveso which had been lost in transit had been found in the French countryside, a Directive was approved that established a system for controlling and regulating the collection and disposal of hazardous wastes moving across frontiers.

For all these reasons – political, economic and geographic – the Community attempted to harmonize a wide range of national environmental regulations. Not surprisingly, this effort led to considerable conflict between those nations which favoured stricter environmental standards and those which did not. The former, most notably Germany, Denmark and the Netherlands, were relatively affluent and had strong domestic environmental movements. Other nations, such as the UK, France and Italy, had weaker environmental pressure–groups and their industries were less willing or able to absorb the costs of stricter environmental controls. Still others, such as Greece and Spain, were even less interested in Community air and water quality standards. Not only were they relatively poor, but they were physically distant from the "core" of the EC and thus unaffected by acid rain emissions or the quality of the EC's major rivers. Further complicating agreement was the requirement of the Treaty of Rome that all Directives be approved unanimously.

Thus it took the Community five years before it could reach agreement on a Directive reducing emissions of sulphur dioxide (Haigh and Baldock 1989: 32–35). The positions of the member states fell into four groups. West Germany, the Netherlands and Denmark were prepared to spend substantial sums on retrofitting their existing plants. However, both Britain and Italy, which were less affluent and whose power plants burned considerable qualities of coal, were not. France and Belgium were relatively indifferent to sulphur emission standards since they relied heavily on nuclear power. Most of the remaining nations were not interested in the Directive since they were not affected by acid rain in the first place.

The Large Combustion Directive, which was finally approved in June 1988, advanced a rather complex formula to reconcile these differences. Emissions of $SO_2$ would be reduced in three stages –1993, 1998 and 2003

– while NOX emissions would be reduced in two stages. In addition, the percentage reductions of each pollutant for each stage varied by country. Thus Belgium, Germany, France, the Netherlands and Luxembourg were required to reduce their $SO_2$ emissions by 40 percent by 1993. On the other hand, Spain was not required to reduce its emissions at all while Portugal was permitted to increase its emissions.

The form of pollution control also led to disputes among the member states. For example, most nations favoured uniform emission standards for water pollutants, since that would impose roughly similar costs on firms throughout the EC. The British, however, argued that since their rapidly flowing rivers could absorb relatively large amounts of pollution without impairing water quality, uniform emission standards were inappropriate; they instead favored water quality standards. "As one British official put it, `Italy economically benefits from the amount of sunshine it receives each year. Why should not our industry be able to take similar advantage of our long coastline. . . and rapidly flowing waters?'" (Vogel 1989: 103). Once again the result was a complex compromise: the emissions of highly hazardous substances would be controlled by uniform emission standards, while less dangerous substances would be regulated by water quality standards.

Notwithstanding the steady growth of EC environmental regulation, the legal basis of EC environmental policy remained somewhat tenuous. Most Community environmental policy could be justified under Article 100 of the Treaty, which authorized the harmonization of all national regulations that directly affected the functioning or establishment of a common market. However in a number of cases, the link between EC environmental regulations and the common market was less clear.

What, for example, did establishing EC standards for drinking or bathing water quality have to do with economic integration? Why should the Community require the member states to protect wild birds? To justify its environmental regulations in these areas, the EC was forced to rely upon Article 235 of the Treaty, which authorized legislation not envisaged elsewhere if it was "necessary to attain . . . one of the objectives of the Community" (Freestone 1991: 136). Since the Preamble to the Treaty of Rome had declared that improving the "living and working conditions of life of the citizens of the EC" was a legitimate Community objective, it presumably followed that the EC could legislate on any aspect of the environment that it chose. Not surprisingly, this somewhat strained legal defence was not entirely persuasive (Close 1978: 461–468).

Moreover the Treaty of Rome, by not explicitly mentioning environmental protection, provided EC policy–makers with no framework for balancing environmental protection with other EC goals, the most important of which was obviously the creation of the common market itself. For virtually any level of environmental regulation was compatible with increased economic integration, providing that it was decided at the Community level. Accordingly, many observers argued that the requirements of a number of EC Directives tended to reflect the "least common denominator" and that therefore the Community had, in effect, subordinated environmental goals to the creation of a common market.

## THE SINGLE EUROPEAN ACT

On 1 July 1987, the Treaty of Rome was revised by the Single European Act (SEA). While the most important purpose of this amendment to the Community's constitution was to facilitate the creation of a single European market, it also introduced a number of important changes into Community environmental policy and policy–making.

Most important, Article 100A of the SEA explicitly recognized the improvement of environmental quality as a legitimate Community objective in its own right. This meant that EC environmental policies need no longer be justified in terms of their contribution to economic integration. The EC now had a firm constitutional basis for regulating any aspect of the environment. Even more important, the SEA stated that in harmonizing national regulations, "the Commission . . . will take as a base a high level of [environmental] protection". This explicitly linked harmonization with the improvement of environmental quality, rather than with, as under the Treaty of Rome, simply economic integration.

Article 130R further declared that "environmental protection requirements shall be a component of the Community's other policies" (Kramer 1987: 651). This provision accorded environmental protection an unusually high priority among the Community's objectives, since no other EC goal was granted a commensurate provision. In practical terms, it strengthened the hands of the Commission's Environmental Directorate (DG XI) in its conflicts with those Directorates whose focus was essentially economic.

To reassure those member states who feared that harmonization would require them to relax existing national regulations, both Article 100A and 130T explicitly granted member states the right to maintain or introduce national environmental standards stricter than those approved by Brussels, provided they did not constitute a form of "hidden protectionism" and were otherwise compatible with the Treaty of Rome (Kramer 1987: 681). The determination as to whether or not a national regulation that affected the completion of the internal market created an open or disguised barrier to trade was left up to the European Court of Justice (Vandermeersch 1987: 559–588).

The Single European Act also facilitated the adoption of environmental regulations by the Council. Prior to 1987, all Community legislation had to be approved unaminously. Legislation approved under Article 130, the SEA's environmental article, still required unanimity. However, the SEA permitted Directives approved under Article 100A – which provides for the approximation of laws concerned with the functioning of the common market – to be approved by a "qualified majority," defined as 54 of 76 votes. This provided an alternative means for enacting environmental legislation, one which deprived any single member state of the power to block approval. In fact, virtually all environmental Directives enacted since the passage of the SEA have been based on 100A.

The Single European Act also expanded the role of the European Parliament, which has generally been more supportive of stricter environmental standards than the Council, in shaping Community legislation. For ten articles of the EC Treaty, the SEA established a "cooperation procedure" under which Parliament has the right to propose amendments to legislation approved by the Council of Ministers. If the Commission chooses to retain these amendments, then the Council must then either reject them unanimously or adopt them by a qualified majority.

The SEA also contributed to the strengthening of EC environmental policy in another, more indirect, way. A primary purpose of the new Community treaty was to accelerate the move toward the creation of a single internal market – a goal which had been formally outlined in a Commission White Paper issued a few years earlier. However, Community officials recognized that the removal of all barriers to intra–Community trade by the end of 1992 was also likely to exacerbate Europe's environmental problems. A 1989 report entitled, <u>"1992" the Environmental Dimension</u>, examined some of the adverse environmental consequences of the completion of the internal market. The most important of these would be a dramatic increase in transportation, which would significantly increase emissions of both sulphur dioxide and nitrogen oxides. In addition, by accelerating intra–community trade, economic integration increased the exposure of member states to the import of environmental "bads" such as toxic and hazardous wastes from other member states. Thus the Community's renewed commitment to economic integration made the strengthening of EC environmental standards even more urgent.

The strengthening of environmental protection within the Community's constitution both reflected and reinforced the public's growing concern with environmental issues that took place throughout Europe during the latter part of the 1980s. Stimulated in part by the Soviets' Chernobyl disaster and a massive chemical spill of toxins into the River Rhine that destroyed a half million fish in four countries – both of which occurred in 1986 – environmental issues moved rapidly to a prominent position on the political agenda in a number of EC Member States. The Washington Post observed:

> Dead seals in the North Sea, a chemical fire on the Loire, killer algae off the coast of Sweden, contaminated drinking water in Cornwall (England). A drumbeat of emergencies has intensified the environmental debate this year in Europe, where public concern about pollution has never been higher. (Herman 1988: 19)

A poll taken in December 1986 reported that 52 percent of the German electorate regarded environment quality as the most important issue facing their nation (Kirkland 1988: 118). In 1987, the German Green Party received 8.3 percent of the votes cast for the Bundestag and increased their number of seats in the legislative body of the Federal Republic to 42. More significantly, in European Parliament elections held in June 1989, Europe's Green parties captured an additional seventeen seats, bringing their total representation to 37 and making them among the biggest "winners" of the first "European" election held after the enactment of the SEA. An EC official publication observed in 1990 that

> Major disasters [and] global problems like ozone depletion and the greenhouse effect, and quality of life issues such as drinking water and air pollution have all contributed in recent years to a "greening" of European public opinion, to a widening consensus in favour of cleaner and more sustainable economic growth. (Environmental Policy 1990: 5).

A survey published by the EC in 1989 reported "strong support for a common EC–wide approach to environmental protection" (<u>Environmental Policy</u> 1990:5).

Since the passage of the SEA, the "momentum for environmental protection [has] accelerated dramatically" (Sbragia 1992: 4). Between 1989 and 1991, the EC enacted more environmental legislation than in the previous twenty years combined. "It now has over 450 regulations in effect and is adding new ones at a rate of about 100 a year" (Bromberg 1992: 5). Not only have many EC standards been significantly strengthened – in some cases approaching American ones – but the EC has also come to play a leadership role in the making of global environmental policy. One example concerns the protection of the ozone layer. In 1987, 31 nations, including the EC, signed the Montreal Protocols in which they pledged to reduce the production of chlorofluorocarbons by 50 percent by the end of the century. However, in March 1989, the EC went a step further, announcing that its member states had agreed to cut production of this chemical by 85 percent as soon as possible and to eliminate production entirely by the year 2000.

The EC's most recent Environmental Action Programme has established four priorities: the preservation of the ozone layer, mitigation of the greenhouse effect, comprehensive regulation of hazardous wastes and fighting tropical deforestation. In 1989, the European Council voted to create a European Environmental Agency, though to date this agency has not been established due to disagreement over where it will be located. Its purpose is to serve as a central information clearing house and a coordinator for national centres of environmental monitoring and evaluation.

However, as the scope of Community regulations has grown, the problem of enforcing them has become more acute. The increased number of Community regulations not only makes the monitoring of their enforcement more difficult, but also more urgent, since significant variations in national compliance threaten to disadvantage industries in some EC member states. The Community itself has no police or enforcement powers. It only knows of a violation if someone complains to it. If it finds the complaint is justified, its final legal recourse is to sue the member state in the European Court. This, however, is a time–consuming procedure; an average of 50 months elapses between the arrival of a complaint and a ruling from the court. The problem of enforcement is further complicated by the fact that while EC Directives are intended to bind national governments, in many countries it is local governmental officials who are responsible for enforcing them.

As of May 1991, the EC had a backlog of 372 cases of non–compliance with environmental Directives and Regulations ("Dirty Dozen...", The Economist 1991: 52). Three–quarters of its disciplinary proceedings concerned four areas of environmental law: birds, bathing water, drinking water, and environmental impact assessments. While the Commission received more complaints about the UK than any other country, this reflected not so much the relative lack of British compliance as the eagerness of British environmental groups to complain to Brussels. In some of the Latin countries, public distrust of government bureaucracies discourages people from complaining in the first place. Spain and Italy had the poorest record of compliance with the decisions of the European Court; the former does not even have an Environment Ministry.

In February 1990, the EC Commissioner in charge of environmental protection publicly complained about unsatisfactory member state implementation of the Community's environmental Directives (Wagerbaum 1990: 465). In June 1990, the European Council acknowledged the extent of the enforcement problem by adopting a "Declaration on the Environmental Imperative," which stated that "Community environmental legislation will only be effective if it is fully implemented and enforced by the Member States" (Wagerbaum 1990: 455). The following month, 130 members of the European Parliament proposed the establishment of a committee on the transposition and application of Community environmental legislation.

A number of suggestions have been advanced for improving national compliance with Community Directives. One is to allow citizens to sue their own governments in national courts; presently the ability of citizens to file such suits is determined by national rather than EC laws. Another is to provide the newly established European Environment Agency with the resources to monitor national compliance, thus freeing the Commission from having to rely upon citizen complaints to determine if its Directives are being enforced. A third is to create a Community "ombudsman". To date, none of these proposals has been adopted, but this may well change in the near future.

## INTEGRATION AND REGULATION

The Treaty on European Union, signed at Maastricht in February 1992, further expanded the Community's legal competence in the area of environmental regulation. Article 130R added another objective to the Community's environmental policy, namely the promotion of "measures at the international level to deal with regional or global environmental problems". Article 130S permitted the Community to adopt "measures concerning town and country planning, land use ... and management of water resources" as well as measures "significantly affecting a member state's choice between different energy sources and the general structure of its energy supply" (Archer and Butler 1992: 116). Finally, Article 130T confirmed the language of the Single European Act which stated that the Community legislation shall not prevent any member state from either "maintaining or introducing more stringent protective measures (provided they were) compatible with this Treaty" (Archer and Butler 1992: 116).

Notwithstanding the ongoing debate over the Maastricht Treaty, it is clear that at least in the area of environmental regulation, the Community is already a federal structure. While implementation remains primarily in the hands of national and local authorities, the role of the Community in formulating environmental rules and regulations has steadily expanded. Not only is Brussels making policy in more and more areas that were formerly decided at either the national or the local level, but the growing importance of international environmental agreements has provided the EC with an additional regulatory role. In areas such as the protection of endangered species, the protection of the ozone layer, and global warming, the EC both negotiates on behalf of its member states and is responsible for assuring their compliance.

At the same time, tension between Brussels and the member states appears to be increasing. The most important source of this tension appears to be between the EC's interest in harmonizing national regulatory standards in order to prevent them from serving as non–tariff barriers, and the persistent efforts of a few member states with strong green movements, most notably Germany, the Netherlands and Denmark, in enacting regulations that are stricter than those of the EC itself.

Through the mid–1980s, many Community environmental regulations functioned as much as a ceiling as a floor. This was notably the case with respect to automobile emissions, without doubt the most contentious area of Community environmental regulation during the last two decades.

The various Community Directives on the lead content of gasoline enacted during the 1970s and the first half of the 1980s specified both minimum and maximum standards. Likewise, the Luxembourg Compromise on automobile emissions, adopted in 1987, both allowed member states to set lower emission levels than those specified in the Directive, and refused to permit any member state to exclude any vehicles that complied with the emission standards of the Directive.

Thus the Community, while attempting to respond to growing public pressures for stricter environmental standards, was equally determined to prevent environmental regulation from interfering with economic integration. When faced with a tension between the two, it chose the latter over the former, much to the frustration of Germany, which wanted to impose both stricter standards on its own vehicles and restrict the import of automobiles from member states with laxer national standards.

In contrast, the Small Car Directive, adopted in 1989 after long and protracted negotiations, succeeded in reconciling stricter environmental standards and economic integration: it significantly strengthened the EC's automobile emission standards, most notably by requiring small as well as large vehicles to be equipped with catalytic convertors, and at the same time made these standards uniform. This Directive represented a major victory for European environmental pressure–groups, as well as an important step forward for European integration; it meant that EC environmental standards no longer simply reflected the lowest common denominator among the member states, but instead could serve as a vehicle for the gradual tightening of regulatory standards.

However, the basic national divisions that have plagued EC environmental regulation from the outset have persisted. Germany, Denmark and the Netherlands continue to insist on their right to establish stricter environmental standards than those established by the EC, even if, or in some cases, because, these regulations serve as trade barriers; however strict the EC's standards, they want to go a step further. On the other hand, Britain, France and Italy continue to place a greater priority on integration: they do not want member states to be allowed to enact environmental regulations that will make it more difficult for their industries to market their products throughout the Community.

The 1988 decision of the European Court in <u>Commission of the European Communities</u> v. <u>Denmark</u> represents an important development in this ongoing dispute between central EC institutions and various member states. The Court upheld the legality of the most important provisions of a Danish bottle recycling law, even though this legislation made it more difficult for non–Danish bottles to gain access to the Danish market. This decision marked the first time that the Court had sanctioned a trade barrier on environmental grounds – even though the Court had previously sustained a number of trade barriers for other reasons, primarily having to do with health and safety. It now upheld a national regulation that clearly interfered with the free movement of goods in the Community on the grounds that such interference was necessary to achieve the environmental goals of a member state. This decision thus represented an important victory for regulation over integration.

While "it will take further cases to show exactly where the European Court draws the line between greenery and trade" ("Freedom ...", The Economist 1989: 22) the political impact of the Danish bottle case has already been felt. In 1989, the German government enacted legislation requiring a compulsory deposit on all plastic and glass bottles. The Commission decided not to challenge the German scheme – although it did demand one relatively minor modification in it: the German government could not require that the deposits only be collected by retail stores. However, two years later, in April 1991, the German government approved a far more ambitious and sweeping recycling law – one "tougher than anything introduced in any other country" ("A Wall of A Waste", The Economist 1991: 73) The objective of the German law was to reduce the amount of waste going into landfill and incineration. Beginning on 1 December 1992, all companies were required to take back and recycle all packaging used during transport, or pay another firm to do so. As of 1 April 1992, the law also covered "secondary" packaging, such as gift wrapping and boxes. On 1 January 1993, all packaging, including sweet and butter wrappers, will be included as well.

The Economist noted "the ferocity of the new obligation is extraordinary. When fully implemented, it will require a level of recycling that not even the most environmentally conscious middle–class community in any western nation has achieved" ("A Wall of Waste", The Economist 1991: 73). Ninety percent of all glass and metals as well as 80 percent of paper, board and plastics must be recycled. Incineration, for whatever reason, is not permitted. The German Environmental Ministry subsequently announced that it planned to extend the recycling requirement to the manufacturers of automobiles and electronic goods.

Not surprisingly, the European packaging industry was "irate", arguing that the German law crossed "the indistinct line between national environmental protection and protection of a more reprehensible sort" ("Free Trade's Green Hurdle", The Economist 1991: 61). Importers specifically complained to the EC that the packaging law included a provision, inserted at the last minute, requiring that only 28 per cent of all beer and soft drinks containers can be disposable. "Packagers claim that this clause was inserted for the benefit of small brewers in politically sensitive Bavaria, who will find it easier to collect and refill the empties" ("Free Trade's Green Hurdle", The Economist 1991: 61). They also charged that the provision requiring companies to collect their used packaging for recycling would discourage retailers from stocking imported goods.

Britain's Industry Council for Packaging and the Environment contended that the rules "restrict the free movement of goods into Germany" ("Free Trade's Green Hurdle", The Economist 1991: 61). Eucofel, a European trade association representing fruit and vegetable shippers, complained its member firms were unable to recycle the wooden crates in which most of the fruits and vegetables imported into Germany were shipped. One firm stated it was told by its German distributor to use "biodegradable" nails in its crates.

Not surprisingly, a number of non–German firms "complained vociferously " to the EC (Thornhill 1991). Nonetheless, fearful of being labelled "anti–green", the Commission has hesitated to take Germany to the European Court. Instead the EC has attempted to produce its own packaging Directive. But harmonizing national recycling laws has proven extremely difficult as both the degree of public enthusiasm for recycling, as well as the existence of the necessary infrastructure to accomplish it, varies considerably among the EC's member states. However, whatever standards the EC ultimately decides on, they are likely to be laxer than Germany's. This in turn will present the Community with a difficult political and legal problem. If the German law is allowed to stand, industries from member states such as the UK will be outraged. But if the German law is declared unconstitutional, both German industry, which has already invested substantial resources in complying with their nation's packaging requirements, as well as the German environmental movement, will be upset. In short, the making of EC environmental policy is likely to remain highly contentious.

## CONCLUSION

The creation of the single European market is an ongoing process. Not only was it not concluded at the end of 1992; it might <u>never</u> be concluded. One important reason is that the regulatory agenda is constantly changing. As new environmental issues emerge, many will present additional potential obstacles for intra–Community trade that could not have been anticipated at the time of the White Paper. As long as both the priority placed on environmental protection and the competitive impact of regulation on industries in different countries varies across the EC, some member states will attempt to enact regulations that in turn will be perceived by other member states as non–tariff barriers. The opportunities are endless: as soon as one kind of regulation is harmonized, another source of contention among the member states or between the member states and Brussels emerge. 1992 was not so much a date as a moving target. And it is a goal whose achievement has been made more difficult by the emergence of environmental protection as a highly visible area of public policy making at both the national and Community level.

The tension between economic integration and environmental regulation can be resolved in one of three ways: first, the ability of member states to impose their own, stricter national environmental regulations can be restricted by Brussels in the interests of economic integration; second, the two can be reconciled by the enactment of strict, harmonized standards; and third, member states can be allowed to establish stricter national environmental laws, even if they interfere with the free movement of goods within the EC.

Clearly the Commission, along with nations such as the UK and France, favours the second alternative. And undoubtedly, an increasing number of environmental regulations will be harmonized. Indeed, to some extent the enactment of stricter laws by the various member states can be seen as part of the dynamic of Community policy–making: these laws help place additional pressure on Brussels to establish stricter, Commmunity–wide standards. But there are also important counter-pressures pushing in the direction of the third alternative. As the principle of subsidiarity assumes increasing importance in the negotiations surrounding the interpretation and ratifaction of the Maastricht Treaty, member states may well be allowed additional opportunities to establish their own environmental standards. How far the EC can or will allow this tendency to go is unclear, especially if these standards interfere with intra–Community trade. What is predictable is continual tension between environmental regulation and integration.

Finally, it is important to place the making of EC environmental policy in a broader, global context. Just as there has been a substantial expansion of the role of the Community in the making of European environmental policy, so are a growing number of national environmental regulations being harmonized at the global level. Yet at the same time, international economic integration is increasingly being threatened by the enactment of national environmental regulations which serve, either intentionally or inadvertently, as trade barriers. In this sense, the challenge faced by the EC is similar to that faced by the GATT: when, and under what circumstances should nations be permitted to restrict trade in the interests of protecting or improving environmental quality? Likewise, many of the disputes over environmental regulations between Canada and the United States under the North American Free Trade Agreement are strikingly similar to those of the EC; the province of Ontario has recently enacted recycling legislation that is similiar to Denmark's, much to the outrage of American bottlers who claim that it violates the terrms of NAFTA. In short, the challenges the EC will face in formulating environmental policy in the 1990s are not unique to it.

# 8
# TOWARDS A COMMON EC ENERGY POLICY

*Svein S. Andersen*

## INTRODUCTION

This article deals with the emergence of a common EC energy policy. What drives the development in this policy area? How are decisions made? How is a common EC energy policy linked to the development of EC institutions and the movement towards European union? The struggle over a common energy policy is a special case of the Europeification of policy–making. It takes place in an area characterized by strong conflicts between a common EC policy, on the one hand, and divergent national policies, on the other. Nevertheless, there has been a strengthening of common EC policies since the late 1980s.

Under what conditions can we expect a development of a transnational authority and common EC policy? The answer to these questions has usually been found within two major theoretical frameworks. One approach is the "realpolitik" perspective. According to this, EC authority develops from below, as the gradual widening and deepening of compromise and consensus. The other approach takes a macro perspective, viewing the strengthening of common policy as increased integration, driven by functional prerogatives in the EC system. None of these perspectives is consistent with the development in the energy sector. However, before we elaborate on the different perspectives, we will briefly summarize the major changes which are occurring with respect to EC common energy policy.

## OVERVIEW AND PERSPECTIVE

Until the end of the 1980s, the EC lacked a common policy in the energy field. This was demonstrated through the oil shocks of the 1970s. However, despite the development of a common energy policy, it continued to be, up until the last few years, nothing but the sum of the member countries' policies. At the same time, parts of the national energy policies and energy industries came close to constituting a counter culture to the EC vision of a free market, with their strong elements of protectionism and monopoly. The coal and electricity sectors have long traditions of this, while the gas sector developed only during the 1960s and 1970s. The exception is the oil industry which, in practically all countries, has strong elements of international orientation, even where state oil companies are strong (Weyman–Jones 1986). One divergent factor relates to the strong monopolistic elements in the down stream sectors in some countries, like Portugal and Spain (White Paper on energy 1988).

The EC is still far from having created a common energy policy. This means that national interests will continue to play a central role in the coming years. During recent years, however, a number of important initiatives have been taken to strengthen supranational influence on the energy policy. What the results will be for member countries is still not clear, but the EC is in the process of working out a number of Directives which may turn out to be very important (Matlary 1991, Lyons 1992, Padgett 1992). As to the setting of the agenda and new initiatives, the trend is clear. The stronger the impact of a common EC energy policy, the less influence the traditional actors, member countries and national companies in the energy sector will have (Padgett 1992).

Initiatives in the field of energy policy on the EC level are increasingly influenced by general efforts at deregulation, environmental policies and supply concerns. This development is further strengthened by the EC treaty reform, which paves the way for a binding cooperation towards a union, even though it is not clear how fast and how extensive the development will be. By the end of 1992 both the Third Party Access (TPA) Directive and the Licence Directive for oil and gas had been blocked.

The evolution of an energy policy is, however, closely related to the development of the EC's supranationality and to the relative strength of the different institutions in the EC decision–making system (Andersen 1992, Andersen and Eliassen 1992). Traditionally two major models have been used. That which explains the development of transnational authority and common policy, emphasizes the gradual emergence of common and overlapping interests. This process is driven by rational actors building coalitions (Morgenthau et al. 1973, Waltz 1979). The lack of overlapping interests between member countries and national energy sectors is consistent with the lack of a common EC policy in the energy sector up until the late 1980s. However, it is not possible to explain the emergence of common policy over the last years in these terms. On the contrary, such a tendency would seem highly unlikely from this down–up perspective since the lack of, or small degree of, overlap is a consistent characteristic of the energy sector.

The other major perspective used to explain the emergence of common policy is that of integration theory, or neofunctionalist theory. This kind of argument exists in different versions. The basic idea is that integration evolves because of the functional requirements of highly interdependent systems, given the need for a higher degree of rationality. The integration of the EC could be regarded as an inexorable process. As an explanatory framework for EC integration, it was abandoned in the 1970s. Later post–neofunctional studies of EC decision–making focused on empirical description and documentation, rather than prediction and generalization (Nye 1968, Keohane and Nye 1977, Moravcsik 1991).

Leaving aside the idea of historical necessity, the neofunctional perspective also contained a scheme for more concrete analysis of policy sectors. In this sense, it represented a pluralist model of international politics. The model accepted that states could be complex actors, as well as taking into account the role of non–state actors. Of the latter type of actor, the most important was considered to be the Commission. Member state actions were regarded as the outcome of various pressures from interest groups in the wider society, also allowing for transnational networks of interests (George 1991: 20–21).

A key concept in neofunctional theory was that of spill–over. The functional spill–over referred to pressures stemming from the interconnectedness of industrial economies. In such systems it was not possible to isolate one sector from the rest. As a result, the successful integration of one sector at the EC level, rested on the integration of others:

> If, for example, an attempt was made to rationalize the production of coal, not just in one economy... it would prove necessary to bring other forms of energy into the scheme; otherwise a switch by one state away from coal towards a reliance on oil or nuclear would throw out all of the

calculations on which the rationalization of coal production was based. (George 1991:22)

However, the lack of a common energy policy in other areas for a period of 40 years after the formation of the ECSC, demonstrates that functional spill–over does not necessarily follow.

The idea of political spill–over involves the build up of political pressures, in favour of further integration within the states involved:

So the creation of ECSC led the representatives of the coal and steel industries in member states switching at least part of their political lobbying from national governments to the High Authority. Relevant trade unions and consumers followed suit. (George 1991:23)

Up until now, the problems relating to the common energy policy in the EC have been only marginally impacted by the ECSC. There has been a lack of progress. However, the changes which have been taking place since the late 1980s are consistent with the notion of political spill–over. The energy policy case demonstrates the interaction between new transnational institutions and authority, on the one hand, and sectoral policy–making, on the other. Issues and decision–making processes are structured from above, changing the rules defining legitimate actors, arguments and resources.

EC energy policy has been driven by the Commission which has exploited institutional rules in order to take the initiative and to redefine the energy sector in relation to the internal market, environmental policy and foreign policy. The areas to which energy is linked all represent areas where transnational institutions have been assigned tasks which the neofunctionalists call inherently expansive (Cameron 1991: 25). This is perhaps most obvious in the case of the Internal Market.

The neofunctionalist argument can be summarized in the following way: "To the extent that inherently expansive tasks (as the realization of the internal market) are assigned to transnational institutions, the responsibility and powers of, and support for, those transnational institutions will tend to increase their power" (Cameron 1991: 25). However, this concept seems to go too far. There is no necessary relationship here. Empirically it is still not clear why certain solutions may be sucessfully implanted in new sectors or how institutions, rules and decisions in other parts of the EC system may structure one specific policy sector. What is needed is a more specific framework for the studying of such processes.

The idea captured by the concept of political spill–over may be a useful starting point, but more as a framework pointing out the direction than as a ready made model. A key dimension to be taken into account is the tension between national and transnational policy–making; an important aspect of this is the interaction between national interests and institutional dynamics at the central EC level. National interests are important, but they have to be articulated and legitimated within a national as well as a transnational context. However, institutions not only provide mandates and regulate actions. The institutional framework of the EC defines actors, issues and resources, as well as possible solutions, in competition with national frameworks (Meyer and Scott 1983, Olsen 1992).

Institutional changes at the EC level alter the relationship between the different perspectives, resources and sources of influence of the organizations and institutions. An example of this is how the majority rule of decision–making in the Council of Ministers, relating to the Internal Market, strengthens transnational authority. If issues are defined as the further implementation of the Internal Market, and here the Commission has room to exercise judgement, this changes the relative weight of the arguments which exist between the transnational interests and the member state interests.

It is hard to find policy areas where the tension between transnational and national interests is stronger than in the energy sector. The outcome of the struggle between these levels is far from determined at this stage. However, even if some countries and industries try to block or slow down the development of an internal market in the energy sector, there are forces of integration at work in the sector independent of such interests. The question is how, under what conditions and in what areas transnational authority and a common policy will emerge.

We shall continue by taking a closer look at the main phases which have occurred until now and how the development of a common energy policy is related to the development of the institutions and transnational authority of the EC.

## UNTIL THE LATE 1980s: NATIONAL POLICIES DOMINATE

Two of the original organizations in the EC were related to energy, especially the European Atomic Energy Commission, but also the European Coal and Steel Union. Together with the European Economic Community, these two organizations form the European Community or EC. Energy was, therefore, an essential part of the EC, right from the beginning. At the same time, the Treaty of Rome negotiations were finalized in the shadow of the Suez War. It seems, therefore, to be a paradox that a common policy in the energy field has been more or less absent until the last few years. National interests have overpowered attempts at establishing a common policy on the EC level.

There are several reasons for this being the case. Firstly, the notion of "energy" covers different forms of energy such as coal, oil, gas, atomic energy and alternative energy sources. It was only after the oil crises in the 1970s, that energy as such came into focus. For the member nations, the national energy sectors have always had a central role to play, and there have been great differences between which sectors were important or problematical in the different countries. Coal, for example, has a strong position in Germany and the UK, relating to local resource

**Table 1**. *Most important indigious productions source.*

| Country | 1972 | 1982 | 1990 |
|---------|------|------|------|
| Belgium | coal | coal | nuclear |
| Denmark | solid fuels* | oil | oil |
| France | coal | nuclear | nuclear |
| Germany | coal | coal | coal |
| Greece | coal | coal | coal |
| Ireland | solid fuels* | gas | gas |
| Luxembourg | hydro | solid fuels* | solid fuels * |
| Netherlands | gas | gas | gas |
| Spain | coal | coal | nuclear |
| UK | coal | oil | oil |

* Solid fuels other than coal
*Source: Energy Balances of OECD Countries*, 1986-87, 1989-90, IEA, 1989, 1992.

extraction in order to create employment. In France, the atomic industry has had a special position, as it has been linked to the military nuclear programme (see Table 1).

This variety of national interests leads us to the other main point, namely that the member countries are in very different situations regarding energy. First of all, it has been the preference of the member countries to solve their problems by themselves. This has dominated EC energy policy. The search for solutions has been, as a rule, dominated by prominent elements of oligopoly and monopoly (EC White paper on energy: European Communities, Commission 1988), and has, therefore, carried greater political weight for national authorities.

What the EC countries had in common was their great dependence on energy, and particularly oil imports (see Tables 2 and 3). This had been increased by the transition from coal to oil which had taken place in the 1960s, since almost all countries were completely dependent upon imports. As a consequence countries were extremely vulnerable to dramatic oil price variations and the security of supply. Such factors were clearly evident during the oil price increases in 1973/74 and 1978. Even if the UK had been self–sufficient from the end of the 1970s, the price effect would have been the same.

**Table 2.** *Self–suffiency in oil*

| Country | 1972 | 1982 | 1990 |
| --- | --- | --- | --- |
| Belgium | 0.00 | 0.00 | 0.00 |
| Denmark | 0.01 | 0.28 | 0.66 |
| France | 0.02 | 0.03 | 0.04 |
| Germany | 0.06 | 0.06 | 0.06 |
| Greece | 0.00 | 0.07 | 0.05 |
| Ireland | 0.00 | 0.00 | 0.00 |
| Italy | 0.01 | 0.02 | 0.05 |
| Luxembourg | 0.00 | 0.00 | 0.00 |
| Netherlands | 0.02 | 0.05 | 0.08 |
| Portugal | 0.00 | 0.00 | 0.00 |
| Spain | 0.00 | 0.03 | 0.02 |
| UK | 0.01 | 1.36 | 1.04 |

*Source: Energy Balances of OECD Countries, 1986-87, 1989-90, IEA, 1989, 1992.*

**Table 3.** *Self–suffiency in energy total*

| Country | 1972 | 1982 | 1990 |
|---|---|---|---|
| Belgium | 0.15 | 0.20 | 0.27 |
| Denmark | 0.02 | 0.12 | 0.52 |
| France | 0.24 | 0.32 | 0.47 |
| Germany | 0.48 | 0.51 | 0.47 |
| Greece | 0.20 | 0.34 | 0.40 |
| Ireland | 0.33 | 0.36 | 0.32 |
| Italy | 0.17 | 0.17 | 0.17 |
| Luxembourg | 0.00 | 0.01 | 0.01 |
| Netherlands | 0.81 | 1.04 | 0.90 |
| Portugal | 0.21 | 0.13 | 0.13 |
| Spain | 0.26 | 0.29 | 0.35 |
| UK | 0.48 | 1.14 | 0.98 |

*Source: Energy Balances of OECD Countries*, 1986-87, 1989-90, IEA, 1989, 1992.

The first oil shock was the strongest. From 1973 to 1975 the growth rate went down from 6.1 percent to minus 0.2 percent, while inflation went up from 7.3 percent to 12.5 percent. The second shock was characterized by a certain adjustment to high prices, but the results were still significant. During the period 1978–1981, the growth rate went down from 3.1 percent to 1.6 percent, while inflation went up from 8.4 percent to 10.7 percent (see Figures 6 and 7). Another expression of the dramatic effect of the oil price increases was that the EC trade deficit went from $ 4.3 billion in 1978 to $ 30 billion in 1979.

The adjustment which took place in the member countries was driven by the individual country's interests. Neither the EC nor the International Energy Agency (IEA) had sufficient strength to establish a joint answer to the oil price shocks which the Western European nations were exposed to. Moreover, the formation of IEA stole some of the thunder from the EC. Even though there was still a great degree of difference between them, the trend of the 1970s was that the member countries were moving in the same direction in some areas. The most important needs were to reduce the dependency on oil prices and to increase security of supply. More and more, the member countries were keeping in step in central areas. In others areas of EC common policy, member countries were not able to come closer together. In energy policy, however, the convergence

**Figure 6.** *Real GDP growth rate changes in two oil shocks*

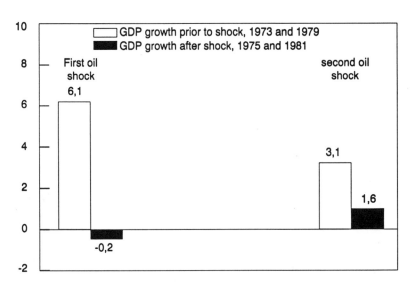

source: *Weyman-jones*:1986:32

of member country policies happened without a super–structure for joint policy.

Nevertheless, the trend towards similar actions could not be changed into a common energy policy formulated at the EC level. On the contrary, the oil price shocks undermined attempts to create a common policy. On the general policy level, the Commission had to settle for opinion, stating EC objectives that it would like to see realized. More than 25 new Directives were passed relating to energy, but these are specific regulations related to increased energy efficiency in specific areas, like the insulation of buildings (Register over gældende EF–retsforskrifter 1992).

The countries were often in different positions in many areas, and national policy was often closely linked to the interests of the oil industry and to trade and economic policies. There were national energy policy complexes consisting of a small number of strong actors with concurring preferences for regulations. These became very evident as the oil crises receded. Another ten years were to pass before attempts at a common policy became evident. So far, the focus of these efforts have mainly been on transportation systems and concession regimes. National consumer

**Figure 7**. *Inflation rate changes in two oil shocks*

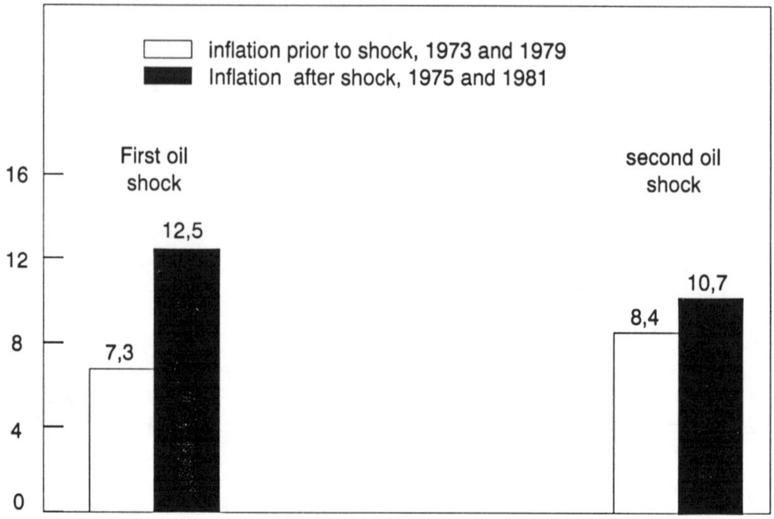

source: *Weyman-jones*:1986:32

prices vary considerably (Figure 8), and this is likely to be the case for a long time to come.

The dominance of national interests in energy policy lasted until the late 1980s, in many ways corresponding to the general power distribution between national and supranational authority in the EC system. Even though the Commission took the initiative, the Council of Ministers was the key decision–making institution. However, rather than expressing a supranational policy, the EC policy was a negotiation arena for national interests. The requirement of unanimity in the Council of Ministers made it easy for some countries to block attempts to establish a joint policy.

## COMMON ENERGY POLICY AND DEREGULATION

The Single Act of 1987, which laid the foundation for the revitalization of the EC and for the fulfilment of the internal market before the end of 1992, contained nothing on a common energy policy. This was no coincidence, as it was regarded as a very problematical area. The energy policy was, however, taken up in a special White Paper on Energy Policy

**Figure 8.** *Gasoline prices versus electricity prices, 1990*

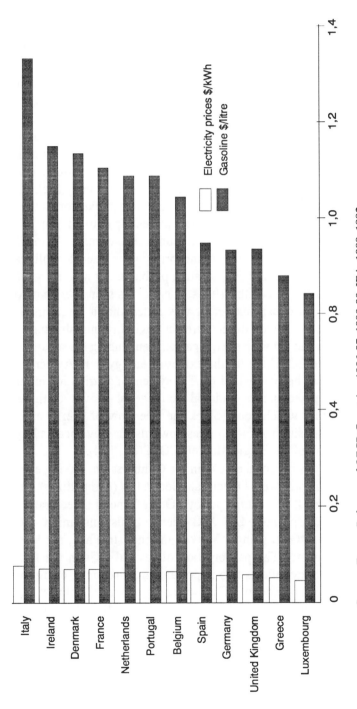

Electricity prices $/kWh
Gasoline $/litre

*Source: Energy Balances of OECD Countries, 1986-87, 1989-90, IEA, 1989, 1992.*

(European Communities, Commission 1988). This study came up with a number of suggestions for a common policy, which were not motivated by what one may call positive objectives related to energy. They were part of a general deregulation policy relating to the realization of the Single Market. After the fall of oil prices in 1986, many of the member countries became less occupied with energy as a strategic commodity. As a result, they were more willing to accept market elements in this area.

The points of departure for the Commission's initiative were Articles 86 and 90 in the Treaty of Rome, regulating state–owned and other monopolies concerning abuses of market power. Such articles seemed especially relevant in the gas and electricity sectors, where the extent of monopolization on the national level was extremely high. To a large degree, these sectors would have to submit to market forces which would lead to greater efficiency and lower prices. Up until this time, energy was partly regarded as a means for national development. As to oil and gas, the security of both supply and price has related to political factors outside the control of EC, creating problems for national goals.

From the end of the 1980s, energy was seen as a commodity in a common European market. It was stated that a single market which functioned well, would create greater flexibility and substitution between countries and between energy carriers, enhancing the security of supply within the EC. Hitherto, the extent of energy delivery across national borders had been very limited. The system of distribution in Europe was not integrated across national boundaries. It was distinguished by monopolies which could block the free flow of energy and use their strategic position to force prices upwards. Energy became linked to the realization of the Single Market (COM (88) 174).

Responsible for the push in the Commission, linking energy to the internal market, were Directorate General IV (competition), and General Directorate XVII (energy policy). Other General Directorates were also involved, especially DG XXI (general customs union and indirect taxation), DG III (Single Market and industry) and, not least, DG XI (environment). The participation of several DGs in the formation of energy policy reflects two important circumstances: energy was being coupled to a number of EC policy areas, and the Commissioners did not have the same degree of control within a policy area which ministers usually have in a national ministry. The Commission passes all motions by majority votes, and all the seventeen Commissioners are involved in all policy fields.

The Commission's suggestions are meant to strengthen the market for the distribution of electricity and gas. The final goal is to get the distribution network to function as a market in which every relevant actor may compete for free capacity. The first stage in this work was to create "transparent prices" and to open transit for distribution companies. The latter gives distribution companies the possibility to use free capacity in pipelines they do not own themselves. These suggestions created a certain tension between the countries and their energy sectors on the one hand and the EC Commission on the other. One may observe that the energy policy in the EC passed from being dominated by countries and companies, to becoming a matter of negotiation between national authorities, industry and central EC organs.

Transparent prices means that gas prices will no longer be secret. Price formulas must be made public in order to create stronger competition. Such a system was established in the UK in 1988, as the new controlling authority, OFGAS, put pressure on the privatized British Gas by threatening to take them to court. A similar Directive was passed by the EC in May 1990. In October 1990, a Directive on the transit of electricity was issued, but only for transport companies. A similar Directive for the gas sector was issued in May 1991. The implementation of these Directives is a slow process (Padgett 1992: 56–59).

The second phase of the liberalization of the EC's electricity and gas markets concerns third party access to the distribution network and access for other distribution companies and large customers to use free capacity in the system. These Directives are presently under consideration, and, in early 1993, the result is uncertain. During the autumn of 1992 a stalemate seemed to arise, particularly in the gas sector. The gas industry and host countries are resisting Commission proposals. The Commission's goals are being watered down in the negotiation process, due to problems with the definition of "free capacity", and to difficulties in securing access for third parties.

On the other hand, the Commission receives strong support from big industrial customers. During a hearing in the European Parliament, the Association for the Chemical Industry in Europe claimed that they could save £ 6 billion if the Commission proposals on electricity and gas were implemented (Dagens Næringsliv, 7 October 1992). In addition, the EC Commission has put considerable weight on these cases, and it is believed that it will ensure that the Directives will be passed in one form or another.

The principle of common carrier, or free access to the transport systems for everyone, created too much resistance for it to be accepted, as this principle presupposes extensive and complicated regulations by the EC. The negotiations between industry interests and the Commission in the Consultative Committee were characterized by strong disagreement. In January 1991, the negotiations ended without the parties reaching an agreement. In the gas sector, Ruhrgas and German interests in particular, were strong opponents (Austvik 1991, Capouet 1992).

The general argument against liberalization voiced by national actors is that energy is too special to be left to market forces. This viewpoint is the factor that underlies national traditions. The exception was Great Britain in the 1980s. Generally, large, strong companies have been regarded as a guarantee of price stability and supply security. It was claimed that the market would undermine such goals. Cheap energy might be a good thing in the short run, but it would not encourage investments in a long–term perspective, and it would lead to increased consumption.

The process from radical Commission proposals, to complicated negotiations and watering down of the orginal intentions, reflects the duality of the Commission's role in the EC decision–making process. On the one hand, it is supposed to be a radical supporter of the realization of the EC's visions. On the other hand, it must try to reach complicated, political compromises. Strong forces at the EC level are not satisfied with national industries, nor with national authorities defending arrangements colliding with EC visions. This means that the Commission's suggestions will often be changed considerably during the long process towards a final passing of a Directive. However, the drive for joint action in the energy sector during the last years is regarded as a victory for the Commission. The question is, however, what the practical implications will be?

During the first years of the liberalization process in the energy sector, the focus was put on the downstream side of the electricity and gas sectors. During the next stage of the Commission's work to create a single market in the energy sector, a Directive regulating concession systems in oil and gas production was proposed, aiming at introducing EC rules about free market access in the upstream petroleum sector. Thus, it will no longer be possible to grant special privileges to national or state–owned companies.

In relation to the licence Directive, the Commission faces fewer strong adversaries among member states than in the areas of electricity and gas transmission. However, at the Council of Ministers' meeting on 30 November 1992, Denmark managed to temporarily block a common position on this Directive with reference to vital national interests. Another important factor may have been Norway's opposition. Norway has the largest oil and gas reserves in Western Europe. It has applied for membership and it is naturally against a final decision being reached in this area before it can participate in the decision–making.

The formal changes in the EC institutions during the second phase of the energy policy from the end of the 1980s were relatively small, but nonetheless important. Among other things, the door was opened for majority decisions in the Council of Ministers. The lobbyists swarmed to Brussels and laid siege to the EC institutions, which indicates that EC institutions and EC policy were in the process of being strengthened compared to national interests. The Council of Ministers was still important, but energy policy was no longer the exclusive domain of member countries and national industry; a negotiation process was being established within the EC central institutions. The Commission was on the offensive, not only because of DG XVII and its responsibility for energy matters, but also because DG IV, responsible for competition policy, was often pushing the Commission. The common energy policy was, therefore, not really a positive energy policy as a follow–up to the strategic considerations DG XVII had in mind, but rather a submergence of these under the Single Market.

## TOWARDS A POSITIVE ENERGY POLICY?

The third phase in the development of EC energy policy started parallel to ongoing deregulation efforts. Again it was not the traditional, national energy actors who were on the offensive, because this time the initiative came partly from forces outside the energy sector also at the EC level. Energy has been increasingly coupled to the environment, security of supply and foreign policy. While security of supply is a traditional problem for DG XVII (energy), environmental concerns have top priority with DG XI (environment). The foreign policy dimension has been pushed forward by the European Council summit meetings, which reflects the developments in Eastern Europe (Matlary 1991, Andersen 1993).

The most important force behind a new energy policy in the EC is the environmental policy (Bergesen 1991, Iversen 1992). An important point is that environmental policy, in contrast to energy policy, is part of the Treaty of Rome, giving it greater weight. The Single Act of 1987 established a foundation for environmental policy in the EC constitution, namely Articles 130R, 130S and 130T.

The goal of Article 130R is to preserve, protect and improve the environment, and to contribute to better health and a rational use of natural resources.

Article 130S concerns decision procedures, and states that in the Council of Ministers motions are to be passed by unanimity. This was changed to qualified majority after the treaty conference in Maastricht, effective from 1 January 1993.

Article 130T states that the introduction of EC regulations in this field shall not deprive member countries of the right to introduce stronger measures.

In addition, Article 100A concerns the creation of uniform and effective regulations in the EC. It states that regulations shall be based on a high level of protection of health, environment and consumer interests. The EC environmental policy comprises air pollution, changes in the climate, water quality, waste disposal, control of chemicals and noise. Pollution and the climate are the fields which until now have had the greatest impact on energy policy.

Demands for reduced pollution, especially $CO_2$ emissions, creates a new context for EC energy policy (COM (92) 226). Demands for reduced energy consumption and a turn towards cleaner energy forms create new price formulas and regulations. Here there are strong coalitions outside the energy sector which drive the process onwards, even though the atomic industry has nothing against stronger rules for $CO_2$ emissions. However, again the actual implementation of the $CO_2$ tax is uncertain, since the Commission has made its realization dependent upon similar measures in the USA and Japan (Euroil May 1992: 12).

Not only is there a strong interest in the environment among the population in the member countries. There are also strong forces within the Commission and in the European Parliament who give environmental policy high priority. Some Directives have been passed to reduce emission from cars and industry, and some are being worked out at present to reduce $CO_2$ emissions and to protect the ozone layer. Duties are most often the result of such regulations. The result of these Directives will be a switch away from coal and oil towards gas. With the exception of France, atomic energy is regarded with much scepticism all over Western Europe.

Another consideration influencing EC energy policy, and which is closely related to the Energy Charter, is the increased attention to the security of oil supplies, resulting from the Gulf War. There is an understanding that this war in the Middle East was not a dramatic one–time event, but could be a symptom of underlying problems which may flare up again. In short: the problem is not a lack of stability in the oil market, but that the Middle East "does not work". Such preoccupations strengthen the view that energy is a strategic commodity, a perspective that is central for the Commission's General Directorate XVII with responsibility for energy questions.

The answer to the uncertainty in the Middle East has, in the short run, been to create a crises depot corresponding to 90 days' consumption, as in the US. In the future, connecting some Arab countries to the EC through agreements might have a stabilizing effect. This will come in addition to the work done on a more effective use of energy in the member countries. An interesting aspect of this is that environmental considerations and supply security, to a certain degree, will converge in the demand for increased efficiency. Limits on the use of energy have a favourable influence on emissions and lead to less dependency on imports. This means that to a certain degree there is a community of interests between environmental and energy interests at the EC level.

A third important driving force is the development in Eastern Europe. An earlier political risk for the EC was the possibility that the Soviet Union would exploit Western dependency on natural gas. This dependency could be used to exert political pressure. Now the situation is quite different. The gas industry in Russia has huge infrastructure problems. There are, for example, great leakages in the pipelines to Western Europe. (Some argue that as much as 30 percent is lost before the gas reaches the market.) Through the Energy Charter, the EC wishes to strengthen the framework for market–based solutions and to offer security to foreign investors. In addition, Russia has large oil resources which could reduce the dependency on the Middle East.

The point of departure was a somewhat unclear political initiative sent to the European Council, the so–called Lubbers Plan. During the Commission's elaboration of this plan, focus was placed on a mixture of foreign policy, aid programmes and energy policy, which in the long run may contribute to lasting and cheap access to energy for the EC. Energy is also one of five sector programmes aimed at assisting the changes in Russia. The last programme aims at using 105 million ECU. About 50 percent will be spent on strengthening security in the atomic industry, 20 percent will be spent on reducing energy consumption, and the electricity and gas sectors will each get around 15 percent.

Through these programmes, the EC wishes to secure its own future supply. By helping Russia in the energy sector, an important contribution will also be made to the implementation of the dramatic changes taking place in this country. If the EC programme can contribute to a successful transformation in the oil and gas sector, it may also function as a model for new institutional solutions in the rest of the economy. The oil and gas sector is one of the few sectors where Russia has export potential, i.e. a source of much–needed foreign currency incomes. However, much of the EC strategy may be understood as help–to–self–help. Moreover, one may perhaps wonder why the EC wants to introduce market–based solutions in Russia, when they have problems with this in their own member countries.

One element of the Energy Charter is that, to a certain extent, there are overlapping interests between national industries and the EC Commission, in contrast to the adversary orientation which is evident in other fields. The Charter is meant to strengthen the market framework prevalent in the West, but there is room for solutions with elements of Western European traditions, i.e. power concentration around large companies. Also, it is unrealistic to imagine market solutions in the energy sectors in the former Eastern Bloc countries. This provides room for a communality of interests between parties which in other areas are strong adversaries.

To sum up: the environmental questions are on the offensive in the EC. Not only are the energy–sector actors in the member countries on the defensive. This is also the case for energy policy actors at the central EC level. In the short run the programme for an internal market has been the most important source of change. However, in the long term perspective environmental policy and Eastern European events may become more important. The tendency is that the more extensive the objectives which may be formulated in the common energy policy, the less control the traditional energy policy actors at the national and EC level will have over developments. The exception is the opening which might be created for Western energy companies in Eastern Europe.

On the other hand, there is a tendency towards watering down radical suggestions made by the Commission in the long and complicated process before motions are passed. Therefore, one should not exaggerate the changes which have taken place so far. However, while the impact of the internal market and environmental concerns may be delayed or temporarily blocked, it seems unlikely that energy can remain unaffected by such factors in the long run. The supply aspect is somewhat different in that both EC authorities and many established actors in the energy industry see attractive opportunities.

The developments during the last years coincide with the strengthening of the EC's supranationality. This happens in many fields, as a number of political decisions are now coming from the European Council, i.e. decisions were earlier taken by state leaders who at the next stage provided a stronger mandate to EC organs. Such initiatives have played a major role in connection with Eastern Europe, not least in parts of the environmental policy, such as limiting $CO_2$ emissions. This tendency meant that important aspects of energy policy were no longer formulated between EC institutions and national energy interests. The premises for the energy policy were introduced in two new ways: firstly, "from above" through general political summit–meeting decisions, and secondly, "from the side" through premises stated by other parts of the Commission than DG XVII, DG IV (competition policy) and, to an increasing extent, DG XI (environment).

## TOWARDS A UNION AND A STRENGTHENED ENVIRONMENTAL POLICY?

After Maastricht, the energy policy actors confront a new challenge through the reform of the EC treaty and EC institutions (Bradshaw 1991, Kuvaas 1992). When implemented it will represent important steps on the way towards a European union. The debate on ratification in the member countries' parliaments demonstrates, however, a widespread scepticism towards the union plans, influencing how fast and to what extent the treaty will be implemented. The gloom characterizing the EC during the last half of 1992 also made it easier for opponents to oppose Directives relating to the Internal Market. Still, if the proposed reforms of the EC decision–making process is passed, then it will probably further strengthen the last years' trends in the field of energy.

A main feature of the new decision–making system of the Maastrict Treaty is the strengthening of the European Parliament. Another is the parallel extension of the right of the Council of Ministers to make decisions based on qualified or clear majority decisions, e.g. in environmental questions. This will enable the EC, to a greater degree, to embrace and strengthen the environmental concerns growing in the whole EC area. In a 1989 survey 75 percent of the EC population thought that the member countries should cooperate on environmental issues (The Commission 1990). However, up to now the work to establish the Single Market has been characterized by the fact that industrial interests have been most successful in getting the Commission's attention. They gained access at an early stage and were able to formulate important premises (Andersen and Eliassen 1991).

The European Parliament will obtain decision–making power in the new system, but it will have extensive veto rights in important fields, i.e. environmental questions. This means that the institution may get important negotiating power in relation to the Commission and the Council of Ministers, especially during the last phase of the EC decision–making process. This will, in all probability, strengthen environmental considerations in the EC. While Parliament was less important, environmental and consumer interests were weak. In this situation, they found each other. There are alliance patterns here which may have a far stronger impact under the new procedures.

The tension between national interests and the EC is the main reason why energy has not become a field of common policy during the revision of the treaty in Maastricht. However, when it was proposed as part of the Maastricht reform the UK was against it due to its strategy to limit the scope of transnational authority, despite the fact that the country has already gone further in the direction of liberalization than the Commission has proposed.

On the other hand environmental policy was incorporated into the Single Act of 1987, further strengthened as a field of common policy by the strengthening of the right of the Council of Ministers to pass motions by majority decisions. At the same time, environment policy initiatives have broad support in member countries. Energy policy is but one of many fields where environmental interests will seek to strengthen their influence.

The Maastricht Treaty could also strengthen the basis for joint EC foreign policy. Indirectly, this may increase the capacity of the Community to deal with energy supply issues. The stockpiling of oil has reduced the immediate effects of supply disruptions stemming from unrest in the Middle East. In a broader perspective, the EC still needs to develop its relationship with the key countries in this region. The lack of a unified position among member countries has complicated this relationship and undermined the position of the EC with regard to the occurence of crises.

A stronger foreign policy concentration may also improve the EC's ability to follow up on programmes of stabilization and reform in Russia.

So far we have focused on factors leading to the Europeification of energy policy. There is, however, reason to believe that national energy policy actors will try to turn back the development which we have seen in the last years, or at least find ways to slow it down. It is still too early to say how this will be done – much will depend on the further development of EC institutions. An important question is to what extent the breakthrough of the idea of supranational decision–making develops. Another question is whether the support for environmental issues will be kept constant when costs become apparent, such as increased duties and taxes. This latter issue will probably depend on the level of economic growth in the EC.

## CONCLUDING REMARKS

This chapter has described the main stages in the development of a common EC energy policy. Although energy has been an issue of great concern, a common policy has been almost totally lacking until recent years. When a common energy policy finally emerges, it will be partly due to the fact that the traditional energy actors are losing their exclusive control over the energy arena.

In this sense, the emergence of a common energy policy demonstrates the momentum of Europeification. While diverse interests may effectively prohibit common policy at one level of integration, it may create increased pressures for harmonization of objectives and policies at a later stage. While there is still great uncertainty as to the effects of new Directives in the energy field, the policy development demonstrates some of the mechanisms which will bridge national and transnational policy–making in a number of policy areas for a long time to come.

Rather than a down–up process based on overlapping interests among actors in the sector, the Europeification initiatives come from actors in the Commission or from actors in other sectors. Initiatives relating to the Internal Market and environment are based on institutions and transnational authority which they try to extend into the energy sector. Policies relating to the security of supply have been based on the emergent need for joint action in foreign policy, triggered by the Gulf War and the break–up of the Soviet Union.

One may characterize the development in the energy sector as political spill–over, but not in the neofunctional sense. In the latter theory, spill–over is based on a concept of interest group politics, where rational actors pursue their interests and there is little concern with contextual factors. The recent development of EC energy policy, on the other hand, demonstrates how interests in a sector become overwhelmed by actors invoking different policy contexts, within a general framework of EC development towards broader and deeper transnational authority. It is the dynamic interaction between several policy contexts, and the impetus of the more general development, which explains the direction of EC energy policy.

Energy is not covered by the Treaty of Rome or in the proposed Maastricht reform, which leaves the Commission with a certain freedom as to how Directives affecting energy should be defined. "Energy" Directives may be handled through the main decision–making procedure laid down in the Treaty, requiring unanimity. However, energy may also be defined in relation to the Internal Market and the majority rule of decision–making (Article 100a) introduced with the Single Act reform. Given the high degree of monopolistic tendencies in the energy sector and the barriers to trade between countries, the Commission here has a strong case for the Internal Market.

The development of energy policy also demonstrates how the impact of the institutional system depends on the general development of the EC. The momentum of the Internal Market made it possible to extend transnational authority into new areas against the will of key actors in these fields. Similarly, the pessimism created by problematic national ratification processes provided more room for opposition and delay strategies. The latter also illustrates the fact that the EC is a dynamic concept, a movement towards ideals. The EC is successful when it makes things happen. However, what will happen in the energy sector, still remains to be seen. There are different degrees of Europeification, and the energy sector is still at the lower end of this scale.

# 9
# EDUCATION

*Erik Beukel*

## INTRODUCTION

Education is not among the policy areas that form the basis of European integration. Ever since the European Community (EC), legally composed of three separate entities, was established in the 1950s, economic issue areas have formed the nucleus of integration in the EC. The most important treaty was the 1957 Treaty of Rome that created the European Economic Community (EEC). This treaty outlined the gradual realization of a common market, a term synonymous with the concept of the internal (or single) market, that is: the free movement of goods, workers, services and capital between the member countries. Thus, as a non–economic issue area, education has not, until the Maastricht Treaty on the European Union, been referred to as an independent subject for common policies. Only a few educational issues, directly related to the functioning of the common market, are mentioned in the Treaty of Rome: provisions for vocational training (Art. 41, 118 and 128) and the provision for mutual recognition of certificates (Art. 57).

However, aspects of the broad educational issue area which are not directly related to these stipulations have, since the early 1970s, been included in the member states' endeavours to set up a common policy–making process. Especially during the early years, when attempts to generate common policies were very tentative and limited, educational cooperation was determined in gatherings denoted "the Ministers for Education, meeting within the Council". Such meetings have formally taken place outside the treaties' framework, with the ministers acting solely as representatives of their governments on the basis of the member countries' constitutional rules. However, they were carried out under a form similar to Council meetings, with a member of the Commission participating but without right of initiative. Both the administrative preparation and the implementation of decisions made at these meetings have used the EC institutional framework, supplemented with intergovernmental organs formally set up as separate units. Thus it may be said that what are looked upon as ordinary diplomatic reunions between ministers for education, have taken place in the "shadow" of the Community (De Witte 1992: 85).

After an action programme in the field of education was adopted by the Community in 1976, educational cooperation outside the Community's original framework has increasingly been combined with references to the Treaty of Rome's few stipulations on education. The body involved in this "mixed" decision–making process, allowing the ministers to adopt acts of Community law and measures of traditional international law at the same time, is the "Council and the Ministers for Education meeting within the Council". In other words, the representatives of the member states wear two hats (van Craeyenest 1989: 127–133). An essential feature of this has been a dynamic interpretation of the Treaty's provisions, first initiated by the Court of Justice in the early 1970s, strongly followed up in the 1980s with the support of the Commission and, since the mid–1980s, applied by the Council as well (De Witte 1989: 9–18 and 1992: 78–83, Lonbay 1989: 373–375). In addition, Art. 235, which stipulates that the Council, under certain conditions, may adopt actions necessary to realize the Community's aims, has been used as a means for expanding the Community's activities in the field of education.

It follows that there has been some kind of institutionalization at Community level, or Europeification, of aspects of the member countries' general educational policies, and the purpose of this chapter is to outline the main features of this process. Analysing the institutionalization of educational policy as a Community issue means examining the process of crystallization of different types of norms, organizations, and frameworks which regulate the way education is dealt with in the EC (Eisenstadt 1972: 414). The focus is on the institutional routines and sets of rules that prescribe behavioural roles, constrain activity, and shape expectations in this field (Keohane 1988: 383, 386, March and Olsen 1989: 21f.)

Two related questions are examined: (1) Which aspects of the educational decision–making process are dealt with? (2) What characterizes the organizational arrangement set up? Does the pattern of activity, established and formed at Community level for dealing with education, relate to predecisional stages of the decision–making process as problem–recognition and information–gathering? Or does it extend to prescribing, enacting and implementing general rules, meaning a direct choice between action alternatives (Lasswell 1956: 2, Lindberg 1971: 53)?

Section 2 reviews the early institutionalization of education as a policy area in the EC. Section 3 considers the marked increase in new initiatives and programmes since the mid–1980s, with a view to expounding the consequences of the strength and character of institutionalization. In Section 4 the analysis focuses on factors influencing the Europeification of education, especially the conditions which initiated the process as well as the factors which stimulated it in the 1980s. Lastly, I will reflect on the prospects for the 1990s.

## THE EARLY INSTITUTIONALIZATION

General education was first mentioned directly as an area of interest to the Community during 1971. In July of that year the Commission decided to set up two bodies which would work on educational issues: a Working Party on Teaching and Education, directly responsible to a Commission member, Altiero Spinelli (Italy), and an Interdepartmental Working Party on Coordination. After that, work was initiated which was designed to collect data on educational issues and elaborate on the need for greater Community effort in the educational field (Suppl. 10/73: 9).

At about the same time the Council, in adopting a series of general guidelines concerning vocational training, stated that the "objective of the programme should be to provide the population as a whole with the opportunities for general and vocational education" (my italics, cf. Suppl. 3/74: 5). More important, the Ministers for Education held their first meeting in November 1971, with Altiero Spinelli from the Commission participating. The resolution from the ministers' reunion stated that the provisions on educational measures in the Treaty of Rome should be completed by increasing cooperation in the field of education as such, and it mentioned that the "ultimate aim" was "in fact to define a European model of culture correlating with European integration" (European Educational Policy Statements 1988: 11). A working party of senior officials from the member countries was set up to consider, together with the Commission, ways in which cooperation in the educational field might be achieved and what the legal bases could be for this. The report of the Working Party was completed one year later, in November 1972 (Suppl. 3/74: 5, Neave 1984: 6–7).

After the ministers' meeting in November 1971, the Commission stated "mit Befriedigung" (cf. Fünfter Gesamtbericht: 7) that from then on, educational issues were to be considered as common policy issues and this would perhaps necessitate the search for common solutions at Community level. In addition, the Commission hoped for a convergence of the member states' educational policies in order to assure a harmonious development in the Community.

From January 1973, education figured for the first time as part of the responsibility of one of the members of the Commission. Directorate General XII on Research, Science and Education was set up, with Ralph Dahrendorf (The Federal Republic) as the responsible Commissioner. Later, in the spring of 1973, Ralph Dahrendorf presented the Commission with a draft proposal concerning the Community's involvement in education, emphasizing how various intiatives could increase mutual understanding and thus help European integration. Among other things, language teaching, improvement of teachers' and students' opportunities to move among the countries of the Community, and the development of the study of Europe as part of the school curriculum were mentioned (General Report 1973: 369–70). Some of these ideas, which were to be termed a "European dimension in education", had been contained in a report prepared by Professor Henri Janne, former Minister of Education in Belgium, and which had been presented a short time before this (cf. Suppl. 10/73).

The following year, in March 1974, the Commission presented the first Communication on education to the Council, "Education in the European Community" (Suppl. 3/74), which elaborated on the fundamental reasoning behind the issues. One of the main arguments is that the promotion of educational cooperation must be an integral part in the overall development of the Community. This does not mean that there must be a common European policy in the education field, in the sense applicable to other sectors. The educational traditions and systems of individual countries are rightly prized and Europe is enriched by their diversity. Thus, the Commission stated, the objective of harmonization would be as undesirable as it would be unrealistic. However, a Community perspective in education is increasingly important, and what is required is a common commitment to the development of educational cooperation and a systematic exchange of information and experience. Among specific proposals mentioned were increasing mobility in education and the development of a European dimension in education (Suppl. 3/74: 6 and 8–15). Generally, the suggestions were similar to the ideas put forward in the reports by Ralph Dahrendorf and Henri Janne.

Later, in June 1974, the Ministers for Education, "meeting within the Council," held their second meeting. In the resolution which they drafted at this meeting, the ministers confirmed the need to institute European cooperation in the field of education (European Educational Policy Statements 1988: 15–16). As the basis for this cooperation, it was stated that education must on no account be regarded merely as a component of economic life and that allowance must be made for the traditions of each country and the diversity of their respective educational policies and systems. A number of priority spheres of action were outlined, and among those not directly originating in the Treaty were: promotion of closer relations and increased cooperation between educational systems and institutions of higher education; encouragement of the mobility of teachers, students and research workers; compilation of up–to–date documentation and statistics on education, as well as the achievement of equal opportunity for free access to all forms of education.[1]

Lastly, the ministers set up an Education Committee, composed of representatives of the member states and of the Commission. The Chairman of the Committee was to come from the country exercising the office of President of the Council.

The Education Committee held its first meeting in October 1974, and its first task was to prepare the Community Education Action Programme which was adopted in February 1976. The resolution on the Action Programme had a dual character in that it was adopted by the Council as well as the Ministers for Education "meeting within the Council" (European Educational Policy Statements 1988: 23–27).

The Action Programme established the Education Committee as a permanent body and the organizational centre of the educational cooperation. The Committee should coordinate and oversee the implementation of the programme and prepare the proceedings of the Council and the Ministers for Education meeting within the Council. Concerning measures to be implemented at Community level, they should be undertaken by the Commission[2] "in close liaison" with the Education Committee. As to the Council and the Ministers for Education meeting within the Council, it was stated that they should meet periodically to follow the implementation of the Action Programme, to establish future guidelines, and to compare their policies.

The exposition of the programme contained six headings:

1. Better facilities for the education and training of nationals and the children of nationals of other member states and non–member countries.
2. Promotion of closer relations between educational systems in Europe.
3. Compilation of up–to–date documentation and statistics on education.
4. Cooperation in the field of higher education.
5. Teaching of foreign languages.
6. Achievement of equal opportunity for free access to all forms of education.

The headings, and the more detailed elaboration under each heading, cover a broad bracket of educational issues. When compared to the resolution adopted in June 1974, the overall similarities are striking. Just one difference should be noted: while the 1974 resolution did not use the term a "European dimension in education", the term was applied and elaborated under heading no. 2. In general, the programme is marked by an extensive use of non–committal wordings and suggestions like exchange of information and experience, study visits, strengthening of contacts, pilot projects, preparation of reports, examination of this or that problem, and so on. It all indicates the exclusive dominance of the predecisional stages in the Community's involvement in the member states' educational decision–making process.

During the following years, the implementation of the Action Programme was characterized by the arrangement of a vast number of pilot projects, meetings, seminars, and the like (Beukel 1992: 27–37). Primacy was given to measures related to the transition from school to work, as indicated by the predominance of resolutions adopted by the Council and the Ministers for Education meeting within the Council through this period (European Educational Policy Statements 1988: 31–33, 41–42, 45 and 79–80). Another significant feature of the implementation was the extensive involvement of administrators of educational systems and labour market institutions throughout the Community (Neave 1984: 43–55). Thus, as there was an unusually high rate of unemployment amongst young people in the member countries after the mid–1970s, one may say that the implementation was dominated by "ractical low–politics needs". One, somewhat belated, indication of this was the first joint session of the Ministers for Labour and Social Affairs and Ministers for Education in June 1983. That reunion had been suggested by the Commission nine years earlier in its above–mentioned communication from the spring of 1974 (European Educational Policy Statements 1988: 95–96, Suppl. 3/74: 7).

Other points from the Action Programme, which were also the subject of several meetings and seminars throughout the Community as well as some ministerial resolutions, included the development of cooperation between institutions of higher education and the introduction of new information technologies. In particular, the last–mentioned issue appeared as a main point in the institutionalization of education after the early 1980s (European Educational Policy Statements 1988: 89–91, 83–86 and 111–112).

Towards the end of the 1970s, from around late 1978 to mid–1980, cooperation experienced a slowdown in that some meetings between the Ministers for Education were cancelled. The reason for this was disagreement over the implementation of a European dimension in education. During that period, however, both the normal work of the Education Committee, as well as several other activities aimed at implementing the Action Programme, continued regardless.[3] It follows that the split at the ministerial level had no consequences on the most important aspect of the institutionalization of European education.

Altogether, both the Action Programme and the extensive measures aimed at its implementation, dealt with predecisional stages of the educational decision–making process. Expressed in terms of organizational development, for the first ten years after the Action Programme was adopted in 1976, the main feature of the institutionalization of education was adaptation in the form of incremental growth (Haas 1990: 97–108).

## NEW FORMS OF EUROPEIFICATION

From the mid–1980s, the institutionalization assumed new characteristics, both with regard to the aspects of the decision–making process dealt with and as to the organizational framework. The primary change is that the Council has adopted independent educational programmes to be implemented by the Commission in cooperation with a number of intergovernmental institutions, established for specific purposes. Another notable change is a new wording applied in resolutions adopted by the

Ministers for Education, giving the term "Europeification" an ideational substance as well.

The three most important programmes, using more than 95 percent of the Community's budget in the field (Eliassen and Mydske 1991: 3, Rosenthal 1991: 273–283), are: (1) COMETT (Community Program for Education and Training in Technology); (2) ERASMUS ( European Community Action Scheme for the Mobility of University Students); and (3) LINGUA, the Language and Training Program.

COMETT I, covering the period 1986–1989, was adopted by the Council (composed of Ministers for Education, without the addition "meeting within the Council") in July 1986. The resolution referred to Art. 128 on vocational training and Art. 235 on supplementary actions (European Educational Policy Statements 1988: 157–163). COMETT II, covering the period 1990–1994, was adopted by the Council (now composed of Ministers for Labour and Social Affairs) in December 1988 and that resolution referred only to Art. 128 (European Educational Policy Statements 1990: 57–63). Whereas COMETT I was endowed with a budget of 45 million ECU, COMETT II has a budget of 200 million ECU, representing almost a quadrupling of the annual budget.

The objective of COMETT is fourfold: to give a European dimension to cooperation between institutions of higher education and industry in the area of new technologies; to foster joint development of training programmes, exchange of experience and optimum use of training resources at Community level; to improve the supply of training at local, regional and national levels; and to develop the level of training in response to technological and social changes. This is to be achieved especially by creating a network of university–industry training partnerships, to be used for transnational exchanges of students, the development of transnational projects for continuing training and multimedia training systems.

ERASMUS I, covering the period 1987–1989, was adopted by the Council in June 1987 (European Educational Policy Statements 1988: 187–193), following long and, at times, bitter negotiations during the seventeen months after the Commission had submitted its first proposal in January 1986. The resolution referred to Art. 128 and art. 235. ERASMUS II, covering the period 1990–1994, was adopted by the Council in December 1989, this time with reference only to Art. 128 (European Educational Policy Statements 1990: 109–113). While ERASMUS I was only endowed with a budget of 85 million ECU, the budget for the first three years of the new period has been more than doubled to 192 million ECU.

The objective of ERASMUS is to substantially increase the number of students spending an integrated part of their study period at an institution of higher education in another member country, generally promoting broadly based, intensive cooperation at all levels between the institutions of higher education. The wider aim is to improve the quality of education and training, ensuring the development of a pool of trained personnel with direct experience of intra–Community cooperation and thereby to contribute to the strengthening of a "People's Europe".

The most important points were outlined as follows: the establishment and operation of inter–university cooperation programmes (ICPs) for exchanging students and teachers; a scheme for student mobility grants to be awarded for at least one term of study in another EC member country; the setting up of a European Community Course Credit Transfer System (ECTS) for the multilateral transfer of course credits, to be connected to the European Community network of National Academic Recognition Information Centres (NARIC).

LINGUA is an action programme to promote foreign language training and skills. It was adopted by the Council in July 1989, referring to Art. 128 and 235, with an estimated budget of 200 million ECU for the period 1990–1994 (European Educational Policy Statements 1990: 89–97). Before its adoption, the programme had been the subject of controversy in the Council in that some countries (Britain, Denmark and Germany) expressed the view that the Commission's original proposal marked an excessive extension of the competence of the EC (George 1991: 210). Hence, the member states' primary responsibility for education and the supplementary character of the Community's measures were emphasized.

Each programme is to be implemented by a committee composed of two representatives from each member state, with a representative from the Commission as chairman. The Commission shall perform the secretarial functions and it clearly has an important role in the implementation of the programmes. Concerning the geographical scope of the programmes, agreements on the EFTA countries' participation in COMETT and ERASMUS were concluded in 1990 and 1991.

Concurrent with the Council's adoption of specific educational programmes in the second half of the 1980s, the Council (now the phrase "the Ministers for Education meeting within the Council" is added) passed resolutions on educational cooperation which placed it in a general European context. Some of these ideas were hinted at in the early

1980s, in the "Solemn Declaration on European Union" signed by the heads of state or governments in June 1983 (European Educational Statements 1988: 99), but the tendency to argue for educational cooperation in terms of European ideas and interests became most evident toward the end of the decade. Often the resolutions were prepared in formal or informal meetings among the ministers where a Communication from the Commission formed the basis of the deliberations.

In May 1988, the Council and the Ministers for Education meeting within the Council adopted a resolution on the European dimension in education which was characterized by a marked attachment to European culture and European ideas; young people should be made more aware of their European identity and learn to understand the value of European ideas as democratic principles, social justice and human rights. To give substance to the European dimension in education, the member states should, within the framework of their educational structures, implement actions emphasizing teaching plans in schools, teaching material, teacher education, and the stimulation of contacts between pupils in different countries. The Commission was asked to carry out various measures concerning exchange of information, teaching material and teacher training (European Educational Policy Statements 1990: 19–21).

The predilection for stressing the role of educational cooperation within a broad conception of the political structure and role of Europe became most evident in a resolution adopted by the Ministers in October 1989, agreed upon around the same time as the seminal events were occurring in Eastern Europe (European Educational Policy Statements 1990: 101–102). After the democratic revolutions in the former totalitarian half of Europe, the need for extending the educational cooperation to the new democracies in Central and Eastern Europe has come into focus, both in ministerial resolutions and Commission manifestations. In the spring of 1990 the TEMPUS (Transeuropean Mobility Programme for University Studies) programme for exchanges in higher education was adopted (Official Journal No. L 131/21–6, 23.5. 1990, Pertek 1992b). In addition, the Europe Agreements, concluded in late 1991, with Poland, Hungary, and the Czech and Slovak Federal Republic include provisions concerning education and training (van der Klugt 1992).

The new forms of Europeification which have developed since the mid–1980s can be elaborated on by stressing six distinctive features:

1. The increased institutionalization of education, moving from only having a bearing on predecisional operations to also including

some educational policy choices, primarily concerning measures which cannot be decided and implemented at single state level.

2. Compared to the early institutionalization when the Education Committee was the organizational centre, the establishment of different organizations for directing and implementing the new Community programmes means that the organizational structure has become more complex.

3. An important aspect of the increased complexity is that the new programmes have a direct bearing on a much broader group of people engaged in European educational systems than the early institutionalization which primarily concerned administrators in the educational and closely related sectors.

4. Therefore, from now on, a greater part of the educational demands and expectations will be directed at the Community. In other words, what has been top–down transgovernmental and supranational initiatives will lead to bottom–up transnational demands.

5. The early institutionalization of education has changed into a kind of <u>Europeification</u> which is rhetorical and ideational as well.

6. The new independent educational programmes adopted at Community level do not affect the overall fact that the predominant institutionalization in the educational field obviously still occurs at individual state level.

Altogether, if a distinct Europeification of educational policies is an essential aspect of an emerging European state, we are very far away from that state. Anyhow, the emerging state – Union or no European Union – will have structural attributes which are different from any other known entity termed "state".

## DYNAMICS OF EUROPEIFICATION

Given the divergent findings as to the growth and character of institutionalization through the period since the early 1970s, it is expedient to divide the analysis of the dynamics of Europeification into two questions. First, how do we account for the early institutionalization which occurred in the first half of the 1970s? Second, how do we account for the growth in institutionalization which has taken place since the mid–1980s, including the specific features of Europeification?

## The initial institutionalization

As to the factors which stimulated the initial phase of institutionalization in the first half of the 1970s, it is difficult to pinpoint the exact sequence of events, but available data seem to provide evidence that the Commission played the decisive role in that specific members of the Commission took the critical initiatives. Thus, in the summer of 1971, Altiero Spinelli led the establishment of two bodies (see above) which were given the role of considering general educational issues and, later in 1971, he also played an active role when the Ministers for Education held their first meeting. During the following years, Ralph Dahrendorf was clearly the active promoter. Yet, it has to be registered that it is evident from the Commission's manifestations that it would have preferred the institutionalization to proceed beyond the measures implemented during the mid–1970s.

The significance of these observations is that the Community's most distinctly supranational institution may be accountable for the early institutionalization of some predecisional stages of the member states' general educational policy. However, the mere initiation of the Community's interest in education, did not mean that the Community then took on the role of prescribing and enacting rules in the general educational field.

Considered in the light of the Treaty's provisions and the then dominant views in the member countries about the role of the EC during the 1970s, the lack of further institutionalization in the field of education is not surprising. The process of institutionalization was not automatic once it had been initiated. The more or less openly expressed desires of the Community's most distinctly supranational institution were not sufficient to carry a strong process of Europeification.

## The new institutionalization and Europeification

Concerning the growth in institutionalization which occurred after the mid–1980s, a more detailed examination (Beukel 1992b: 14–19) indicates that factors directly related to the Community system did not play a significant role. The dynamics of the new Europeification have to be looked at by examining changes in the Community's environment, that is, changes which have confronted the member states and the Council with challenges which they reacted to by strengthening the extent of educational institutionalization.

*Economic structures*

During the late 1970s and early 1980s, changes in international economic structures altered the EC countries' options. Long–term changes in the economic strength of different countries and regional groupings reached a critical point. Most important, since the relative economic position of the United States had declined through more than a decade, it was no longer a viable option for Europeans just to follow in the wake of the United States and adapt to the economic policies of that country. In the early 1980s, the Reagan administration's economic policy was strongly criticized by European politicians, including people who otherwise supported the American–West European partnership. Besides this, there were several other economic bones of contention on both sides of the Atlantic Ocean which prompted European decision–makers to question a continuing European reliance on American economic leadership (Ginsberg 1989: 270f.).

As to the European position in the international economic structure, different indicators and trends pointed to different conclusions (Patel and Pavitt 1989). It was an oversimplification to simply denote the developments as indicators of Europe's decline, but there was widespread talk of Euro–sclerosis in the early 1980s. The European countries which were members of the EC began reconsidering their economic possibilities and strategies. Various elites in governments, business, and the Commission during the first half of the 1980s, began contemplating new economic, technological and political strategies that could reinvigorate European integration and meet different challenges (Sandholz and Zysman 1989).

Evaluated in this context, the Community's new institutionalization in the educational field can be seen as one part of a more extensive endeavour to reinvigorate Europe in response to changes in international economic trends which became apparent in the early–to–mid–1980s.

Another dynamic factor relates to the consequences of the changes in communication and information technologies that may be encapsulated by the phrase "from industrial society to the information society".

The essential point is that, while the technology of industrial societies is based on mechanical systems aimed at mass production, the technology of today is becoming increasingly knowledge based. The post–industrial society is a knowledge society (Drucker 1989: 173–250) where knowledge as the social centre of gravity is shifting to the knowledge worker who collects and uses information in order to comply with heterogeneous demands in society (Toffler 1990: 368–371). Critical economic processes are dependent on information–based organization; the use of systematic information, fantasy and other abilities which are culturally conditioned. Flexibility, knowledge and education are rewarded in a way very different from that used in the traditional industrial society, involving increasing interdependence among governments, business enterprises and citizens across national boundaries.

For educational systems, this has far–reaching consequences. They must be open systems as transnational and interdisciplinary activities become much more significant, and the basis for strictly national educational systems is undermined (Ørstrøm Møller 1990: 106ff. and 136–139). The economic, educational and cultural interplay between educational institutions and economic life in different countries is being strengthened. The socio–political content and meaning of these processes clearly needs a more systematic elucidation. Anyhow, the new institutionalization of education is closely related to the growth of the information society.

*Political structures*

European wishes for a more independent European role in relation to the American ally and vis a vis the Soviet opponent have been one of the motives for European integration ever since its initiation in the early 1950s. During the Carter administration (1977–1981) and the first Reagan administration (1981–1985), many Europeans shared a more or less undefinable feeling of uneasiness that the American Soviet policy was too confrontational. However, ten years earlier, many Europeans had been apprehensive spectators of the Soviet–American détente. Where the Soviet–American relationship was concerned, and regardless of whether the incumbent administration in Washington stressed confrontation or détente, Europeans thought that their interests were being disregarded. As noted in an Indian proverb – quoted by Pierre Hassner in a study of Europe and the contradictions in American policy (Rosecrance 1976: 72) – two fighting elephants will trample the grass, but it is equally true that two loving elephants will do the same.

It all meant that, from the early 1980s, more and more Europeans across the political spectrum expressed the view that Western Europe and the Community ought to move away from their traditionally passive political role of just complaining – "Americans decide, Europeans complain" – towards a more active and independent role. This occurred at the same time as among European elites – authors, journalists, politicians – began identifying a common European identity, an all–

European "Europeanness", described by noting its historical roots and its cultural and political characteristics, often in rather woolly terms (Buzan et al. 1990: 50–57). Central Europe was rediscovered, and the Soviet military and political hegemony in Eastern Europe was being increasingly questioned, not least by political groups which, a few years earlier, had perceived Europe's problems solely in terms of détente, disarmament and opposition to nuclear weapons, and the consequent political actions as simply a matter of opposing the United States.

The growing quest and support for a European cultural and political identity through the 1980s, and the related greater interest in Europe's role in relation to the United States and the Soviet Union, implied positive attitudes to the concept of Europeification.

## PROSPECTS FOR THE 1990s

A starting point for evaluating the prospects for continuing institutionalization and Europeification of education, is to note the obvious similarity between the stipulations on education in the Maastricht Treaty and several resolutions adopted by the Ministers for Education since their first resolution was passed in June 1974 (Beukel 1992a: 90–91). Widespread opposition to further integrative steps has become apparent after the Danish referendum in 1992 and it is particularly strong in Northern member countries. However, as the Community's involvement in the member countries' educational policies is not among the reasons for this opposition, this points to a general conclusion that the institutionalization of education will continue, including the evolution of a still more open trans–European system for higher education (Pertek 1992a). On the other hand, the organization and content of teaching in primary schools will not be institutionalized on Community level. There is no doubt that many member countries strongly oppose that.

At the same time, it is worth noting that the range as well as the character of the Community's involvement in educational issues hold several potential seeds of conflict which could erupt between member countries and between transnational political groups. One matter in dispute might be the more exact definition of a "European dimension in education" which is a natural candidate in the educational field for the stronger scepticism vis a vis institutionalization at the Community level.

The new slogan in Community politics is closeness, meaning that decisions have to be taken as closely as possible to the citizens. This will definitely be applied as an argument in this battle over integration, as will the Community's obligation to contribute to the development of quality education and to respect the member states' responsibility for the content of teaching and the organization of education systems.

All these arguments can refer to stipulations in the Treaty on the European Union. Moreover, they may lead to divergent conclusions concerning the expediency of new Community measures in the educational field. Therefore, when we look at the Europeification of education today, the same comment can be made as that expressed by a British researcher twenty years ago (Shonfield 1972): Europe is moving to an unknown destination.

## NOTES

1   The ministers indicated the problems concerning the extension of the new cooperation in the field of education by stating that the "cooperation must not hinder the exercise of the powers conferred on the Institutions of the European Communities". It is also worth noting that the Council the same day adopted a resolution on the mutual recognition of diplomas, certificates and other evidence of formal qualifications, cf. European Educational Policy Statements 1988: 19.

2   The Programme applied the peculiar wording that the "Commission is invited to undertake...".

3   This may be seen from the extensive review in a general report of the Education Committee, "agreed to in substance" by the Ministers for Education at their session of 27 June 1980, cf. European Educational Policy Statements 1988: 49-71.

# 10
# IMMIGRATION AND THE
# EMERGING EUROPEAN POLITY

*Yasemin N. Soysal*

This chapter presents an analysis of the emerging form of the European polity from the perspective of a weakly institutionalized and relatively marginalized policy area. Since the 1960s, there has been a steady increase in the number and variety of policy areas incorporated into the authoritative realm of the European Community. Immigration, along with other social issue areas such as health and social welfare, remains a relatively less developed and formalized policy area with a limited set of policy instruments, despite its apparent bearing on the creation of the Community's Internal Market. Yet, the very construction of immigration as a weak formal policy area can be seen as indicative of the emerging mode of the European polity. Reflecting upon the immigration regimes of both the EC and its member states, I aim to delineate some of the elements of this emergent polity.[1]

My discussion of the EC immigration regime is informed by two premises. First, much of the literature on the EC conceptualizes the Community either as a transnational administrative unit or as a policy–making body. The role of transnational organizations as norm–setting or model–generating agencies does not generally inform discussion of the EC. In this capacity, the Community contributes to the institutionalization of a transnational discursive agenda, a cognitive map and legitimated goals, available for pirating by the member states (cf. Anderson 1991). My analysis views the EC as a normative rule–producing arrangement, as well as a policy–making organization. Thus it scrutinizes institutional processes that are operative beyond formal authoritative structures and decision–making.

Second, most studies of the EC focus on strong national actors and their interests as the major determinant of the evolution of the EC's action and policy. In contrast, I stress global–level factors, such as the increasingly institutionalized discourses, principles, and regimes that provide models for and constraints on actions and policies of the EC and member states (cf. Meyer 1980). As regards immigration, two normative principles of the global system are crucial: the principle of national sovereignty and the principle of universal human rights. These two principles, celebrated and codified in various international conventions and treaties, constitute the basic components of the post–war immigration regimes. This implies, on the one hand, expanding "responsibilities" charged to the nationstates vis–a–vis the foreign populations living within their borders on the basis of human rights. On the other hand, it means increasingly pronounced regulation of immigration and increasingly restrictive border controls as elemental to the national sovereignty. The development of an EC immigration regime cannot be understood independently of this global context.

## COMMUNITY POLICY AND IMMIGRATION

The 1957 Treaty of Rome provides for the free movements of persons within the European Community without any nationality distinction. This provision, however, excludes persons originating from the non–EC countries, who currently constitute the majority of the immigrant populations in Europe. There are about 13 million foreign immigrants living in the Community countries. Eight million (2.5 percent of the total EC population) of these foreigners are non–EC nationals, mostly from North Africa, Turkey, Yugoslavia, and the Indian subcontinent. Germany and France have two–thirds of the non–EC foreigners. Luxembourg and Belgium, on the other hand, have mostly EC foreigners. One–third (4.2 million) of the total number of foreigners are in the host countries' labour force, making up 6.7 percent of the EC labour. About 2.4 million of these foreign workers are from non–EC countries; almost half of them work in Germany (Martin et al. 1991).

Currently the EC is experiencing large migratory flows from non–EC countries, almost reaching the levels of immigration in the 1970s. The number of legal immigrants in Community countries rises by some 400,000 a year. The two major migrant groups are asylum seekers and the family members of previous guestworkers. The average annual flow of asylum seekers between 1989 and 1991 to the EC countries was more than 350,000 (SOPEMI 1992). In 1992, asylum applications mounted to 500,000 in Germany alone. A very low proportion, no more than 10 percent, of the asylum seekers are actually accepted to refugee status. Nevertheless, most of them find employment during the three to five years their claims are being considered and eventually remain in the host country. There are also an estimated 3 million immigrants without a legal status, although official numbers are hard to assess ("The Other Fortress Europe", The Economist 1991).

Until the mid– 1970s, when labour recruitment came to a halt, migratory flows from third countries were not part of the agenda at the Community level.[2] In 1974, the question of migrant labour was identified as a "key factor of social policy" in the "Action Programme in Favour of Migrant Workers and Their Families". However, it was not until 1985 that the Commission took a more active and formal approach to immigration issues and adopted "Guidelines for a Community Policy on Migration". The guidelines stated the goals of establishing a common position among member states on immigration and coordinating their national legislation regarding foreigners. The Commission was not successful in introducing a formal framework or procedures to realize these goals.[3] Nevertheless, the "Guidelines" marked the inauguration of immigration as a legitimate EC issue area.

The 1987 Single European Act defines the Community as "an area without internal frontiers", requiring the abolition of all intra–EC border controls as a step toward the free movement of people. The White Paper, issued along with the Act, proposed a body of measures about immigration, leading toward the realization of the EC as a unified territory by the end of 1992. The measures included the coordination of visa policies, the status of third country nationals, and the rules for granting asylum and refugee status. In addition, a policy declaration by the member states affirmed their willingness to cooperate on these issues. The goal underlying the proposed measures was to introduce the control of EC's external boundaries to realize the abolition of internal boundaries, without necessarily any implications for a common Community immigration policy (Callovi 1992). The most important initiative taken upon the European Act was the Schengen agreement. Signed initially by France, Germany, Belgium, Luxembourg, and the Netherlands, the agreement provides for the elimination of common border controls on persons and goods, and for cooperation in matters of security and policing. Accordingly, the citizens of the signing countries and the foreigners who legally reside in these countries no longer need visas within the zone covered by the agreement. Third country nationals are included in the free movement, but they do not acquire the right to seek residence or employment.[4]

With the 1991 Maastricht Treaty, immigration has gained a prevalent status as an EC issue area. The Treaty clearly urges common action to harmonize certain aspects of immigration as a prerequisite for the principle of free movement of people within the Community to be realized after 1992. Despite its EC–flavoured language, the Maastricht Treaty did not generate a full–fledged Community policy with formal structures regarding immigration and immigrants. Concerning long–term immigration and the right of asylum, national–level legislation takes precedence over the EC rules and regulations, even though concerted action among member states is suggested and planned. A common visa policy is to be agreed on by the Council acting in unanimity until January 1996 and by a qualified majority thereafter. Each member state, however, still retains its own legislation regarding the status of foreigners as well as its own laws with respect to naturalization and immigrants' rights. The Treaty carefully distinguishes between the long–term goal of establishing EC rules regarding the status of third country nationals and the more limited, short–term goal of harmonized visa and asylum policy through intergovernmental action.

The insistence on intergovernmental negotiation and national resistance to the development of legally binding Community laws and institutions are not restricted to the immigration policy area. Given the general emphasis on negotiations as the basis for decision–making and frequent references to the sovereignty of member states, the Community has been characterized as a weak policy–making authority. Anchored in a classical nation state model, both realist and rational–choice approaches regard the Community as nothing more than the simple aggregation of member states' interests and agendas (Moravcsik 1991; Garrett 1992a, 1992b).[5] The proponents of these approaches conclude that the EC has not transcended or supplanted the sovereignty of its member states since tasks and decision–making have not been raised to and reorganized at the transnational level.

The realist or rational–choice perspectives would privilege the nation state sovereignty and look upon group interests as the major hindrances to the codification and institutionalization of immigration as a Community policy. So it follows that even though member states may engage in intergovernmental cooperation, immigration remains under the exclusive formal authority of the national states, without circumventing their sovereignty. The commission has the right to propose, amend, and enforce legislation, but the governments of the member states retain the final approval of EC laws. In the end, it is the Council of Ministers (or, more precisely, the twelve ministers from the member states) who make the final decisions regarding the EC's position on immigration. Furthermore, distinctive national practices and organizational structures may create difficulties regarding harmonization and regulation of immigration policy and legislation at the EC level.

Contrary to such views, the EC actually generates much standardization and organizational activity at the European and national levels, both in terms of policy outcomes and policy–making processes. There are two striking trends that do not fit the weak image of the EC constructed in the literature. First, despite the lack of formal, authoritative rules and structures at the EC level, there is an increasing "harmonization" in policy in many areas at the national level (Soysal, forthcoming). The EC member states are having a hard time coming up with a common immigration policy; there are no direct, formal binding rules at the EC level and there is much national resistance to any direct interference by the EC. Nevertheless, an examination of the individual member state policies reveals that there is already considerable standardization across countries. Restrained and prompted by several inter– and transnational instruments (the conventions of the UN, ILO, European Council, and the EC itself, and bi– or multilateral treaties), the European states have granted an increasing set of rights and privileges to their immigrant communities. Consequently, the EC's foreign immigrants constitute a legitimate category with a well–defined set of rights and entitlements.

Second, over the years, the EC's agenda has extended impressively to include several new issue areas. Though not incorporated within the formal decision–making mechanisms and the jurisdiction of the EC, many immigration and immigrant related issues have now become part of the supranational agenda and discourse: entry and residence, employment and working conditions, trade–union and collective bargaining rights, social security, family reunification, education of immigrant children, associative and participatory rights, as well as individual and collective freedoms. The multiplication of EC issue areas has been accompanied by an increase in the rate of organizational expansion. In the last decade, more and more commissions or committees have been established to deal with new domains of policy. The significance of these committees is not necessarily that they formally, or effectively for that matter, influence policy– or rule–making at the EC level. It is in that they create a complex network of advisory bodies, extensively incorporating non–EC and non–state actors into a multilayered system of interaction, and contributing significantly to the creation of a common discourse and understanding.

These two trends, standardization of policy and expansion of the EC's agenda and organization, point to a "Europeification" of policy beyond the simple aggregation of national agendas even in the relatively unformalized area of immigration. They are evidence of an organizational and discursive complexity that challenges the traditional formulations of nation state sovereignty. In the following sections I elaborate on these two trends to consider "Europeification" in policy and discourse, and pursue their implications for the emerging form of the European polity.

## STANDARDIZATION IN IMMIGRATION AND IMMIGRANT POLICY[6]

Too deeply entrenched in national sovereignty, the regulations governing the entry and stay of foreigners remain one of the least standardized aspects of immigration policy. Still, there are general principles upon which all member states agree; family reunification and political asylum are recognized as inalienable rights. Even though there is no formal EC policy or legislation regarding family reunification or asylum seeking, they are defined as inalienable rights in several international fora and accepted as such in national conventions. Currently, none of the EC member states allows immigration for economic reasons, except in the cases of seasonal or frontier–zone employment and people with special skills. Entry into the EC states is restricted to immigrants who qualify on humanitarian grounds, namely family members and political refugees. Despite common national–level efforts to curb immigration by administrative action, member states find it very hard to contain new migratory flows justified on humanitarian grounds.[7]

Although in principle political asylum is accepted as a right, application procedures for asylum vary across member states. Belgium, the Netherlands, and the United Kingdom have the most restrictive policies regarding "spontaneous" asylum seekers not in possession of an entry visa. Germany has the most liberal asylum rules; the 1949 Constitution guarantees legal privileges for asylum seekers that include entitlement to shelter and sustenance during legal review.

National legislation regarding the residency of immigrants in host countries also displays some variation. Residence permits are initially given for temporary periods, usually one year, with the possibility of yearly extensions. Permanent residency (residency for an unlimited period) can be obtained after residing and/or working lawfully in the host country for a period of time. Immigrants also have to wait for a period of time before applying for the citizenship in the country in which they reside.[8]

However, formal citizenship is no longer a prerequisite for many membership rights and entitlements. Well over half the foreign population in the EC states has permanent residency – a status that carries with it an extensive set of rights and privileges originally reserved for the national citizenry.

In many European host countries, the membership status of resident non–citizens is not significantly different from that of citizens, in terms of the rights and privileges they hold. Foreign immigrants are entitled to full civil rights and equality before the law. They enjoy freedom of religion, expression, assembly, and association, though sometimes constrained by national security considerations.

The status of permanent resident also allows access to a set of social rights and services (education in public schools, health benefits, and welfare and social insurance schemes) almost identical to those available to citizens, or to EC nationals. Also, political immigrants are entitled to various social services and rights, including education and cash assistance (in Denmark, Belgium, the Netherlands, and Germany), even while their application for a refugee status is pending.[9]

As regards economic rights, engagement in professions and access to labour markets are regulated by a set of work or residence permits defined by the existing laws governing immigration. This is what most differentiates non–EC immigrants from EC nationals, who are exempted from such restrictions. After staying and/or working legally for a certain period of time, however, non–EC immigrants no longer need a work permit or can obtain a time–unlimited permit. In that case, they are entitled to take up any gainful activity and in law their status is barely distinguishable from that of citizens. The major exception is civil service employment, which is reserved for citizens for national security reasons. Certain professions that are connected with the exercise of public authority, such as being a judge, may not always be open to non–citizens either, although this holds true for the EC nationals as well.

The right that distinguishes national citizens from foreign immigrants, and the EC immigrants for that matter, is the right to vote in national elections. None of the member countries allows non–citizens to participate in national elections. Local voting rights, on the other hand, have been extended to non–citizens in various European countries since the 1970s (Denmark, Sweden, the Netherlands, Ireland, and Norway). In other European countries, local voting rights have been a topic of public debate since the 1980s, and such controversies have gained momentum locally as the debate has intensified throughout the European Community. Still, the main channels of political participation for foreign immigrants remain indirect – alien assemblies or advisory committees, which may be formed both at national and local levels, and unions or work councils at the workplace. All EC countries have some form of consultative arrangement for immigrants, although the role and functioning of these arrangements differ among host countries.

As this brief review shows, whereas policies on immigration control vary across member states, there is considerable resemblance in terms of the rights and status they grant to immigrants.[10] In accordance with the increasing codification of the status of non–citizens in international instruments and treaties, the EC countries have already extended similar sets of rights to their immigrants. There are several international codes and charters that specify principles of immigrant treatment within a "human rights" framework.[11] These codes and charters provide important guidelines and models that bind EC or member state legislation and practice, thereby leading to standardization of the category and status of the international migrant.

The EC itself has produced a set of charters and legislative acts establishing various measures and agencies regarding the integration of immigrants. For example, acting upon the Directives of the European Conference on Local Powers of 1964, several foreigners' assemblies and advisory councils were established throughout Europe, between 1968 and 1978. The EC Commission's recommendation of 1962 was taken by many national governments as a basis for creating specialized social service centres for foreign workers and their families. Similarly, during the early 1970s, participation rights for foreigners at the workplace were mainly introduced by the expansion of European Community law and practice. A more recent introduction, the 1989 Community Social Charter requires member states to guarantee living and working conditions and treatment of workers from non–member countries and their family members to be comparable to that of the nationals of the member state.

More directly, using its authority to engage in international treaties, the Community has made agreements with third countries, bringing the rights of non–EC foreign workers within the legal framework of the EC. These agreements entail non–discrimination provisions in regard to social security, working conditions, and pay, under which the workers from the signatory countries and their family members can claim benefits on the same terms as EC citizens (Callovi 1992).[12]

The EC member states still try to protect their membership by controlling inflows of foreigners. At the same time, constrained by European and global–level discourse, arrangements and laws, they grant an expanding range of rights and privileges to immigrants. Foreign immigrants in Europe now comprise a well–defined category, sustained by a wide array of organizational and administrative structures, state instruments, and budgets. Consequently, even the EC member countries, who are traditionally emigrant countries and have not necessarily had prior experience with immigration, emulate the existing models and accommodate similar categories. In Italy, for example, the legislation passed in 1990 to regulate the hiring and treatment of immigrant workers incorporated many of the guidelines put forth in the ILO's 1975 Convention on Migrant Workers. The legislation guarantees equality of treatment and rights to all legally resident foreigners and their families, provides access to social and health services and housing, and emphasizes maintenance of cultural identity in schools. It also proposes to create a committee for immigrant workers' problems at the Ministry of Labour and Social Affairs, with representation from the immigrant groups themselves – by now a quite common organizational feature in many European countries.

## INSTITUTIONAL MECHANISMS OF "EUROPEIFICATION"

Like most other transnational instruments, the EC charters and codes in general do not entail formal legal obligations or enforceable rules. Nevertheless, they are more than mere principles or guidelines; by setting norms and constructing legitimate models, they enjoin (informal) obligations on the member states to take action (Donnelly 1986, Finnemore 1990, Nadelmann 1990). They define goals and levels of competence, and compel nation states to achieve specific standards. The "Europeification" process, in this sense, is one of gradual transnationalization and standardization through consensual organizational activity, generating a common discourse, if not necessarily common action, justified and propounded by a network of national/international experts, bureaucrats, academicians, and public interests.

The institutional mechanisms that generate such common discourses, frameworks, and models can be indirect, involving mimetic and normative processes. DiMaggio and Powell (1983) identify three mechanisms that contribute to institutional isomorphism and diffusion: coercion, imitation, and normative processes. Coercion would involve imposition of the rules and principles of stronger EC member states on the weaker ones. The primary example is that of the European Monetary Union, which requires the poorer member states to meet imposed criteria in order to attain the level of economic performance of the richer ones. Alternatively, the rules and principles of more successful and dominant countries are sometimes imitated, even in the absence of coercion. Member states may adopt certain principles and models to affirm their membership within the larger European Community and to deal with the uncertainties of an emerging supranational political structure. An example of this process is the adoption of several EC rules and regulations by the members of the European Free Trade Agreement, and by the membership–anticipating countries, such as Turkey, Hungary, Czechoslovakia. Lastly, the diffusion process may involve the emergence of common models through the elaboration of networks and cooperative arrangements, and the normative enactment of these models. Thus, in general, "Europeification" as a process entails learning, comparing differences in national situations and patterns, evaluating the strength and weaknesses of national systems, and finally reorienting and changing national practices (cf. Van Dijck 1989). Through this process, European–level standards, norms and discourses emerge, against which national practices are themselves evaluated.[13]

Much of the EC activity involves regular and extensive information exchange and consultation. At multiple levels of "decision–making", a variety of actors – national administrators, national consultants, European bureaucrats, interest representatives, transnational experts – are engaged in advising and architecting the Community programme and policy. Several groups of experts and academic specialists, hired on a contractual basis, conduct studies on behalf of the Commission and give advice on budgetary, legal, technical, and administrative, as well as substantive, aspects. In 1987, there were about 550 committees of experts and 250 regulation and management committees responsible for the technicalities of the implementation of EC decisions. In recent years, there has been an expansion of the consultative committees and advisory efforts in the field of immigration. In 1989, the EC formed an ad hoc immigration group to examine national positions on the entry and movement of third country citizens, as well as appoining a group of experts to study integration issues. The Maastricht Treaty establishes a coordinating committee of national government officials to make recommendations regarding immigration, asylum rights, and visa requirements. There is also a permanent European research network on immigration sponsored by the EC, with a long–term programme of integrated research. Through their participation in collective projects, committees, and meetings, these different–level actors develop common discourses, understandings and models, which in turn contribute to the "Europeification" and "harmonizing up" of various aspects of cross–national policy.

As models and rules are generated and elaborated at the European level, there is also organizational expansion and activity at the nation state level. The member states continually create new administrative units to cope with different aspects of the EC agenda and programme. Belgium, for instance, most recently established a national office that is solely responsible for political refugees. In 1991, both Italy and Spain formed new administrative units specializing in immigration. And the non–EC immigrant sending countries are compelled to establish corresponding organizational structures, which add to the number and variety of actors operating at the European level. In 1990, for example, Turkey established a secretary of state responsible solely for immigration, with the goal of "defending and furthering the rights and status of Turkish citizens living within the European Community".

The expansion of Community organization and activity also contributes to the shifting of pre–existing national agendas or reorganization of political activity at the transnational level. In response to the elaboration of the EC as a supranational political structure, immigrant associations increasingly become centralized and coordinated at the European level. They establish umbrella organizations and fora to coordinate their activities and to pursue a Europe wide immigrant policy. Through international conferences, meetings, and networking activities, they form common platforms and programmes of action.[14] Several of these organizations have been established since the mid– 1980s, SOS Racisme having the most widespread recognition and network. Another transnational immigrant organization, the Council of Associations of Immigrants in Europe (CAIEUROPE), comprising 2530 associations Europewide, seeks to obtain a consultative status and a liaison to the European Community. It has introduced initiatives concerning the rights of immigrants to be included in the European Social Charter. MIGREUROPE, another supranational effort, attempts to link all organizations involved in immigration and refugee issues, with the intention of exchanging information and cooperating to further positive Europewide immigration and asylum policies.

## IMMIGRATION AND THE EMERGING FORM OF THE EUROPEAN POLITY

In a recent article Philippe Schmitter (1992) challenges us to imagine the "futures of the Europolity". If we were to take EC action and policy-making on immigration as symptomatic of the emergent form of European polity, the picture revealed would be an interesting one: a weak authoritative structure with almost no formal enforcement mechanisms (except the decisions of the European Court), but an increasing amount of activity, organization, and standardization built upon this weak structure. The trend in immigration policy has not been to replace national legislation by a set of authoritative EC rules, but rather to specify certain abstract principles, which in turn create a common discourse of policy and practice. So far, much of the EC activity regarding immigration has involved the production of "non–binding" declarations that outline basic principles, typically framed within the globally institutionalized ideologies of human rights and national sovereignty. These two global doctrines are often invoked in the Community texts and provisions. The Maastricht Treaty and other EC conventions state that immigration issues will be dealt with in compliance with the "international commitments" regarding human rights and the "humanitarian traditions" of the EC states. The same treaties and conventions also affirm that it is the "right and duty" of the member states to take measures to control immigration.

The nature of EC policy–generating mechanisms and activities offers clues to the emerging mode of the European polity. This is a polity whose normative basis and legitimization are located in the wider supranational level, and whose realization still rests with the member nation states (cf. Meyer 1980). The model is one in which the larger system assumes the role of defining the rules and principles, and submitting the responsibility to the subunits, the member states in this case. This model still privileges the nation state as the major agent of public functions and goods, while advantaging the supranational institutions as the locus of legitimacy and basis of these functions. Nation states remain the primary caterers of social functions, while the definition and nature of these functions are increasingly determined at the transnational level.

This model of polity does not involve a centralized, authoritative organization (it is not necessarily accompanied by state–building at the supranational level). Nevertheless, it generates immense organizational activity, involving various actors and levels, mainly toward creating binding discourses and norms, but not necessarily toward formally binding, enforceable rules. Much of the authority of the EC does not come from an established hierarchical structure that can enforce rules, but from the dominance of cultural/cognitive models. The European–level discourse and norms penetrate national systems and set out models through various, indirect institutional mechanisms. Models, discourses, and norms generated at the European level are further accompanied by organizational expansion at the national level. In this way, the formal authority of the member states is not challenged, and distinctive, national organizational structures and practices remain intact.

One caveat: In his eloquent trajectory of the emergent form of the "Europolity", Schmitter (1992) projects "several Europes", where multiple institutions at multiple levels (supranational, national, and subnational) will act autonomously to perform public functions and produce public goods. Thus, whereas immigration policy remains within the realm of member states' responsibility, in some other issue areas EC institutions may perform a more prominent role by taking over the functions and authority of the national units. Especially in the economic and monetary policy area, the EC's authority is more firmly established, the rules are binding and the requisite supranational institutions are being developed. The point I want to emphasize here is that by focusing only on more formalized policy areas, most projections about the structure of the EC undermine the cultural/cognitive component of the emergent model, which facilitates a supranational polity independently of supranational authoritative structures.

Although the member states remain as formal authoritative units, in this new model, the sovereignty of the nation states is circumvented in two major ways (cf. Schmitter 1992). First, the incorporation of increasing numbers of issue areas into EC charters, conventions, and protocols creates a legitimate ground for policy and action at the transnational level. By defining immigration as a policy issue, for example, the Maastricht Treaty licenses the EC and the Commission to legitimately propose laws and policy in this area. In Maastricht, several other chapters are introduced as new EC issue areas: consumer protection, health, education, training, "trans–European networks" (telecommunications, transportation, and energy), industrial policy, and culture. Any EC legislation regarding these policy areas requires unanimity, which is hard to achieve given the rather controversial nature of these issue areas. However, by introducing these policy areas as separate chapters in the Treaty, the Commission acquires a more legitimate ground for making proposals and setting the agenda for further action, independently of national agendas and bypassing national interests.

Second, the incorporation of new fields of policy into the EC agenda also circumvents the sovereignty of member states by creating legitimate grounds for demands by actors at different levels, thereby significantly amplifying the range of the EC's organizational activity. A growing number of European–level interest associations and networks try to influence EC–level rule–making independently of national hierarchies and institutions. More important, this transnational process empowers new actors and induces legitimate claims and interests. Not only immigrant organizations, but also trade unions, social service organizations, regional authorities, cities, and nations without states (Catalans, Basques, Bretons) have been organizing across national borders and seeking representation vis–a–vis the EC, further reaffirming the autonomous institutional existence of the Community.

The mode of the emergent European polity, as suggested here, is by no means a weak one. Even when they are simple non–binding declarations, the EC Commission's proposals and guidelines are important agenda setters. They exert influence on national legislations and sub–national claims. They provide a basis for the claims of immigrants; they shape the platforms of immigrant organizations as well as other public interests. They generate transnational activity and stir publicity for immigrant issues. Even though the Maastricht Treaty is not yet ratified, European immigrant organizations have already started launching demands in regards local voting rights, a par with EC citizens. Also, the status of "European Citizenship", introduced by the Maastricht Treaty, has generated much discussion around the question of who qualifies for it. The European Parliament, the Commission, and the immigration communities all have expressed concerns about the exclusion of non–EC nationals from the "People's Europe". Around the time of Schengen discussions, the EC ministers had to make a declaration and assure the concerned parties that their practice and programmes are "in accordance with the international commitments regarding asylum and the humanitarian traditions of our states". The intensity of concerns and claims and the amount of organizational activity pertaining to immigration are indicators of a "Europeification" already in process.

The emphasis in the literature on the formal policy–making structures and processes of the EC overlooks its role as a norm–setting, model–generating organization and disguises the emergent forms of polity in Europe. The evolving European system, especially in "peripheral" issue areas such as immigration, needs to envision a multiplicity of discursive and institutional mechanisms beyond the confines of formal authoritative structures and "decision–making" processes.

## NOTES

1  I use the term regime to refer to a set of principles and rules, and accompanying organizational structures, around which immigration policy is constructed. See Krasner (1983) for a general discussion.
2  The next four paragraphs draw upon Callovi (1992).
3  In 1987, a Commission decision establishing a procedure for "prior communication and consultation on migration policies in relation to non-member countries" was repealed by the European Court of Justice, upon appeals by Germany, France, the Netherlands, Denmark, and the United Kingdom.
4  By December 1992, the Schengen group is yet to actualize the agreement. The agreement still has to be ratified by the Parliaments concerned (only France and Luxembourg ratified the accord), and it has not received the support of full EC members. Furthermore, the original January 1993 deadline for eliminating passport checks on travelers crossing internal EC frontiers has been postponed because of disagreements among member states about the interpretation of the 1987 Act. The United Kingdom, Ireland, and Denmark claim that the Act still allows the right to maintain border controls.
5  The realists conceptualize the nation-states as "real actors" with a unitary set of interests and agendas, whereas the rational-choice perspective defines the nation-state as an aggregation of individuals and/or groups with self-motivated and calculable interests. See Schmitter (1992) for a review and critique of these approaches in regard to the European Community.
6  This section draws upon Soysal (forthcoming).
7  The complex and multiple set of human rights arrangements can generate interesting instances, as exemplified in the following case. Early in 1992, a Sudanese political refugee in Germany fled to the UK seeking asylum, for fear of racial persecution in Germany. The British government decided to send him back to Germany, his first port of entry; however, a British high-court judge ordered the government to halt the deportation in accordance with the European Convention on Human Rights, accepting that in Germany he might be in danger of attack by neo-Nazis (*The Economist* 1992).
8  The duration of stay required for permanent residency is 2 years in Denmark, 3 years in France, 4 years in the United Kingdom, 5 years in Belgium and the Netherlands, and 8 years in Germany; and for eligibility for citizenship it is 5 years in Belgium, France, the Netherlands, and the United Kingdom, 7 years in Denmark, and 10 years in Germany.
9  Obviously, the substance of welfare rights differs considerably from country to country, depending on the existing national social systems. The Netherlands and Germany have very comprehensive systems; while in the southern member states, the welfare system is rather recent and remains poorly developed. The

differences among national social systems make the availability of social provisions to immigrants unequal across member countries.

10 The ways these rights are organized and realized differ across countries, mostly owing to different understandings and organization of the relationship between the individual and the state in particular polities, as well as different national institutions of citizenship (see Soysal, forthcoming).

11 Some examples of international instruments that provide standards specifically applicable to international migrants are the ILO Convention Concerning Migration for Employment (1949), the ILO Recommendation Concerning the Protection of Migrant Workers from Underdeveloped Countries and Territories (1955), the ILO Convention on Migrant Workers (1975), the Council of Europe's Social Charter (1961) and Convention on the Legal Status of Migrant Workers (1977), and the UN Convention on the Protection of the Rights of All Migrant Workers and Members of Their Families (1990).

12 Currently the EC has agreements with five immigrant sending countries: Turkey, Algeria, Morocco, Tunisia, and Yugoslavia.

13 Although the EC functions much like other transnational organizations, the geographical closure of its collectivity, the intensity and expanse of its actions, the formal recognition of its jurisdiction, as well as its professed intent to create a "Community" make it more effective to generate standardizations and models (as opposed to other transnational arrangements).

14 The Europewide networks are not confined to immigration of course. European trade unions, business associations, consumer groups, academics, and farmers also have their own networks. All these groups operate to ensure and strengthen their claims vis-a-vis the Community.

# 11
# EUROPEAN POLICING

*Ellen Ahnfelt and*
*Johan From*

---

## INTRODUCTION

This chapter deals with the growth of new forms of police cooperation between the members of the European Community.

There has been a considerable expansion in European police cooperation both within and outside the Community since the 1970s. The most dynamic and ambitious elements in this development are the forms of cooperation which have developed between the member states in parallel with the structural changes which have taken place within the Community.

In order to throw light on the development of European police cooperation, it would be opportune to focus on three parallel processes: cooperation within TREVI, the Schengen Agreement, and cooperation within the framework of the Maastricht Agreement. TREVI represents the Community's forum for consultative police cooperation which was established as the result of German and British initiatives in 1975. The negotiations leading to the Schengen Agreement were initiated in the mid– 1980s, the objective being a reduction in border controls between France, Germany and the Benelux countries, and collaboration on so–called compensatory measures. The Maastricht Treaty encompasses a more extensive and more formalized cooperation in the area of Justice and Home Affairs than has hitherto existed, as well as the establishment of Europol. Common to all these endeavours is that they embrace all or some of the EC member countries, that the cooperation takes place at an intergovernmental level, and that they are all, to various degrees, consociate with EC institutions.

The questions which it is intended to address are the ways in which these cooperative structures are linked to EC institutions, how close this association is, and whether it would be possible to talk of a Europeification of policy areas. Has the development of police cooperation, from the establishment of TREVI in 1975 until the launching of Europol, led to an integration of policy formulation in this field, i.e. through a closer linkage to EC institutions and the wielding of stronger influence on the part of the Community?

Police activity may at the outset be characterized as <u>high politics</u>, a policy area which has traditionally been seen as the prerogative of the state (Hoffmann 1965). A Europeification of police cooperation would therefore represent the elevation to EC level of a policy area in which the influence of the individual state has traditionally been very important.

According to classical political theory, a monopoly of the legitimate use of force is a fundamental characteristic of the nation state, and in democratic countries the police force represents the state's central implementing agency in the internal exercise of legitimate power. The strong connection between the nation state and control of the police force, and between police functions and the area of state jurisdiction, at once constitutes a barrier both to cross–border operational police cooperation, international cooperation on a political level, and in particular to supranational cooperation involving the relinquishing of power and control at the national level.

It is also possible in this context, however, to speak of high and low <u>policing</u> as a parallel to high and <u>low politics</u> (Brodeur 1983). This signifies that certain police functions which do not directly affect the integrity of the state are more readily transferable from the national level to e.g. an institution within the Community, while responsibility for areas such as the maintenance of law and order as well as security, is strictly retained at the national level. It should therefore be possible to visualize a comprehensive international police cooperation which goes beyond an informal level in "low policing" areas, without necessarily implying Europeification of core national politics.

In order to shed light on these problem areas, the historical development of TREVI, the Schengen Agreement and the Maastricht cooperation will be described here. Attempts will also be made to identify certain key features relating to the way in which the development process has unfolded, as well as which interests have been of significance in this process. An important issue in this connection is the degree to which integration within the EC, the Internal Market, and the reduction of border controls have represented a driving force in the development of police cooperation. It is assumed that the most important interests are partially related to the development of police cooperation as such, and partly to integration within the Community.

The points at which the processes interconnect will be returned to, but it would seem advantageous to take as a point of departure that the Single European Act (SEA) which incorporated the formal decision to establish the Internal Market involving an unrestricted flow of goods, services, persons and capital before the end of 1992, represents a watershed in the process in the sense that the integration of the EC hereafter becomes prominent as a driving force in relation to the development of police cooperation. Simultaneously with the creation of the SEA, the twelve member states made a political declaration to the effect that when the implementation of <u>unrestricted movement of persons</u> had been accomplished, it should be followed up by cooperation on the entry and residence of persons from third countries, as well as the introduction of measures in the combat against terrorism, drugs, illegal trade in art and antiques and other organized crime. Among other things, this laid the foundation for linking police– and immigration policy–areas.

The growth in international police cooperation from the 1970s and onwards is often understood in an exclusively rational context; fresh initiatives and forms of cooperation are seen as functional and necessary responses to the increase and development of international crime. It is the underlying assumption of this study that international crime constitutes <u>one</u> driving force in the development of police cooperation and that there are strong interests involved, but that this in itself is an inadequate explanation both of the dynamic growth in police cooperation since 1970 and the possibly closer linkage with EC institutions.

It may be argued that the increase in international crime, or the perception of an increasing threat from crime, has been of significance in legitimizing intensified police cooperation. International crime is not novel, and while terrorism and drug–related problems represent areas which have accelerated the development of international cooperation, other areas of crime with international ramifications, such as environmental crime and trafficking in women, have not brought about the introduction of corresponding preventive measures (Anderson 1989).

Political and public awareness are a prerequisite if international crime is to trigger initiatives in police cooperation (Gregory and Collier 1992). These may, however, be induced if the threat of crime is linked with other factors and interests. With regard to police cooperation within the EC, two factors are presumptively of particular importance. First, there is the reduction of border controls in the expectation that the reduction of such controls will encourage a cross–border flow of criminal activities within the EC, which legitimizes compensatory control measures. Second is the wish to secure the Community's external borders against internationally and globally organized crime, but in particular to control immigration from the poorer regions to the south and east of the EC in order to prevent illegal immigration and an increase in the number of applications for asylum on false premises (Bigo 1992).

It has here been assumed that integration within the EC also makes itself felt as an <u>independent</u> driving force in the development of police cooperation in the sense that an enhancement of police cooperation at the EC level may in turn act as a means of promoting integration. Police cooperation can reinforce the process of integration in several ways: by providing the basis for reducing border controls as described above, but also because integration is augmented when new policy areas come under the Community's authority; in particular does this apply to policy areas which have traditionally been central to state control.

Influence over the development of police cooperation can be of importance to the EC system for several reasons. The attainment of power and influence over functions related to control and implementation as progressively new policy areas are incorporated in the EC, is integral to EC rationale. EC crime, for instance in the form of fraud directed against the Community, is an increasing problem. Furthermore, problems related to the Community's external borders and the growing identification of the Community as a single unit which is being threatened from outside by increasing criminal activity and illegal immigration, also promote a speeding up of the centralization of police cooperation. Furthermore, institutional development at the Community level will strengthen the EC as a unit in relation to its constituent members.

## BACKGROUND

The three processes which have been selected as a point of departure represent a segment of current cooperation in the area of justice and police in Europe. There exists an extensive and many facetted cooperation within and among EC member states as well as with other countries. It occurs on several levels encompassing practical, informal day–to–day police cooperation across national boundaries as well as intergovernmental cooperation of the kind with which this study is concerned. There are many examples of more or less formalized bilateral cooperation. There is the central role played by Interpol, and within the Council of Europe there exist various fora and organizations such as the Pompidou Group with its interdisciplinary and interministerial approach to drug problems, in which, moreover, many East European countries participate. Nor are TREVI, Schengen and the envisaged Maastricht cooperation the only organs operating in this field within the Community; for instance there is CELAD, which represents a forum for EC cooperation at ministerial level, also in matters relating to drugs. The EC also has its own forms of cooperation in the field of immigration, with certain similarities to TREVI and which, in terms of the Maastricht Agreement, is to be coordinated with police cooperation.

Despite the close nexus between policing and the individual state, bilateral and European police cooperation has long traditions. Although crime has increasingly assumed the character of an international phenomenon, the police also in earlier times had an operational need for cross–border cooperation. Such cooperation as took place during the first half of the present century was, however, little known to the general public, by and large being of an informal nature and independent of formal agreements and conventions (Fijnaut 1992). Since 1956, Interpol has been the key organization for international police collaboration. Under the auspices of the Council of Europe, two important criminal law conventions were formulated towards the end of the 1950s; the European Council's Convention on Extradition (1957) and a corresponding Convention on Legal Aid (1959). As far as the European Council was concerned, however, police collaboration has always been secondary to judicial cooperation. It was not before the beginning of the 1970s that development in the area of police collaboration really gathered momentum, and this cooperation came to be expressed in innovative ways. In general, the process has moved in the direction of according formalized cooperation greater significance, an increased degree of politization, and an increase in the number of organizations now working with a broader spectrum of issues as opposed to those confining themselves to one specific type of crime.

## POLICE COOPERATION PRIOR TO SEA: TREVI AND THE RELATIONSHIP TO INTERPOL

At the initiative of the British and the Germans, TREVI was established by the Council of Europe in Rome in 1975 as an intergovernmental forum for the EC Ministries of Justice and Home Affairs, and designed to coordinate counter–measures against terrorism. The need for separate police cooperation within the EC had been discussed since the beginning of the 1970s, and the establishment of a Europol was already being debated in Germany at this time. It was, however, the extent of politically motivated terrorism experienced by several of the member states in the mid–1970s which led to the creation of TREVI. TREVI may be seen partly as a functional response to the threat of terrorism, a threat which was aimed at a high political level and which was perceived as a blow directed against the social order itself; partly as a result of dissatisfaction with Interpol, the established international police organization, and also as a first important step on the way to the creation of a separate police structure for cooperation, closely linked to the political level within the Community.

Dissatisfaction with Interpol stemmed from several factors. Even if Interpol is defined as an international organization, it is still partly characterized by its origin as a more or less private international association of chiefs of police which first saw the light of day in 1923. Consequently, resistance to a politization of the organization has been fierce (Fijnaut 1992). In the 1960s, Interpol was moreover strongly criticized for being ineffective and bureaucratic, incapable of fulfilling the need for practical police cooperation in Western Europe. Such criticism emanated particularly from the UK and Germany, while in France, and perhaps in particular within the ranks of the French police, Interpol enjoyed high status, partly because the organization was strongly French–dominated. The most important reason for the EC electing to establish TREVI instead of upgrading Interpol was nevertheless the problematic role played by the latter in relation to terrorism. Interpol's statutes precluded the organization from dealing with cases having political, religious or racial overtones, and this hampered cooperation on measures aimed at combatting terrorism. It was not until 1984 that the statutes were subjected to a reassessment or reinterpretation which enabled Interpol to deal with issues related to terrorism (Anderson 1989). Irrespective of this is the fact that Interpol was and is a world–wide organization representing many different types of regimes, and the EC countries did not have confidence in the organization's ability to deal with terrorism with the necessary degree of confidentiallity.

The two countries which took the joint initiative in creating TREVI, the UK and Germany, nevertheless have widely differing attitudes towards international police cooperation. The UK has shown greater enthusiasm for combatting certain types of crime of a strongly international character such as terrorism, than in police cooperation of a more general character. She is also more concerned to secure the Community's external borders than to further inter–EC police cooperation, and her attitudes are generally more characterized by pragmatism than by vision (Walker 1991). The belief that the state should retain full control of the police force is deep–rooted, and it is such practical matters as the rising level in international crime and crime directed against the EC which are forcing the member states to combine their efforts. Germany, on the other hand, has played a crucial role both in the debate on European police cooperation and its development for more than twenty years. As mentioned above, a Europol had already been discussed in the 1970s, though not necessarily in the context of the EC. Germany's central placement on the European continent, the high level of professionalism of her police force, as well as the need for well regulated, formalised cooperative arrangements as a means of rehabilitating the German police force after World War II, have been advanced as reasons for Germany's eagerness in promoting European police cooperation (Fijnaut 1992).

TREVI's existing organizational structure which was already established in 1976, has three coordinating levels; ministerial, top civil servant and the working group level. The working groups are composed of civil servants and police officers, and are responsible for preparatory work on matters to be discussed at higher level meetings, as well as for carrying out research and planning at the request of the politicians. TREVI does not have its own permanent secretariat. TREVI ministers and senior level officials get together in advance of meetings of the European Council, and the Presidency of TREVI follows the Presidency of the EC.

As has already been remarked, TREVI is a purely intergovernmental forum, and it was not until 1991 that the Commission and the Secretariat of the Council of Ministers was permitted to participate as observers in the working group TREVI 1992, which was responsible for preparatory work on the removal of border controls within the Community. Responsibility for parliamentary and public control of TREVI has been vested in each member country. TREVI has right up to the present been a tightly closed forum, and as such has maintained the traditions from earlier forms of police cooperation. Access to information on the activities of the organization has therefore been limited, both on the part of the EC and at the national level.

From 1975 up to the present, TREVI's ambit of functional responsibility has been gradually extended from combatting terrorism and exchanging information, to embracing general police matters, international crime, and post–1992 compensatory measures. These areas are the responsibility of the working groups TREVI I, II, III and TREVI 1992.

TREVI III, which is responsible for dealing with international crime (illegal drugs trafficking, the weapons trade, computer crime, armed robbery, money–laundering), was established in 1985. The direct cause of this extension of TREVI's responsibilities is not entirely clear, but it may be linked to growing acknowledgement of the complexity of international crime, a stronger tendency to regard international crime as a threat to the internal security of Europe, or a step on the road of greater European integration (Fijnaut 1991).

Parallel to the extension of TREVI's mandate, the organization's leadership structure was strengthened. From 1986 and onwards, TREVI has been headed by a troika consisting of the present, past and in–coming presidents. Up to 1989, the three countries providing the leadership troika also contributed secretarial services. Since then, the two countries "on each side of" the troika have also been responsible for TREVI's secretarial functions, so that these are now taken care of by a "piatnika" secretariat.

## SEA AND ITS SIGNIFICANCE FOR POLICE COOPERATION

As delineated in the first part of this chapter, the SEA's and EC countries' declaration on closer cooperation concerning entry and residence for persons from third countries, combatting terrorism, drugs, illegal trading in art and antiques and other organized crime, as follow–up on the intention to introduce free movement of people, had considerable import as a fresh stimulus to police cooperation and for closer coordination of police, immigration and judicial cooperation. This significance was expressed in various ways for example SEA can be seen as a catalyst in relation to the Schengen Agreement which will be discussed later in this chapter.

In 1988, the Council of Europe established the so–called Coordinators' Group. According to the Palma Report it was designed "to coordinate, stimulate and promote all the work being performed at intergovernmental and Community level in relation to the free movement of people" (Koordinatorgruppen Fri Bevegelighet for Personer 1989). Both the member countries and the Commission were represented in this group. The group's first report, which was presented to the Council at its Madrid meeting in June 1989, clarified which instruments had competence in the various areas of responsibility related to the control of persons, necessary measures, and a timetable for their implementation. The proposed measures for vitalizing police cooperation were not revolutionary in themselves, but on a somewhat generalized level they contained a proposal to extend the applicability of the police recommendations contained in the Schengen Agreement which were being negotiated at this time, to all member countries (Fijnaut 1992).

The Coordinators' Group singled out TREVI, the Ad Hoc Group on Immigration and the Judicial Cooperation Group, the latter organized as part of the European Political Cooperation, as the most important responsible fora, thus opening the way for later linkages between these. In a subsequent report submitted to the European Council meeting in Maastricht, the Coordinators' Group recommended that the cooperation in the judicial area be given a structrual framework which could promote greater efficiency, a recommendation which is being followed up by the Maastricht Treaty.

Simultaneously with the creation of the Coordinators' Group in 1988, TREVI was instructed to assess what impact the removal of border controls would have on international crime, and this resulted in the establishment of the working group TREVI 1992. Its mandate was later expanded to include the planning and preparation of necessary compensatory measures in this connection. The resultant Programme of Action was adopted by the TREVI Ministers in 1990, and has subsequently provided the groundwork for the organization's activities.

The programme of Action is based on "the Minister's conviction that new coordinated measures are called for as a follow up of the Single European Act, as is the intensifying of security measures at the external borders of the EC". The programme is also intended to ensure that the responsibility for implementing these measures is evenly divided among the member states. It embraces all the measures which the twelve member countries have agreed upon, but without the existence as yet of the legal basis for implementation of all the measures. The recommendations have a great deal in common with the measures contained in the Palma Report. TREVI 1992 has, since the presentation of the proposal, had the overall responsibility for coordinating the implementation of measures in the individual countries, as also for dovetailing the work of the other TREVI–groups in this sphere. It has thus become the most important group within TREVI.

The responsibility for laying the basis for the removal of border controls led to the Commission being given observer status in TREVI 1992, and at TREVI's meetings at the Senior Officials level whenever these dealt with issues related to the establishment of the Internal Market. The Commission thus achieved what it had frequently requested but repeatedly been denied ever since the establishment of TREVI in 1975. The grounds for refusing to allow the Commission to participate had all along been the strong emphasis on TREVI's intergovernmental status, and the crucial significance of the police and the judiciary for the sovereign state. There was moreover considerable scepticism among the member countries at the time when the Commission was admitted to TREVI 1992, and at the first meetings the representatives of the Commission and the Secretariat of the Ministerial Council were consigned to inconspicuous back benches.

The relationship between the Commission and TREVI has differed markedly from the relationship between the Commission and the EC's intergovernmental cooperation on immigration, which was initiated in 1986. Here the Commission has all along participated as observer, and has for example been involved in formulating proposals to the EC's convention on asylum (the Dublin Convention). The explanation probably lies partly in the fact that immigration cooperation was established at a different stage in the development of the EC, and partly that cooperation on immigration came to be so strongly emphasized as a common problem for all member countries after the decision to create the frontier–free Internal Market.

The Programme of Action includes proposals on which areas of cooperation between the police and security services within the Community ought to be strengthened, methods of cooperation, and the precise modus of implementation.

The most important areas of cooperation were to be combatting terrorism, drug trafficking, organized crime and illegal immigration; cooperation in the technical and methodological spheres; and the conduct of joint training programmes. With regard to the drug trade, the programme provided the basis for the EC's network of liaison officers, and it was proposed that those member states which did not already have national narcotics units should investigate how these could be brought into being. On the basis of a British proposal, the programme also proposed that TREVI should investigate the conditions for the establishment of a drug combatting unit at European level, the European Intelligence Drugs Unit (EDIU). The plans for EDIU are in practice the same as those now constituting the premises for the creation of the first stage in Europol, the Europol Drugs Unit (EDU).

Part of the follow up of the Programme of Action was a plan for a step by step establishment of EDIU. Germany proposed that at some stage in the process, EDIU should also be accorded executive police authority. However, this proposal aroused so much opposition among the representatives of the other eleven member countries that it was omitted from the plan which was put before and adopted by the TREVI Ministers at their Luxembourg meeting in May 1991.

This meeting took place immediately prior to the May 1991 Luxemburg EC summit, at which Chancellor Kohl proposed the establishment of Europol with an appreciably wider range of powers than those envisaged for EDIU. He won approval for the proposal that this possibility should be further looked into. Responsibility for this was given to the TREVI Ministers, who in turn delegated it to TREVI 1992. As a consequence of this and because of the short time available (it was to be presented to the Council of Ministers at its meeting in Maastricht in the autumn of 1991), the Europol proposal was to a large extent based on the existing plans for EDIU.

Independently of the projected European Union, TREVI had towards the end of the 1980s undergone such transformation with regard to its assigned tasks and ambit of responsibility that a revision of the organization's degree of formalization and structure was indicated. The lack of a permanent secretariat hampered the exchange of information within TREVI in terms of both quantity and quality. During Spain's chairmanship, a permanent secretariat had been proposed but not adopted. Furthermore, there was an increasing need within TREVI for greater openness, commensurate with the organization's ever expanding area of responsibility.

The implementation of the Maastricht Treaty will call for a transformation of TREVI to the extent that it is unclear whether it would be correct to say that it will survive. The Community's institutions will be accorded greater influence. Police cooperation forms part of the planned collaboration on matters affecting Justice and Home Affairs, and will come under the jurisdiction of the Council of Ministers. Hence, the Council will be replacing the ministerial level in TREVI. The Commission will be given observer status in all TREVI working groups, which will presumably continue to exist, and the Secretariat of the Council of Ministers will be taking over the secretariat functions. Also to be established is a new coordinating agency for the entire area of cooperation, the so–called K4 Group (in accordance with Article K.4 of the Maastricht Treaty, where the group is defined). TREVI's tasks and activities will thus be adapted so as to fit into a new structure resulting in closer links with the Community, as well as with other areas of policy, first and foremost immigration. It would thus be correct to say that if the Maastricht Treaty were to be adopted, TREVI's days as a closed forum exclusively for police cooperation are probably numbered.

A certain disagreement persists as to the role which TREVI has actually played in relation to police cooperation in Europe, probably partly because the organization has been so opaque to public scrutiny, and partly because attitudes vary as to what should have priority in the field of police cooperation, for example political coordination versus operational cooperation. TREVI has premarily been a consultative organ at the political level, an informal organization without executive powers. It has been indicated that TREVI has been no more than a symbolic forum producing rhetoric at the macro–level (Benyon 1992). A more prevalent view is that TREVI has played a significant role by accentuating the importance of police cooperation, and that the working groups have had relatively important practical functions. The development of TREVI, from being a forum for cooperation in combatting terrorism to being accorded responsibility for laying the groundwork for the reduction of border controls between member states, has, in advance of the Maastricht Treaty, transformed itself into a tool crucial to the development of the Community.

## THE SCHENGEN AGREEMENT

The Schengen Agreement has as its goal the creation of a Europe free of internal borders, as set out in the Single European Act, and has thus a completely different point of departure from TREVI. The initiative in connection with the Schengen negotiations was taken by Chancellor

Kohl and President Mitterand with the aim of accelerating the laying of the foundation of a "citizens' Europe", and the establishment of the four freedoms (Schutte 1991). The original Schengen signatories were Germany, France, and the Benelux countries. Schengen's historical roots lay in earlier joint action between these countries, as the agreement is partly based on the Saarbrucken Agreement on reduced border controls between France and Germany since 1984, and partly on the Benelux Union since 1958. Prior to the Schengen negotiations, this Union represented one of the most important attempts in Europe at reducing border controls.

The Schengen Agreement represents intergovernmental cooperation for the gradual removal of border controls, preceding the establishment of the Community's Internal Market. Cooperation is based on two conventions, the first being the Schengen Agreement signed in 1985, and the second the subsequent Implementation Agreement (Schengen II) entered into in June 1990. The Schengen Agreement thus has a different and more formalized legal foundation than TREVI, with police collaboration representing only one element of joint action.

Italy, Portugal, Spain and Greece later signed the Agreement, so that today only Denmark, the United Kingdom and Ireland among the EC member states, are not included. There are several reasons for the reluctance of these member states to sign the Agreement, the chief of these being that measures governing border controls and compensatory measures are mutually interconnected in the Schengen Agreement, and these countries do not for the time being wish to dismantle border controls.

The rationale behind the Schengen Agreement is the notion of compensatory measures: when the borders are opened for the free flow of people and goods, internal security can only be maintained if the border controls are compensated for by the introduction of alternative measures. Conversely, compensatory measures in the form of intensified internal controls should not be implemented until the external border controls have been removed. This coupling has made the Schengen Agreement into a bargaining card against those countries which are reluctant to eliminate border controls.

The Schengen Agreement is usually deemed to have served as an important stimulus with regard to integration within the EC. The participating countries have described the negotiations as experiments in the devising of models for, among others, police cooperation. This cooperation has been likened to a laboratory, a first proof, a recipe book etc., for the reduction of border controls and for integration. This function has had an important bearing on the member countries during the preparatory stage of the Agreement, and has to a large extent served to legitimize the negotiations. The Schengen cooperation may consequently be seen as a precursor to closer cooperation in the areas of Justice and Home Affairs within the entire Community. The Convention embraces a number of key measures relating to areas which have traditionally been strictly reserved to the state, and represents the most ambitious attempt thus far towards the evolution of a model for European police cooperation, as well as towards its formalization. The agreement encompasses cooperation on several levels: it covers legal and constitutional issues inclusive of allowing policemen to operate on other countries' territory, an advanced information system, the Schengen Information System (SIS) is to be launched, and there is the additional intention of promoting cooperation in the area of research into specific forms of crime (Benyon 1992). Agreement between the member states on the aim of collaboration, namely the abolishing of border controls, has evidently made it possible to agree on measures which had been unacceptable in other contexts.

The attitude of the signatories to the Schengen Agreement towards the significance of the Agreement contains a certain element of contradiction in that, as already mentioned, attempts have been made by one side to use the Agreement as a bargaining chip, as one has not been willing for Schengen membership to be granted unless the entire Agreement, including specifically the decision to eliminate border controls, is accepted. On the other hand, its value as a forerunner has been emphasized, and it is underscored that the Schengen cooperation has no intrinsic value, and that it is not the intention that it should become a permanent organization for international police collaboration. It would be ideal if Schengen "disappeared", and that the principles enshrined in the Agreement were to be extended to the Community as a whole. One example that this has already happened, is in connection with the Dublin Convention, the EC's Convention on Asylum which was signed in June 1990. It coincides to a large extent with the Schengen Agreement, but goes further in harmonizing the legal framework in the area of asylum.

Even though the Schengen cooperation does not embrace all the member countries in the Community, the linkage to the EC–system is in some respects closer, and at any rate different, to that of TREVI. One factor in this connection is the ideological agreement with regard to integration and the reduction of border controls. The EC Commission has participated in the negotiations on the Schengen Agreement through the presence of the Commissioner for the Internal Market, Martin Bangemann, as observer. He played a very active role in this connection, and hence the Commission has been able to ensure that the collaboration falls within the EC legal framework and that it is in conformity with the EC's intentions (Morén 1991). The Schengen Agreement is valid only "as long as it is in accordance with EC legislation" (Art. 134). The Convention also makes clear that if a European Convention on the elimination of border controls is adopted, it will replace, incorporate or modify the Schengen Agreement (Art. 142).

Negotiations concerning the Schengen Agreement ran into difficulties on several issues. While France was strongly opposed to granting foreign policemen any authority whatever on French soil, Germany argued for the right to pursue criminals across borders. Extradition, visa collaboration and a common policy on asylum were other areas of contention. Also the agreement as to where the Schengen Information System should be located was contentious.

Negotiations on Schengen II were originally finalized in December 1989, but the signing was delayed as a result of the developments in Eastern Europe. For instance, Germany felt that it first needed a clarification of its role in relation to control of its borders with East Germany, and in particular the issue of controlling the influx of immigrants from other Eastern European states (den Boer 1991).

At this stage, powerful criticism was levelled at the Agreement, both by the Parliament of Europe and at the national level. In the European Parliament, two socialist members put forward a resolution addressed to the national parliaments of member states, recommending that the Schengen Agreement not be adopted until both the national parliaments and the European Parliament had been more fully informed, and been accorded the right to participate in the negotiation process. The resolution was adopted by 88 votes against 41 (den Boer 1991). Several of the national parliaments had earlier expressed concern that sensitive issues had been negotiated without political or parliamentary control. The critics pointed out that the Schengen Agreement negotiations had taken place behind closed doors, and that it had not been presented to the national parliaments before negotiations had been finalized. Several countries were moreover dissatisfied with the Agreement itself. Also the status and significance of the Agreement for EC cooperation was criticized. In a leading article in the Dutch newspaper, NCR Handelsblad, dated 13 December 1989, it was argued that the crucial problem with the Schengen Agreement was lack of appreciation of the significance of police collaboration and cooperation in the legislative area within the constitutional EC structure (den Boer 1991). The leader emphasized that the Commission does not have its own Directorate for these areas, which traditionally constitute a corner stone of national sovereignty. Lack of democratic control was underscored since the European Parliament is a weak institution, and the national parliaments were in danger of being kept in ignorance. This criticism was an important contributary cause of the delay in the signing of the Agreement. However, after some hesitation, the negotiations were resumed in March 1990, and the Agreement was finally signed on 19 June of the same year. In the final version, more emphasis was placed on, for example, the protection of the individual's rights and the status of refugees than in the draft version of December 1989.

The Schengen Agreement will only come into force when the five original member states have ratified the Convention. By the end of 1992 France and the Benelux countries of the original signatories, together with Spain and Portugal, had done so. At that time, the Schengen countries intended that the Convention should become effective on 1 July 1993, and hence that control of persons at the borders of these countries should cease at that date. According to the text of the Convention, the Agreement is to come into force three months after the completion of the process of ratification. In May 1993, it had still not been ratified by Germany. Precisely what independent role the Schengen Agreement will play in future police cooperation and in the elimination of border controls, is therefore still uncertain. The Schengen Information System is, however, currently being established.

## EUROPOL AND COOPERATION IN THE FIELDS OF JUSTICE AND HOME AFFAIRS IN THE MAASTRICHT TREATY

The Maastricht Treaty, or the Treaty on European Union, which was adopted at the meeting of the European Council held in Maastricht from 9 to 10 December 1991 and signed on 7 February 1992, introduces several important changes in EC police collaboration, cooperation within related policy areas, and the institutional links between them. The most significant alteration with regard to police collaboration in Europe is undoubtedly the creation of Europol, which is at present being established, but cooperation in the domains of Justice and Home Affairs as delineated in the Maastricht Treaty also has important implications.

The preamble to the Treaty declares the goal of developing close cooperation in the area of Justice and Home Affairs. During the Maastricht negotiations, Germany strongly advocated that the arrangements for such cooperation should be incorporated in the supranational EC, but this did not get the necessary support of the other member states, and the provisions were placed in the so–called third pillar, with the consequence that this aspect of cooperation will be coordinated at intergovernmental level (see Figure 3).

Cooperation on visas, however, is an exception here, as the regulations governing visa policies have been subsumed under the EC's supranationality as one of the Community's new policy areas (Section III, Art. 100 C). The regulations on visa policies are more far–reaching than in the other new policy areas, thus underlining its importance for the EC. The adoption of uniform visa regulations is seen as a precondition for a reduction of controls at the Community's internal borders, again underscoring the crucial significance of immigration policy for the EC.

Within the European Union, it is the Council of Ministers which will decide which third world citizens will require visas for entering the Community (Article 100 C). Resolutions on visas have for the time being to be unanimous, but from 1 January 1996 it will be in the Council's power to make decisions on visas, with a qualified majority. As in other policy areas, such proposals have to come from the Commission after a round of hearings in the European Parliament. In the event of a crisis situation arising in a third country with resultant major influx of citizens from that country, the Council of Ministers may, at the request of the Commission, introduce visa requirements with a qualified majority for a period of up to six months. Before 1996, uniform visas will have been introduced throughout the Community. Article 100 C emphasizes that the Commission is obliged to lay recommendations from a member country affecting this area before the Council, if requested to do so by a member state.

This common visa policy may be regarded as a precursor paving the way for other judicial and internal affairs being brought under the supranational Community, as the text of the Treaty specifies that the Council of Ministers can decide that the rules on procedure contained in Article 100 C shall also be applicable to other measures in a number of third column policy areas. This applies to policies affecting asylum, immigration, the combatting of drug related crime, international fraud, and judicial cooperation in civil matters. Such decisions have to be unanimous.

The EC's new intergovernmental cooperation in the fields of Justice and Home Affairs is justified on the grounds of a need for closer cooperation if the goals of Union are to be realized, in particular those related to the free movement of people (Section IV, Article K).

The following policy areas are to be encompassed:

1. Asylum policy
2. Rules governing border crossing and border control
3. Immigration policy, and policy regarding nationals of third countries
    (a) Conditions for entry, and movements by nationals of third countries within the borders of member states;
    (b) Conditions governing residence of third country nationals within member countries, including regulations governing family reunion and the right to gainful employment;
    (c) Combatting illegal immigration from third countries, unauthorized residence, and employment while within the borders of member states;
4. Combatting drug addiction
5. Combatting international fraud
6. Judicial cooperation in civil matters
7. Judicial cooperation in criminal matters
8. Customs cooperation
9. Police cooperation

These important and sensitive areas are being linked and accorded a higher degree of formalization in relation to the EC's institutions than earlier, even though such cooperation is to continue having the status of being intergovernmental. Status in relation to the EC as well as the degree of organization had earlier varied from area to area. While police cooperation has been the responsibility of TREVI without any participation on the part of EC institutions (apart from the Commission's observer status in TREVI 1992), immigration issues have been taken care of by the so called Ad Hoc Immigration Group, in which the Commission has had observer status since its inception in 1986. In the field of immigration cooperation, the Dublin Convention, among others, has been successfully negotiated to a conclusion. EC cooperation in civil and criminal law matters, has been formally organized as part of the European Political cooperation, which also takes place at intergovernmental level. Combatting drug abuse has been the responsibility of CELAD (European Community Drugs Coordination), which is an EC ministerial coordinating group, while the Community's customs cooperation has been organized through MAG, later MAG 92 (Mutual Assistance Group), since the end of the 1960s.

In addition to the stipulations relating to the third pillar, two concluding declarations are incorporated in the Agreement concerning respectively police cooperation and asylum policy. The declarations can be seen as a political addendum to the text of the Treaty, and reveal something about the relative importance attached to the different areas within the pillar. Matters related to asylum were to be given high priority, and aspects of asylum policy were to be harmonized before the beginning of 1993 (Declaration on Asylum). This is in turn linked to the goal of removing internal border controls and, as a precondition, reinforcing the external ones. As far as The Declaration on Police Cooperation was concerned, Germany received political support, the partners expressing agreement on the objectives which form the basis for the proposals forwarded at the meeting of the Council of Europe in Luxembourg in 1991. It was at this meeting that Chancellor Kohl first put forward his proposal for the establishment of Europol, a proposal which was appreciably broader in scope than the one which was ultimately adopted.

Cooperation in the fields of Justice and Home Affairs is hence to take place at the intergovernmental level, after the introduction of the Maastricht Treaty. The different policy areas will, however, become more closely integrated, and the relationship to the EC's institutions will furthermore undergo alteration. The Maastricht Treaty formalizes the framework for the cooperation which has evolved in the various sectors since 1975, and facilitates uniform and partly closer ties to the EC system in these areas.

A "new" Council of Ministers with responsibility for the entire area is to be established. As a result, the highest political level for police cooperation will be the Council of Ministers instead of the EC's Minister of Justice or Home Affairs serving in their capacity as TREVI ministers. Through the Council, the member states are to keep one another informed and to consult one another in order to coordinate their actions within the relevant areas (Article K.3). The member countries are also to establish a network of mutual cooperation at the administrative level. However, by virtue of being a fully intergovernmental Council, its decisions will have to be unanimous.

It will be the responsibility of the Council of Ministers to establish uniform attitudes and to promote all forms of cooperation which further the Union's objectives. It will have the power to <u>adopt joint measures,</u> and at the same time resolve that measures aimed at implementation can be adopted with qualified majority. Furthermore, the Council is to <u>draw up resolutions in preparation for conventions.</u> The regulations governing convention proceedings will require a two thirds majority unless the convention itself determines otherwise. Article K.3 C moreover permits conventions to incorporate regulations which would authorize the European Court to interpret such conventions, and to pass judgment in cases of dispute. This signals that the cooperation on judicial conventions, as has been previously mentioned, is to be strengthened, as was proposed by the Group of Coordinators. It is also generally recognized that police cooperation is being hampered by the lack of progress in harmonizing legislation within the Community.

The Commission's position will be enhanced in many respects. It has been determined that the Commission is to be fully involved, even though the cooperation is to be intergovernmental. More precisely, the Commission will, in line with the consitutent member countries, have the right to initiate policies in the areas of asylum, border control, immigration policy, narcotics, countering international fraud, and judicial cooperation on civil matters. With regard to cooperation in the spheres of criminal matters, customs cooperation and police collaboration, only the member states will be entitled to initiate proposals to the Council of Ministers. However, the Commission will not be without influence here, either as it has been accorded observer status in appropriate fora. In the sphere of police cooperation this implies that the Commission will no longer be confined to having observer status in relation to TREVI 1992, but also in all extant TREVI Working Groups. As to the wielding of influence, its lack of expertise in this domain is evidently a greater problem for the Commisson than its lack of powers of initiation.

A <u>new coordinating organ</u> covering the entire area of cooperation is also to be established, beneath the Ministerial Council level. This is the Coordination Committee for Justice and Internal Security, K.4, in accordance with Article K.4 which provides for its establishment. In addition to its coordinating functions, the Committee shall make pronouncements to the Council and have a preparatory role in relation to the fields of justice, internal security and joint visa policy.

The Committee shall operate within the entire area of cooperation, and is accorded a very broad sphere of operation. In practice the existing Group of Coordinators will take over the functions of the K.4.

The Maastricht Treaty also to some extent explicates the role of the European Parliament. The Presidency of the Commission shall progressively keep the European Parliament informed on current progress in the area (Article K.6). The Parliament is furthermore to be consulted on the principal aspects of activities, and the Presidency shall ensure that Parliament's views are duly taken into consideration. This implies that matters relating to Justice and Home Affairs constitute a domain in which the Parliament will have a minimum level of influence. According to the wording here, the right to be consulted is the Parliament's original medium of influence. The European Parliament, partly by virtue of SEA (1986), and partly through the Maastricht Treaty, has in some areas been accorded more influence in that different procedures have been established. The Parliament can raise queries and make recommendations to the Council, and is to make an annual review of progress in the area of Justice and Home Affairs.

## EUROPOL

As has previously been emphasized, the establishment of Europol represents the most significant step so far in elevating regular police cooperation to EC level, as Europol is, or is intended to become, a police institution while simultaneously forming an integral part of the EC Union. Europol has a lengthy prehistory. Since the 1970s, Germany has attempted to initiate a reorganization of European police cooperation, and the creation of a Europol Unit (Fijnaut 1992). Views on whether the unit should be part of intergovernmental cooperation or be subordinated to the EC's institutions have, however, differed, and the relationship between Europol and Interpol, as well as the role to be played by Interpol, have been the subject of debate.

Chancellor Kohl's proposal at the Luxembourg meeting in June 1991 for the establishment of Europol should be seen against the background of Germany's earlier interest in the matter, and the already existing plans for the prospective EDIU (European Drugs Intelligence Unit) under TREVI. The projected EDIU expresses a desire on the part of the other European EC countries, with the UK in the forefront, to create a European police unit, but specifically organized at intergovernmental level without operational functions, and confined to the field of narcotics. Kohl's proposal may hence be seen as a political manoeuvre to take up and develop these plans in line with Germany's interests. The German

Europol proposal was presented towards the end of the negotiations, and came as a complete surprise to a number of the other delegations. What was envisaged was a unit for combatting terrorism and organized crime. There were to be two stages in the establishment of the unit, which at first was to be confined to the exchange of information but later also to have an operational mandate. At the conclusion of the Luxembourg meeting, the other countries gave their approval to the German aims, in the same way as in the concluding declaration on police cooperation at Maastricht. Responsibility for preparing the text of a final agreement to be negotiated at Maastricht was assigned to the incoming Dutch Presidency, who in turn delegated it to TREVI.

As was described above, the result was that the EDIU plans came to form the basis of Europol's first stage, Europol Drugs Unit (EDU), an information and possibly research unit, with responsibility for drugs related matters. The link with the EC is, in like manner to the other cooperation within the third pillar in the Maastricht Treaty, intergovernmental, but with closer links to the EC's institutions than was the case with earlier police collaboration.

The decision to establish Europol may mark the first step on the road to a more operational police cooperation between the EC member states, but it is by no means a foregone conclusion that the unit will ever have practical functions devolved upon it. In the Maastricht Treaty, Europol is only loosely defined, and its responsibilities are limited to the exchange of information. Police collaboration is one of the nine areas regarded by the member states as "matters of common interest, to achieve the objectives of the Union, in particular the free movement of persons", and has been defined as "police cooperation for the purposes of preventing and combatting terrorism, unlawful drug trafficking and other serious forms of international crime, including if necessary certain aspects of customs cooperation, in connection with the organization of a Union–wide system for exchanging information within European Police Office (Europol) (Articles K.1 and K.1 [9])". In the final declaration, Europol is not explicitly mentioned. A number of areas relevant to an expanded cooperation are, however, listed, and the member states commit themselves to considering a broadening of the framework for such cooperation during the course of 1994.

Tasks which were accorded particular mention in this connection are: assistance to the national authorities responsible for investigative and security tasks in order to facilitate coordination, the establishment of data–bases, engaging in crime analysis and undercover work, as well as developing investigative methods, the collection and systematization of national preventive programmes with a view to sharing information in order to organize these at a European level, extra training, research, forensic techniques, and anthropometry.

The Maastricht negotiations resulted in the TREVI ministers, in collaboration with the Commission, being charged with the task of taking the necessary steps in establishing Europol (EDU) as quickly as possible. Within TREVI, the responsibility for establishing Euoropol was given to a separate Europol group under British leadership, in which the Commission also took part. The Group has worked in accordance with a so–called "fore–runner principle". Various participating countries assumed the main responsibility for preparing a report on certain aspects of the activity, and the various sections were then coalesced into a report which was presented at the meeting of the TREVI ministers and the European Council in June 1992. At this meeting, agreement was reached on a number of important issues, but by no means all.

What was adopted at a Dutch suggestion was to create a <u>Europol Project Team</u>, which was to undertake the practical planning. It was also determined that Europol and the European Information System (EIS) in their final form should be based on a convention requested by Denmark, and that a provisional start, based on an agreement at the ministerial level, should be made as from 1 January 1993. The question as to the geographic location of Europol's permanent base was postponed, as also the matter of Europol's working language.

The Europol project team was established early in the autumn of 1992, with provisional headquarters in Strasbourg, and under German leadership. In September, representatives of five nations participated, Denmark not yet having decided whether to participate or not after the Danish electorate had returned a negative verdict on the Maastricht Treaty at the referendum held earlier that month. Whether both the customs authorities and the police were to participate was for the time being left to each individual country to decide. The team worked according to a "two stage strategy", involving one model for information–sharing until the European Convention had been worked out, and another which was to take effect afterwards. It will take a minimum of two to three years to negotiate the Convention, and it was therefore expected that Europol's final structure would not be established before 1994 at the earliest. The project team anticipated that before this time a steadily increasing need to solve a variety of crime related problems within the Community, such as the laundering of money, and fraud and environmental crime, would have arisen, and that this would lead to various political decisions with the likely result that there would be too many rather than too few tasks for Europol.

The relation between Europol and the Schengen Information System had not been finally settled at this juncture; it had not yet been decided whether Europol should have direct access to SIS. Europol's provisional placement was to coincide with that of SIS.

The Europol project team is at present very much concerned to elucidate the issue of parliamentary control of Europol. It has, however, not yet been determined whether it should be vested in the EC Parliament or at the national level, but the degree of contact with the former is increasing. The Parliament has established a separate committee for civil liberties and internal affairs, with the Europol project as its point of departure, and this committee has to date produced two reports on Europol.

In sum, there remain many uncertainties pertaining to Europol's future role and status. Europol owes its existence to the intergovernmental cooperation on Justice and Home Affairs envisaged by the Maastricht Treaty, but its establishment will be independent of whether or not the Treaty is finally adopted. Whether Europol is to be integral to the intergovernmental EC, the extent of influence from the EC institutions, and in particular the Commission and the Parliament, is still indeterminate. Much will depend on how much expertise the Commission manages to acquire in this area, as well as on the evolution of the Community itself. Precisely which responsibilities the unit may be charged with has not yet been finally determined, nor whether it will be entrusted with operational responsibility. In the meantime, the Europol project team, the provisional Europol unit, has become a factor to be reckoned with in influencing future European police cooperation, both with respect to speeding up the political negotiations on a Europol Convention, and more generally. It is probable that this participation, under German leadership, will strengthen Germany's role and serve to advance her views in the further development of the Community.

## CONCLUSION

It is the contention of the authors that the development of TREVI, the Schengen Agreement, the Maastricht cooperation and Europol demonstrates that, from the mid– 1970s and up to the present, there has been a certain measure of Europeification of police collaboration between the member states. TREVI, the Schengen Agreement, and the Maastricht cooperation all fall within the framework of the EC, and function at intergovernmental level. Interconnection with the Community's institutions is a common feature of these processes, but the various EC institutions participate in various ways and to a varying extent. TREVI represents the EC member states' coordinated police collaboration, and has carried out assignments partly on behalf of the European Council, and after being given responsiblity for laying the foundation of a removal of the EC's internal border controls, the Commission has had observer status in TREVI 1992. The Commission has participated as observer during the Schengen negotiations, and has ensured that the Convention has been in line with the Community's integration ideology as well as with European legislation. The European Parliament has adopted a sceptical attitude towards the Schengen cooperation because of a perceived lack of parliamentary control. However, not all of the EC countries are participating.

Under the Maastricht Agreement, the interrelationships between these areas of activity will become closer and more formalized. Police cooperation will be linked to other policy areas with implications for border issues, primarily immigration policy and judicial cooperation. The domains of Justice and Home Affairs are to be subordinated to the Council of Ministers, and the Commission will acquire increased influence in police matters by virtue of its observer status in the appropriate committees. The Parliament is to acquire a certain degree of control by virtue of its consultative function. A new coordinating body is to be established for the entire area falling under the Ministerial level, K 4. In short, the foundation is being laid for a higher degree of integrated policy formulation than before.

This study confirms the significance of EC integration as a driving force in the evolution of police cooperation within the Community. The Single European Act and the reduction of internal border controls between member states have had implications for both TREVI and the Schengen Agreement, as well as for the linkages of policy areas and the increased degree of formalization envisaged by the Maastricht Agreement.

In the Maastricht Treaty, the creation of Europol is seen to be crucial. Establishing Europol was initiated in the autumn of 1992, and is the most visible expression of an intensified police cooperation within the Community.

Europol epitomizes the difficulties the Europeification of police cooperation will encounter, and points up the conflicts implicit in the transfer of various police tasks to a supranational level. For example, when Chancellor Kohl at the Luxemburg meeting proposed the establishment of Europol as an operational unit, he wanted the unit to combat terrorism, a task for which TREVI had earlier been established to deal on a strictly intergovernmental level. As a result of the rivalry between the various parties, the first step towards the creation of Europol was confined to the establishment of an information unit in the area of combatting drug trafficking, but without operational mandate. This serves to demonstrate that, not surprisingly, it is easier to achieve political agreement on the Europeification of low policing tasks than on high policing areas such as terrorism.

# Part III
# The Future of Europe

# 12
# THE EC IN EUROPE'S FUTURE ECONOMIC AND POLITICAL ARCHITECTURE

*Finn Laursen*

## INTRODUCTION

Talk about Europe's political architecture has become fashionable in recent years, especially after the revolutionary changes which occurred in Central and Eastern Europe in 1989. The discussion did start somewhat earlier in connection with the work of the Conference on Security and Cooperation in Europe (CSCE). However, as the Soviet dominance of Eastern Europe vanished, a completely new situation emerged in Europe after 1989. Gone were the bipolar structures of the Cold War. It became possible to imagine new, all–European structures.

When Commission President Jacques Delors spoke to the European Parliament in January 1989, he referred to Gorbachev's concept of a "common European House", but said:

> ... I would say that our vision is of a "European Village" where understanding would reign, where economic and cultural activities would develop in mutual trust. But if I were asked to depict that Village today, I would see in it a House called the "European Community". We are its sole architects; we are the keepers of its keys; but we are prepared to open its doors to talk to our neighbours. (Delors 1989)

Delors saw a European village of different houses. Obviously the European Community was an important house in that village. However, the European Free Trade Association (EFTA) was still there, as were the Soviet Union, the Council for Mutual Economic Assistance (CMEA or COMECON), and the Warsaw Treaty Organization.

It was the view of the Commission in 1989 that internal EC development should take priority over enlargement. Thus the idea of various kinds of special partnerships with the neighbours was envisaged, including first of all "a new, more structured partnership" with EFTA countries, but also trade and cooperation agreements with Central and Eastern European countries. These "flexible proximity policies", according to Delors, would also extend to the Mediterranean countries and North Africa.

Since January 1989, however, things have changed profoundly and rapidly in Europe. The EC has negotiated the European Economic Area (EEA) agreements with the EFTA countries, and "Europe agreements" first with Poland, Czechoslovakia and Hungary, and now with Bulgaria and Rumania. The Soviet Union has ceased to exist, and so have the Warsaw Treaty Organization and COMECON. The Baltic states have become independent, as have Slovenia and Croatia but a cruel civil war is pulling Bosnia–Herzegovina apart, and threatening to expand to other parts of the Balkan area. The Community itself has negotiated the Maastricht Treaty which, when and if ratified, will deepen the internal EC integration process further. Moreover, the formal list of countries applying for membership in the Community – or the European Union (EU) to be established by the Maastricht Treaty – now includes five EFTA countries: Austria, Sweden, Finland, Switzerland and Norway, as well as three Mediterranean countries: Turkey, Cyprus and Malta. In addition, the new political leaders of the Central and Eastern European states also have their eyes set on Community membership.

This suggests a major shift between 1989 and today; from an image of the European architecture as a village with the EC as the centrally located house to one where the European system is increasingly becoming the EC itself, enlarged to include all or most EFTA and Eastern European states and some Mediterranean ones (Ludlow 1991). This, at least, was the case until the Danish referendum in June 1992, when a small majority of the Danish electorate voted "no" to the Maastricht Treaty. During the second part of 1992 the situation in Europe was one of great uncertainty in respect to deepening and widening of the EC. The Edinburgh meeting of the European Council in December 1992 accepted the Danish request for clarifications and opt–outs from the Maastricht Treaty, increasing the likelihood of a "yes" vote in a second referendum in Denmark in 1993. The Edinburgh summit also decided to start membership negotiations with Austria, Sweden and Finland early in 1993 (European Council 1992). This has clarified the situation somewhat, but many uncertainties still lie ahead.

**Figure 9.** *Kinds of international cooperation and integration*

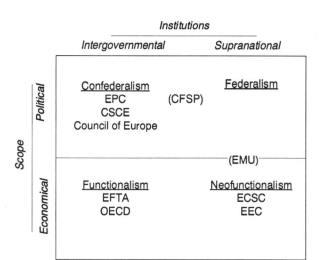

In this paper we will outline and analyse these important changes in the Community's integration process and how it affects the European economic and political architecture. First, however, it may be in order to outline a few concepts that can help organize the discussion.

## INTEGRATION AND COOPERATION OPTIONS

States contemplating participation in schemes of international cooperation or integration face various choices in respect to the scope of cooperation and the capacity of the joint institutions they create. To simplify matters somewhat, they may limit cooperation to either economic or political issues or they may include both. In respect to institutions, an important decision is whether to stick to classical intergovernmental cooperation or accept supranational institutions. The four main possibilities are illustrated in Figure 9.

The European Coal and Steel Community (ECSC) and the European Economic Community (EEC) both constitute examples of the neofunctionalist strategy of integration. They created cooperation in economic areas and have established supranational institutions. However, when the members of the European Communities (EC) started cooperation in the area of foreign policy in 1970, through the so–called European

Political Cooperation (EPC), they based this on a purely intergovernmental kind of cooperation. The European Free Trade Association (EFTA) established intergovernmental cooperation in the economic area, an example of functionalism.

The neofunctionalist strategy is also referred to as the "Community method". It includes the right of initiative of the independent Commission, which is expected to represent the Community interest, the possibility of decisions in the Council of Ministers by qualified majority, and a legal system that has primacy and direct effect, including a Court of Justice, which makes binding decisions. It is interesting to notice that EFTA, which did not originally accept anything like the Community method will, as a result of the recent European Economic Area (EEA) agreement, establish an EFTA Surveillance Authority and an EFTA Court which, in certain areas, will have powers comparable to those of the EC's Commission and Court of Justice. A vindication of the Community method, one may say.

In the political area the application of the Community method has turned out to be much more difficult. A first effort in the early 1950s, the European Defence Community (EDC), failed. This partly explains why the EPC was developed on an intergovernmental basis. An important issue in the Maastricht Treaty negotiations was whether the new Common Foreign and Security Policy (CFSP) should be based on the Community method. Ultimately, this will not be the case. However, the Commission will get a non–exclusive right of initiative and, under certain conditions, some majority decisions may be made, but the Court of Justice will not be competent within the CFSP. It can also be said that the CFSP straddles the threshold between intergovernmentalism and supranationalism, but the intergovernmental element dominates. This is different from the economic areas, the first pillar of the Maastricht Treaty, where supranationalism is strengthened further, especially in respect to Economic and Monetary Union (EMU).

To the extent that the European Union (EU), created by the Maastricht Treaty, becomes the focus of the future European architecture, this difference between supranationalism in economics ("low politics") and intergovernmentalism in foreign and security policy ("high politics") will have some implications. Optimal cooperation may be easier in areas of "low politics" than in areas of "high politics" and different styles of architecture seem to emerge in the economic and political areas.

# THE PROCESS OF DEEPENING: FROM THE SEA TO THE MAASTRICHT TREATY

The attractiveness of the EC to its neighbours is largely due to the new momentum of European integration which became apparent from the mid– 1980s. In particular, the Internal Market Programme of the EC, which in principle has led to free movement of goods, services, capital and people from January 1993, has got the industry in EFTA countries to turn towards the EC and increase their investments in EC countries to be sure to be part of that Internal Market (Laursen 1990b, 1991b).

The Single European Act (SEA), which was adopted in 1986, linked the Internal Market project with institutional improvements, firstly through the introduction of qualified majority voting in the Council to complete the Internal Market (Laursen 1990a).

The SEA entered into force in 1987. Its new rules of qualified majority voting with respect to the Internal Market, helped get the necessary legislation adopted. The Internal Market project made enough early progress to give the EC new momentum.

However, the EC's new momentum did not stop with the Internal Market. At the Hannover meeting of the European Council in June 1988, a committee was established to study "the objective of progressive realization of economic and monetary union" (EMU). This committee, chaired by Jacques Delors, produced a report in 1989 (Committee for the Study of Economic and Monetary Union 1989). On the basis of this report, it was decided at the meeting of the European Council in Strasbourg, December 1989, to call an Intergovernmental Conference (IGC) to consider the realization of EMU.

The idea of having a second Intergovernmental Conference on European Political Union (EPU) emerged soon afterwards. It was discussed at an extraordinary meeting of the European Council in Dublin in April 1990, on the initiative of President Mitterrand of France and Chancellor Kohl of the Federal Republic of Germany, and it was confirmed by a meeting of the European Council in Dublin in June 1990. The two intergovernmental conferences then started in December 1990 in Rome.

The European Council of Maastricht in December 1991 concluded the negotiations of the two IGCs and adopted the Treaty on European Union, also known as the Maastricht Treaty (European Communities, Council and Commission 1992).

In many ways, the Maastricht Treaty continues the logic of the SEA, especially with respect to EMU, which is a part of the treaty (Laursen and Vanhoonacker 1992). The treaty includes various institutional reforms. In particular, the role of the European Parliament is enhanced in various ways. First of all, Article 189B creates a new procedure which will give the European Parliament a real veto on legislation in certain areas. In the future, the Parliament will also have the right to approve the President and other members of the Commission.

The Maastricht Treaty has a three–pillar structure. The first pillar, the European Community, includes the EMU and various reforms and developments of the existing Communities. The second pillar is about a Common Foreign and Security Policy (CFSP) and, as such, a development of EPC. The third pillar is about cooperation in the areas of Justice and Home Affairs. With the exception of visa policy, which is included in the first pillar, the latter includes asylum policy, immigration policy, combatting drug addiction and fraud on an international scale, judicial cooperation in civil and criminal matters, customs cooperation, and police cooperation.

If ratified by the two remaining countries, the UK and Denmark, the Maastricht Treaty will constitute a further deepening of European integration. The first pillar will move the EC from the Single Market to Monetary Union, including a single currency by 1999 at the latest.

## THE EUROPEAN ECONOMIC AREA

As mentioned, it was in January 1989 that Jacques Delors offered "a new, more structured partnership with common decision–making and administrative institutions" to the EFTA countries (Delors 1989).

There can be no doubt that the Commission offered this partnership as an alternative to membership. The Commission wanted to complete the 1992 Programme of the Internal Market and move on to further deepening of integration, in particular Economic and Monetary Union (EMU), before taking in new members.

The official EFTA answer to the Delors initiative was positive. In general the EFTA countries said that they wanted the greatest possible realization of free movement of goods, services, capital and persons within the European Economic Space (EES), as the combined EC–EFTA area was called at the time (Later the name changed to European

Economic Area). Institutionally, no alternatives should be excluded a priori (EFTA Bulletin, April–June 1989).

Formal negotiations started in June 1990, after exploratory talks. Elements of a package deal started emerging gradually towards the end of 1990, including agreements on decision–making and institutional set-up. A joint meeting at ministerial level on 19 December 1990 outlined the future decision–making structures. It made a distinction between a "decision–shaping phase" where there would be "a continuous information and consultation process" and decision–taking which would be by consensus between the two sides (Europe Documents, No. 1683, 15 January 1991).

With respect to competition policy, a joint ministerial meeting on 13 May 1991 decided that there must be "a system ensuring equal conditions of competition including state aids throughout the EEA". The creation of an "independent EFTA structure (with equivalent powers and similar functions as to those exercised by the EC Commission)" was therefore necessary (Europe Documents, No. 1712, 22 May 1991).

In the autumn of 1991, the final problems with regards to fish, transit through the Alps and EFTA financial contribution to "cohesion" within the EC were finally resolved. However, the story was not finished there. The ECJ was asked its opinion about the draft agreement. To the surprise of many, the ECJ decided that the draft agreement was incompatible with the Treaty of Rome (European Communities, Court of Justice 1991). The negotiators therefore had to get back to the negotiating table at the beginning of 1992. In the end, the proposed EEA Court had to be dropped. Instead the EFTA side will establish an EFTA Court. The EC will retain its institutional autonomy. The final agreement on this was reached in February 1992 (Sweden, 1992). The ECJ found the new agreement compatible with the Treaty of Rome (European Communities, Court of Justice 1992). It was signed in Oporto, Portugal, on 2 May 1992.

The EEA Agreement consists of 128 articles, 49 protocols and 22 annexes. Through this agreement the EFTA countries will take over about 950 Directives, 160 regulations, 120 decisions and 300 non–binding instruments, amounting to about 14,000 pages of legislation.

The EEA differs from the EC in various ways: it is not a customs union, but an improved free trade area; it does not include the Common Agricultural Policy (CAP), nor common foreign policy nor taxation. It gives no real participation in decision–taking to EFTA countries, and there is no transfer of competences. It establishes a two–pillar structure, where each side has to agree to new EEA–wide legislation. There will be no majority voting on the EFTA side.

Except for membership, the EEA constitutes the closest relationship with the EC currently available. The next closest relationship is constituted by association agreements. Here we have new association agreements with countries in Central and Eastern Europe, and older ones with Mediterranean countries.

## ASSOCIATION AGREEMENTS WITH CENTRAL AND EASTERN EUROPE

Prior to 1988, the USSR and its allies in Eastern Europe did not formally recognize the EC. There were of course trade relations between the EC and the members of CMEA but various factors, including quantitative restrictions on the EC side, limited trade. Only one of the Eastern European countries got a formal trade agreement with the EC, namely Rumania in 1980, in recognition of its independent stance vis–a–vis the USSR at the time.

Things started to change after Gorbachev came to power in the USSR. On 29 June 1988, the EC and the CMEA formally recognized each other's existence. The Eastern European countries could now establish missions at the EC (Maresceau, 1992). It was Hungary, which had gone furthest in the area of economic reforms at the time, which got the first agreement on trade and commercial and economic cooperation with the EC on 26 September 1988.

Later, other trade and cooperation agreements were concluded with Poland, the USSR, the German Democratic Republic (GDR), Czechoslovakia, Bulgaria and finally with Rumania. Because of German unification in 1990, the agreement with the GDR never became operative.

Soon after the first trade and cooperation agreements were negotiated between the EC and the Eastern European countries, things started moving very quickly. The collapse of the Communist regimes in Eastern Europe in 1989 called for more assistance from the West to facilitate the reform process. The summit meeting of the Group of Seven (G–7) in Paris in July 1989 asked the EC Commission to coordinate assistance from the 24 members of the Organization for Economic Cooperation and Development (OECD) for reforms in Eastern Europe; initially, this focused on economic assistance to Poland and Hungary, which led to the establishment of the so–called PHARE (Poland–Hungary Aid for

Reconstructing the Economy) programme by the Commission in September 1989 (Ungerer 1990). In September 1990, the Council adopted the regulation that allowed the PHARE programme of economic assistance to be extended to Czechoslovakia, Bulgaria, Yugoslavia and Rumania. In order to receive aid, the countries had to establish pluralistic political regimes, including free elections, multiparty systems and respect for human rights, and they had to establish market economies.

The idea of moving from trade and cooperation agreements to association agreements emerged quickly. In August 1990, the Commission proposed the possible conclusion of association agreements, called "Europe agreements", with the Eastern European countries. It was decided that negotiations should be started with Hungary, Poland and Czechoslovakia. Conditions in Bulgaria and Rumania were not considered satisfactory at the time. However, negotiations with these two countries might follow later when the necessary political and economic conditions have been established. In the case of the Soviet Union, the idea in 1990 was that the existing trade and cooperation agreement offered an appropriate framework for relations (European Communities, Commission 1990a).

The Commission's August 1990 Communication suggested that "Europe agreements" should have a common framework, including:

- political dialogue,
- free trade and freedom of movement,
- economic cooperation,
- cultural cooperation,
- financial cooperation,
- institutions of association.

However, within the common framework, specificity and differentiation were foreseen as taking the specific political and economic situations of the different Eastern European countries into account.

Apart from allowing a political dialogue, the agreements were, first of all, to aim at gradually establishing a free trade area. Later, "consideration can be given to the free movement of services, capital and persons". The Commission also suggested that the approximation of laws should be carried out in many areas to facilitate economic interactions.

The official opening of negotiations with Hungary, Poland and Czechoslovakia took place on 20 December 1990 and agreements were concluded in December 1991, confirming the general structure of what the Commission had proposed. These agreements are to establish a political dialogue at the highest level, and realize a free trade area over a ten–year transition period. For industrial products, many tariffs were abolished from the entry into force of the agreements. Asymmetry is foreseen; the EC will abolish tariffs faster than the three associated countries. There are special protocols on agricultural products, textiles and coal and steel. The agreements also include such points as safeguard measures, anti–dumping rules and rules of origin. Furthermore, there are rules on free movement of labour, establishment, services, capital movements, and competition policy. Measures in some of these areas will need further development through the Association Council. There will also be economic, financial and cultural cooperation. The institutions established are of the classic pattern: Association Council, Association Committee, and a Parliamentary Commission (Lucron 1992, Maresceau 1993). Similar agreements have now also been concluded with Bulgaria and Rumania. The one with Czechoslovakia will now have to be renegotiated due to the formation of the two independent Czech and Slovak Republics in January 1993.

## THE MEDITERRANEAN ASSOCIATION AGREEMENTS

Turkey established an association agreement, known as the Ankara Agreement, with the EC back in September 1963 (and which has been in force since December 1964). However, the agreement never worked to Turkey's full satisfaction, partly because of the military intervention in Turkish politics in 1980 and partly because of political problems within the EC, especially after Greece joined in 1981 (Laursen 1991, 1992).

The objectives of the Association agreement were: (1) the progressive establishment of a customs union; (2) alignment of economic and social policies, including the progressive achievement of free movement of workers; and (3) financial cooperation. The agreement also foresaw membership of the EC at a later stage. The 1963 agreement was supplemented with an Additional Protocol in 1970. This set the rules for establishing a full customs union over a period of 12 to 22 years from 1 January 1973. It added economic cooperation and started the second phase of alignment of policies (Cendrowicz 1991).

Achieving the customs union turned out to be rather difficult. There have been problems on both sides. A great increase in Turkish export of textiles to the EC in the late 1970s led the EC to insist on "voluntary" export restrictions (VERs). Turkey, on the other hand, was not able to follow the schedules laid down for tariff dismantlement.

The EC has failed to enact free movement of workers and the Fourth Financial Protocol, negotiated in 1980, has remained blocked since then for various political reasons.

Cyprus has an association agreement with the EC which goes back to the time of the first enlargement. It was signed on 19 December 1972 and entered into force on 1 June 1973. This agreement provides for the gradual elimination of trade barriers and the creation of a customs union in two stages (European Communities, Commission 1990b). The first stage of the customs union should have ended in June 1977 but it was extended until the end of 1988. A protocol signed in October 1987 provided for the implementation of stage two, which was divided into two phases. The first phase is due to run until the end of 1997 and it should complete the customs union as regards tariffs. At the same time, trade in agricultural products will be expanded through the reduction of quotas. Through financial protocols, there is also financial cooperation between the EC and Cyprus.

Malta's association agreement with the EC was signed on 5 December 1970. It entered into force on 1 April 1971. The original agreement provided for two five–year stages leading to a customs union. The first stage, however, was extended by an agreement in March 1976, by an Additional Protocol in October 1977 and by a Supplementary Protocol in December 1988 (Malta 1990).

Creating customs unions with the three Mediterranean countries has thus turned out to be more difficult than originally expected. This should dampen the expectations in respect of the possibilities for Central and Eastern European countries.


## CONCENTRIC ECONOMIC CIRCLES

What we have seen in the economic area is an edifice with the EC at the centre surrounded by concentric circles. The first circle is the EEA Agreement. The next is the association agreements, including the older ones with the Mediterranean countries and the newer ones with Central and Eastern European states. Beyond the association circle, there will still be countries having trade and cooperation agreements. This circle now includes the Baltic countries and Albania, which may move into the association circle. More recently, in June 1992, the Commission suggested negotiating "Partnership and Cooperation Agreements" with the ex–USSR states, including the members of the Commonwealth of Independent States (CIS) and Georgia. This new category of agreements will include mixed agreements, including political dialogue, most favoured nation (MFN) treatment, economic, financial and cultural cooperation. The longer term perspective of Partnership and Cooperation Agreements is a gradual rapprochement in a wider area of cooperation, while association agreements may help third countries achieve the aim of membership. The situation is illustrated in Figure 10.

Both the first and second circles around the EC include states which have applied for membership in the EC. What then are the possibilities of "graduating" to join the central group in this architecture? It should be understood that the possibility of "flunking" also exists. Should Denmark fail to ratify the Maastricht Treaty, it may have to join the EEA. The Swiss failure to ratify the EEA Agreement leaves it with the Free Trade Agreement of 1972 and some other bilateral agreements.

Moreover, in connection with this economic architecture, we should be aware of the likelihood of an inner core within the EC, moving faster than some members. Some members may not meet the Treaty's convergence criteria for the third stage of EMU by 1999, and the UK and Denmark have opt–outs with regard to the EMU. The UK established an opt–out clause with respect to social policy at Maastricht. Add to that the Danish clarifications and opt–outs at Edinburgh, and it becomes clear that some multi–speed integration is likely (European Council 1992; Laursen 1993).

## THE ENLARGEMENT ISSUE

The Turkish Government applied for membership of the EC on 14 April 1987. The Council of Ministers then requested an opinion from the Commission. This opinion was finally sent to the Council on 18 December 1989. It was the view of the Commission that no membership negotiations with Turkey should be considered until at least 1993 (European Communities, Commission 1989).

The Commission's opinion basically stated that one should look at both the capacity of the applicant and the EC itself to absorb new members. On the latter point, it was recommended that the Internal Market should be completed before the EC contemplated admitting new members. With respect to Turkey, it was argued that the Turkish

**Figure 10.** *Economic architecture of Europe*

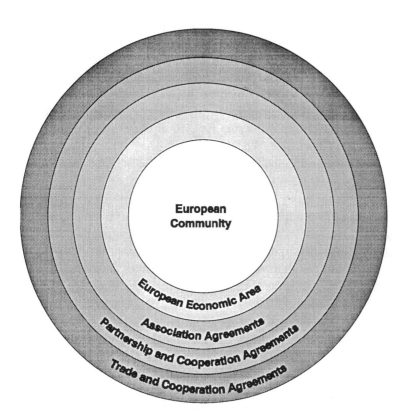

economy was not yet ready for membership. Despite a high rate of growth in Turkey, there was still a great gap. This was partly due to high population growth in Turkey. Turkey also had high inflation and unemployment. More than 50 percent of the work force was still employed in agriculture. Industrial development had only taken place under a high level of protection. Therefore, the Commission feared that Turkey might not be able to live up to the obligations that follow as a result of membership. Turkish membership would put extra pressure on the structural funds, and free movement of workers would be a problem as long as unemployment remained high in the EC.

The Commission also dealt with the political context, saying that the human rights situation and respect for the identity of minorities had not reached the level necessary for a democracy. In addition, reference was made to the Turkish military presence in Cyprus.

The broad lines of the Commission's opinion were endorsed by the Council on 3 February 1990.

The Cyprus Government decided to apply for full membership of the EC on 4 July 1990. The government argues that Cyprus is well prepared for membership. Per capita income in Cyprus today is higher than in Portugal, Greece and Ireland. In addition, the government has decided to facilitate membership by harmonizing its legislation with that of the EC (Republic of Cyprus 1991).

Malta has also applied for membership in the EC. The application for membership was submitted to the President of the Council on 16 July 1990.

The remaining applications for membership have come from EFTA countries. The institutional limitations of the EEA agreement was one of the reasons for their applying. Had the Cold War still been a part of the European political landscape, the EFTA countries would just have had to accept this, at least the neutral EFTA countries. However, following the 1989 revolutions in Eastern Europe, the EFTA neutrals were able to ask themselves whether membership was becoming a politically more realistic and attractive option. Only membership would allow them to become equal partners in what was perceived as a very successful European integration process within the EC.

Austria was the first EFTA country to decide to apply for membership. It applied in the summer of 1989, before the formal EEA negotiations had even got started. Sweden followed in July 1991, and Finland and Switzerland in the beginning of 1992. Norway was the latest EFTA country to apply, submitting its application in November 1992.

The Commission produced a preliminary internal report on enlargement in November 1991, during the IGC negotiations, but prior to the Maastricht summit (European Communities, Commission 1991). The report argued that the Community as it existed was "insufficiently developed to meet the challenge of enlargement". The EC's institutions were "over–complex and lacking in democratic legitimacy". The EC's financial resources were close to exhaustion.

The report divided the applicants and potential applicants into three groups: EFTA countries, the Mediterranean countries and the countries of Central and Eastern Europe. The EFTA applicants did not pose major economic problems. Neutrality could perhaps pose a problem, but less so after the 1989 revolutions. As a NATO country, Norway did not pose any security–related problems. No applications from Iceland and Liechtenstein were expected to be forthcoming in the near future.

Concerning the Mediterranean countries, the report was relatively pessimistic. The Commission's opinion on the Turkish application remained valid. In respect to Cyprus, "the current division of the island represents an insurmountable obstacle to accession". Regarding Malta, three sets of problems were noted. The political parties on the island were divided on the issue of EC membership, with the Socialists being against it. Next, there was a "lack of administrative infrastructure" which raises severe doubts about Malta's ability to fulfil all the obligations associated with membership. Finally, as a neutral and non–aligned country, Malta's "foreign policy remains very different from the European mainstream" (European Communities, Commission 1991:11). Concerning Central and Eastern Europe, it was clear that the three front runners were Hungary, Czechoslovakia (which has now split into two countries), and Poland. The EC should set down both political and economic conditions for membership. The political conditions should include free elections, the rule of law and protection of civil and human rights, as well as the administrative capacity to implement Community legislation. Economic conditions should include a competitive market economy, financial markets, currency convertibility and free trade with the other members.

More specifically the applicants should accept the finalité politique of the EC, including the notion of "an ever closer union between the European people (sic)", Community goals such as EMU and CFSP, and "methods and mechanisms appropriate to realise European Union". On one point the report was very specific: "Neutrality would be incompatible with such common policies which are likely ultimately to lead to mutual military assistance, membership of WEU/NATO, joint military forces and planning, etc." (European Communities 1991:14).

The report also dealt with institutional questions in connection with enlargement.

The Maastricht summit in December 1991 only issued a short statement on enlargement, saying that "any European State whose system of Government is founded on the principle of democracy may apply to become a member of the Union". This, of course, implied that applicants would have to accept the Maastricht Treaty, including provisions on EMU and CFSP. Negotiations on accession could start as soon as the Community had terminated "its negotiations on Own Resources and related issues in 1992". Therefore, finalization of the Internal Market, ratification of the Maastricht Treaty and agreement on the so–called

Delors II budget plan were the preconditions for starting enlargement negotiations. The European Council in Maastricht also invited the Commission to prepare a report on enlargement for the Lisbon summit in June 1992.

The Commission report to the Lisbon summit was much shorter and more "diplomatic" than the November 1991 internal report. The June 1992 report started by stating the assumption that enlargement would take place on the basis of the Maastricht Treaty. It then referred to the new context: "In the past enlargement took place in a divided continent; in future, it can contribute to the unification of the whole of Europe" (Europe Documents, No. 1790, 3 July 1992).

Among the conditions and criteria, we find the usual ones: democracy and respect for fundamental human rights, acceptance of the Community system and capacity to implement it, competitive market economy and an adequate legal and administrative framework. Applicants should also accept and be able to implement the CFSP. In general, membership implies acceptance of the Community's acquis.

From an economic point of view, it was expected to be easy to fit the EFTA applicants, as well as Cyprus and Malta, into the Community system. With regard to the CFSP, "specific and binding assurances will be sought from [applicants] with regard to their political commitment and legal capacity to fulfil the obligations" (Europe Documents, No. 1790, July 1992:4).

The Lisbon report argued that each new accession will magnify the risk of overload and paralysis because of the increased number of participants and the greater diversity of issues. It suggested that a more rigorous application of subsidiarity as well further reforms to reduce the "democratic deficit" would be necessary.

The section on institutions was largely a list of questions. The Commission did not, at this point, venture to give answers of a concrete nature.

Regarding specific countries, the Lisbon report confirmed that membership for Turkey would raise serious difficulties at the moment. However, "The Community should take all appropriate steps to anchor [that country] firmly within the future architecture of Europe". The division of Cyprus was mentioned as a problem. The question of neutrality of some EFTA countries was "a particular concern". In respect to Central and Eastern Europe, the report emphasized the existing "Europe agreements", with new ones under way with Bulgaria and Rumania, and the new trade and cooperation agreements with the Baltic republics and Albania. However, the Commission agreed that these countries, which are not yet ready for membership, "have political needs which go beyond the possibilities of existing agreements". The Commission therefore expressed its belief that "new means should be created for this purpose, building on the existing "architecture" of European organizations, so as to create a "European political area" ( Europe Documents, No. 1790, July 1992: 7). The concept of a "European political area" was not developed in detail. One possibility, but not the only one, would be "a confederation based on the Council of Europe".

The Conclusions of the Presidency from the European Council in Lisbon, confirm that negotiations with the EFTA applicants will be opened as soon as the Maastricht Treaty is ratified and agreement has been reached on the Delors II package. No further deepening was considered necessary before this first enlargement: "The European Council agrees that this enlargement is possible on the basis of the institutional provisions contained in the treaty on the Union and attached declarations" (Agence Europe, 28 June 1992).

With respect to the Mediterranean applicants, the European Council stated that relations should be developed and strengthened by building on the association agreements and by developing the political dialogue. Regarding Central and Eastern European countries, "cooperation will be focused systematically on assisting their efforts to prepare the accession to the Union which they seek" (p. 6).

The current EC enlargement policy thus suggests enlargement in two or three phases, where the latter phases may be many years in the future. The Lisbon summit opened the possibility of a relatively quick enlargement with some EFTA countries. However, even here, the future is uncertain. In some of these countries membership may well be voted down in referenda when it comes to the ratification of accession treaties. For Central and Eastern European countries, it may take many years to fulfil the requirements. Various forms of association agreements and trade and cooperation agreements may solve some of the economic problems and help prepare some of these states for membership later. In the meantime, GATT may, and should, provide a general framework for trade relations between all European states. Poland, Czechoslovakia, Hungary and Rumania are already GATT contracting parties. It can be expected that other Eastern European and CIS states will join in the future. However, since they all give high priority to their relations with the EC, the economic pole of attraction in Europe, the economic architecture of Europe will remain one of concentric circles around the EC. This leaves open questions relating to wider political, including security, structures in Europe.

## THE CFSP AND THE WEU

The new CFSP, the second pillar of the European Union, will encompass all aspects of security policy, including "the eventual framing of a common defence policy, which might in time lead to a common defence". The Western European Union (WEU) will become the defence component of the new European Union. At the same time, it will become the European pillar of NATO. The new defence policy shall "be compatible with the common security and defence policy established" within the Atlantic Alliance.

As mentioned earlier, the CFSP will basically remain intergovernmental, but it takes two steps towards applying the so–called Community method. Although the Commission is not given the exclusive right of initiative, which it has in the Community today, and which it will retain in the Union's first pillar, it will be allowed to make proposals within the framework of the CFSP. Secondly, the treaty includes a small opening for majority voting within the CFSP. A distinction is made between systematic cooperation and joint action. Gradually a number of areas will be included under the heading of joint action. The areas to be covered by joint action will be decided by the Council "on the basis of general guidelines from the European Council". It is then stipulated that "the Council shall, when adopting the joint action and at any stage during its development, define those matters on which decisions are to be taken by a qualified majority". Such a majority "shall require at least 54 votes in favour, cast by at least eight members".

According to a declaration by the European Council, areas of joint action will include the following ones, as from the entry into force of the treaty: the Conference on Security and Cooperation in Europe (CSCE) process, the policy of disarmament and arms control in Europe (including confidence–building measures), nuclear non–proliferation issues, and the economic aspects of security, in particular control of the transfer of military technology to third countries and control of arms exports.

At the moment the WEU has ten members. Greece joined recently, as a result of the Maastricht Treaty negotiations. However, two EC members, Ireland and Denmark, are not likely to join in the foreseeable future. Denmark and Ireland have become observers. European NATO countries which are not members of the EC have been invited to become associate members of the WEU.

The defence policy dimension was one of the issues raised by Denmark after the "no" vote in the referendum in June 1992. As a result, the "decision" reached by the European Council in Edinburgh included the following:

> ... nothing in the Treaty on European Union commits Denmark to become a member of the WEU. Accordingly, Denmark does not participate in the elaboration and the implementation of decisions and actions of the Union which have defence implications, but will not prevent the development of closer cooperation between Member States in this area. (European Council 1992)

## THE WIDER EUROPEAN POLITICAL ARCHITECTURE

There will also be some wider European organizations which will deal with political cooperation. These include the Council of Europe. Some Central and Eastern European countries have now joined this organization, which may have certain roles to play in the future, particularly with respect to human rights.

Practically all European states now take part in the CSCE, which has been developed through the Paris Charter of November 1990 and the new institutions created by that charter (CSCE 1991). The Charter of Paris confirmed the importance of human rights, democracy, the rule of law, economic liberty and responsibility, friendly relations among participating states, and security. It claimed that "Europe whole and free is calling for a new beginning" (p. 198). The institutions outlined by the charter included meetings of Heads of State or Government, a Council of Foreign Ministers, which is to meet at least once a year and a Committee of Senior Officials which will prepare the meetings of the Council and carry out its decisions. Furthermore, a CSCE parliamentary assembly was established. It was also decided that a Conflict Prevention Centre should be created in Vienna and an Office for Free Elections in Warsaw. Finally, a Permanent Secretariat was established in Prague. However, the CSCE remains a large organization, still based on a consensus approach. Following the break up of the USSR it now has 52 members. Although this organization may be able to contribute to confidence building and conflict prevention in some cases, it is clear that some Central and Eastern

European states are looking for more. One observer summarized the CSCE's weakness in this way:

> Despite the recent improvements made in the CSCE's procedures, CSCE members can do little other than convoke emergency meetings when faced with a threatening situation, whether within or between member states. The requirement that all substantive measures have the consensus approval of all member governments allows one dissenting party to veto any proposed action. (Weitz 1992b)

The CSCE cannot offer the kind of security guarantees that are central to NATO or even the WEU. It does not possess military forces to enforce its decisions. It is not unfair to say that the CSCE was unable to do much in relation to the crisis and civil war in Yugoslavia (Weitz 1992a).

Indeed, some of the Central and Eastern European states have expressed a wish to join NATO, and NATO responded by establishing the North Atlantic Cooperation Council (NACC). Through this organization, these countries can take part in deliberations, without getting the full security guarantee which members get. The first meeting of the NACC took place in December 1991. Apart from the sixteen NATO countries, the following eight countries from Central and Eastern Europe took part: Bulgaria, Czechoslovakia, Estonia, Hungary, Latvia, Lithuania, Poland and Rumania. There was also a representative from the Soviet Union present at the meeting who announced that the USSR had ceased to exist (Von Molthe 1992).

## AN ELLIPTICAL POLITICAL ARCHITECTURE

As mentioned in the introductory part of this chapter, the distinction between economics and politics has been an important one in the history of European integration. The EC has basically been an economic entity. Political cooperation among the members of the EC remained a distinct endeavour. Even in the European Union to be created by the Maastricht Treaty, the CFSP will remain weaker than the economic part in the first pillar. Moreover, the Union will apply the Western European Union (WEU) to develop a defence policy.

With respect to security, we have, therefore, an architectural design which is different from the one in the economic sphere. If the Maastricht Treaty enters into force, the new European Union (EU) with its CFSP will become the central part of this architecture, with the WEU forming an inner core defence organization (see Figure 11). However, the European

**Figure. 11** *The political architecture of Europe*

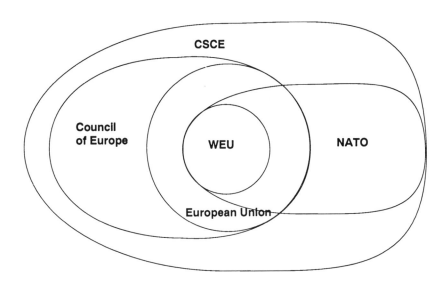

security architecture still clearly includes NATO, which has extra–European members, most significantly the United States. The United States and Canada are also members of the CSCE, as are the ex–Soviet republics, including the Asian ones. This explains the elliptical nature of parts of the European security architecture.

However, the future role of NATO may gradually diminish (Hoffmann 1992). This possibility, and the weakness of the CSCE, provide additional reasons why Eastern European states look towards EU membership, and why many Europeans would like to give the EU a strong defence dimension.

## CONCLUDING REMARKS

Looking back to our concepts of intergovernmental and supranational cooperation, it is clear that most of the new European architecture will be of an intergovernmental nature and thus fairly weak. Supranational institutions will largely be limited to the economic area of the first pillar of the Maastricht Treaty. However, if the European Union of the Maastricht Treaty is realized and new countries can join, then economic integration in Europe can be both deepened and widened. This is the optimistic scenario. However, as we have seen, there are many problems to be overcome. The ratification process remains to be completed and monetary problems to be solved. Current economic stress makes it difficult for the EC to be generous towards Eastern Europe and the Mediterranean countries, and major economic improvements will have to take place in those countries before they will be able to fulfil the economic conditions of membership.

If we look at the political architecture, the future development of the CFSP and the WEU will be of decisive importance. Will the intergovernmental conference (IGC), foreseen for 1996, allow further deepening of integration in the foreign and security policy areas? As the case of Yugoslavia has shown, the current security structures of Europe are very weak. The Maastricht Treaty constitutes a step forward, but only a relatively minor one.

# 13
# THE EC AND CENTRAL AND EASTERN EUROPE

*Jaroslav Jaks*

## THE TRANSFORMATION PROCESS IN CENTRAL AND EASTERN EUROPE AND THE EC

The radical changes which occurred in Central and Eastern Europe at the end of the 1980s and the beginning of the 1990s brought a new dimension to the traditional understanding of the concepts associated with the words "Europe" and "Europeification". The consequences of these changes, especially after the unification of Germany, have been a strong and increasing influence on the complicated political and economic structure which came into being in the 1940s. The connection between the EC and Central and Eastern Europe has been one which has always flowed from the West to the East. The reason for this has mainly been the economic and political dominance of the European Community at the heart of Europe.

The second half of the 1980s produced some positive results for the EC, despite rivalries between the member states and the structural challenges being created from outside Europe. Moreover, in spite of deformation of the West caused by onesided propaganda and isolation from the outside world, these results were, in fact, witnessed by the citizens of Eastern Europe. As a result, it was hardly surprising that, after the radical changes that occurred in Eastern Europe, Western Europe became the political and economic model on which the post–communist reforms were based. The connection between the EC and the social transformation in Eastern Europe is very important and it is impossible to reduce it to a mere institutional framework. As a result, economic, technological, political and security cooperation with Western Europe has become, not one of several possible alternatives, but almost the only option open to the new political elites in Eastern Europe. Therefore, in this sense, it is possible to speak of a relationship between the priorities in the Eastern European countries and those in the Western European countries.

In the former socialist countries, it is possible to witness, in the newly created value systems, a higher degree of political and economic Europeification than that which is apparent at the legislative level. The existence of such a gap is only natural at such an early stage of development and it was reduced by ratification of the Association Agreements which Hungary and Poland have signed with the EC. Moreover, the successor states to the CFSR, the Czech and Slovak Republics, will also sign these agreements. It is likely that, if they manage to fulfil the pre–negotiation conditions, this process will also occur in other countries in Central and Eastern Europe and the Baltics. However, the idea that any of the transformation states will be granted full EC membership in the course of this century, is more than unlikely.

From the point of view of the transformation states of Central and Eastern Europe, the phenomenon of Europeification means more than just the building up of legislative and institutional connections with the EC. Europeification also means the formation of a spiritual link, the sharing of common values and a functioning market economy. These things are all of vital importance for Eastern Europe in the creation of new political, economic and technological structures based on the model of Western democracy. In this sense, the Europeification process in Eastern Europe is different from that in the Western European countries. Many of the Western European countries are already full members of the EC or they find themselves on the verge of realizing this goal. For these states, increased orientation towards the EC is something which is fairly easy to accomplish, due to the fact that they possess compatible economic and political structures. However, in Central and Eastern Europe, such structures have yet to be created and this process may take longer than expected. The EC is now facing historic challenges created by the transformation countries and their political elites. As John Pinder says, "The European Community faces historic choices in its relations with its neighbours to the East. It is in the interest of the Community that pluralist democracy and market economy should prevail throughout Europe" (Pinder 1991:1–2).

In connection with this, one may ask how deep the interest of the EC and its individual members really is in the Europeification of Central and

Eastern Europe. Moreover, one should also question how great a price they are willing to pay to achieve this Europeification. This refers, not only to financial costs, but also to the short–term slowing down of the EC's own integration process. Is it possible that Germany could become a model of reserved cautiousness rather than the dynamic force which it is currently? The internal development of the EC which was, until 1989, shaped by the "comfortable" realities of a divided Europe and a divided Germany, now faces a completely new situation. Despite some optimistic declarations by the EC, it is still too early to express, with any certainty, the consequences which the changes in Central and Eastern Europe and Yugoslavia will have on the behaviour of the EC itself. It seems that, in the years or perhaps decades to come, the EC will be more interested in the consolidation of its current membership and its possible widening to include the countries of ESVO. With the advent of 1993, there is also the problem of coordinating the establishment of the Single European Market and the formation of the European Monetary and Political Union.

To consolidate today's "capitalistic" Europe has had a higher priority than to risk what it has achieved by its premature opening (Nye, Biedenkopf and Shiina 1992). However, it would be in the EC's interest to quicken the speed of its transformation, with an eye to the changes occurring in the East. One could argue that the democratisation process in Central and Eastern Europe has, since the middle of 1989, completely changed the international environment in which the EC operates.

The public and the politicians in Western Europe must be made aware of the fact that, in the future, the Community and its member states must alter the way in which they relate to other states. It would be an illusion to believe that Western Europe could remain an island of wealth and peace, while the young democracies of Central and Eastern Europe face the danger of political defeat, economic backwardness, ethnic conflicts and maybe even a bloodbath. No wall can protect the democracies of Western Europe from the consequences of an unsuccessful reform movement in the East (p.71).

It is necessary to declare openly that the so–called Maastricht process did not offer any sort of real consolation for the transformation states of Central and Eastern Europe. In fact, it contributes nothing at all to the Europeification of the decision–making system and political thinking in the transformation economies. The path which the EC is now taking is in line with what has been occurring since 1984: it is focusing mainly on internal development problems. This pattern is bound to be intensified as the critical elements of the Maastricht Treaty and the principle of subsidiarity assert themselves. It should not be forgotten that the EC helped bring about the birth of democracy and market economy in Central and Eastern Europe.

Max Jakobsen, the former Finnish Ambassador to the United Nations, clearly defined the problem in a recently published study:

> So far, the response of the Community to the challenge, posed by the desperate economic and political chaos in the Eastern half of the Continent, has been half hearted. Intellectually and emotionally the Brussels Commission is still a West European institution. It has been preoccupied with the task of forging a political and monetary union out of the present Community. Indeed, in some ways, the EC seems to be bent upon creating a "Fortress Western Europe" designed to protect its members against an influx of cheap goods and cheap labour from the East. The dilemma posed by the issue of widening versus deepening has not been resolved by the Maastricht Summit (Jakobsen 1992)

In September 1992, President Bush made an offer to Hungary, Poland, and Czechoslovakia, during the pre–election period in the US. This offer concerned the creation of a free trade zone but it is unlikely to result in any immediate economic solutions for any of the parties involved. It was, in fact, more of a provocation directed at the EC. The first reactions from Hungary were quite enthusiastic. However, only the future will show what will remain of this "gunpowder" shot emitted before the US presidential election, and in what way the young, fragile, Eastern European democratic elites will articulate their economic and foreign policy interest. Will they remain faithful to the exclusive alternative of a united Europe? The answer to that question is dependent on the amount of goodwill shown by the EC itself, especially with regard to the opening up of product markets.

In an attempt to solve their political, economic and social problems, the transformation states will themselves have a key role to play. It is also very important that they build a flexible relationship with the EC and utilize all parts of the Association Agreements. Giles Merrit is correct when he says,

> ...both the EC countries and the Eastern Europeans will do well to see their relationship as a flexible one that can be improved without formal ties being necessary. The Eastern Europeans will have to work hard to align their new market economies with EC practice and standards and the EC nations must open the doors to their markets wider still. Access to the Community market place will be of vital importance to the recovery of Eastern Europe. (Merrit 1991)

Europeification concerns not only the economic, but also the political institutional connections. When forming a permanent and stable connection between the national institutions of the transformation countries and the EC, it is necessary to take into account the difficulties involved in the formation of a functioning democratic political system.

> Taking into account the political, economic and social realities of the years 1989 to 1992 in the countries which went through transformation, we must stress the following: it is necessary to touch upon the preferential political role, the creation of the balanced political system out of the present outburst of sometimes vested interest enforced by democratically entitled but not overly experienced politicians, especially in the regions. In any event, it is politics, the political sphere in the widest sense of the word, which today more than in the future, determines the first signs of the success of the reform process just now beginning. (Jaks 1992)

When looking at the decision mechanisms, it is important to examine the declared and pursued political aims and institutional structures of cooperation and contacts which exist between the EC and the Eastern European countries. However, what is perhaps of greater importance is the compatibility of the existing economic structures and the degree to which the business interests are complementary. Up until now, a strong degree of asymmetry has been prevalent in these areas.

The Eastern European market buys under 5 percent of all exports from the EC. Germany is the main exporter to Eastern Europe while France, the UK and Italy have only marginal exports to this area. An important role is played here by Austria, although she is not yet a member of the EC. Is this situation liable to change within a short term perspective? When considering the fact that the EC takes almost 50 percent of all Eastern European exports, a disintegration of this market would prove to be extremely detrimental for the transformation countries. In markets such as agriculture, coal, steel and textiles, the transformation countries could be capable of penetrating EC markets. This situation is a very delicate one for the EC and the Community is being somewhat overcautious, concerned, as it is, with its own political and economic problems. In the end, it has little left to offer except sympathetic political support for the newborn "capitalists".

The association countries produce products which are possibly a threat to the EC economy. Moreover, about 40–50 percent of their net exports go to EC countries. This implies that their level of exports to the EC is not of minor importance. Almost certainly, the EC countries would not be thrilled by an influx of Eastern European competitors into their markets, even if many believe that Eastern European products will not be able to compete. However, it is unrealistic to believe that this is going to happen, despite the complaints of politicians in the transformation states who are impatiently criticizing the EC for the way in which it is dealing with these issues. Instead of criticizing the West, those in Eastern Europe should perhaps focus their energy on building market economies which meet with EC standards. With the right structural changes to those products which they export to the EC, the transformation countries would gradually be able to reduce the importance of the most sensitive issues. This would probably also widen the spectrum of new competitive products and services being produced in Eastern Europe.

## THE ASSOCIATION PROCESS AND THE BASIS OF EUROPEIFICATION

The EC reacted very quickly to the changes in Central and Eastern Europe, not only through material and technical help (PHARE), but also also on the institutional (BERD) and legislative (Euroagreements) levels. The intensity of contact between the national government levels of all the transformation countries (not only those which have signed the Association Agreements) and the EC, has increased in an unprecedented way. This has added a new quality to East–West relations.

In the Eastern European countries, attitudes towards increased contact with the EC were initially of a euphoric nature. However, this was mainly because the countries involved had insufficient knowledge about the complicated decision and feedback mechanisms which exist in the EC system. A certain level of sobriety and professionalism is now dawning in the East. The Eastern European countries no longer expect to solve all their domestic and transformational challenges in Brussels. A new phase of Europeification has begun, based on knowledge of the situation which exists on both sides of the fence. This has allowed an evaluation of the possibilities and barriers which exist. It is the new–found knowledge of these complicated issues inherent within the EC system, which is of vital importance and sometimes even a source of disappointment for the political elites and people of Central and Eastern Europe.

The association process to which the association countries have bound themselves will provide important support for the national governments and the transformation process. It is probable that the countries that have already entered the agreement will have an advantage over those that have not entered. This is mainly due to the long term fragility of the political structures and market economies in Central and Eastern Europe. Moreover, by citing their "European obligations" to them, it will be easier for the political elites to overcome the general public's fear of reform. At the same time, it is important that they do not use their European connection as an alibi when internal problems arise, such as insufficient political consensus. This is, therefore, a natural starting point for all decisive transformational changes. However, there is the danger that it might inspire an antipathy towards "Europe" and further strengthen already strong national trends.

The Europeification process will probably, on the basis of the Euroagreements, cause the transformation countries great problems of obligation. These problems will surface as the gradual opening up of the economies proceeds and the environment becomes more competitive. There will not always be a synergetic effect, especially in the sectors where the EC is going to have certain social costs. In this sense, the association countries will also be a source of "progressive" conflicts. The means by which this should be overcome will depend on the intensity of mutual political will directed, in the long term, towards the European Union.

The key for a successful association process in the transformation countries lies in the degree of European orientation which is present in the public's political conscience. In the future, it is likely that a strong, dominant and positive spill–over association will not only be strengthened by the political elites, but also by the interest sectors in the public which favour Europeification. It would be a mistake to regard such an orientation as given. In this matter, it is possible to learn about the motivations which act against the EC and about the changing attractiveness of the association process. It is only through this that full membership of the EC for the transformation countries, may become a reality. From this angle, the Europeification process for transformation countries is actually almost identical with the process of "Westernization". In both cases, the goal is to establish communities that will be based on Western economic and democratic values. The attractiveness of orientation towards the EC has, undeniably, a greater intensity in the transformation states than the attractiveness which the reform process has in the West.

Besides the Association Agreements, there is another important factor in the process of Europeification. To a certain extent, this factor is independent of the dynamics of the association process. Despite this, it forces the partner countries in the selected sector into a onesided adoption of the "aquis communitaire" of the EC. Here it is the so–called Single Market which is being referred to. The Single Market contains provisions for creating an area of free movement of capital, people, services and goods. It came into being on 1 January 1993. The challenge of "1992" naturally concerns all of the EC partners, the people of Japan and the USA and the EFTA countries. The concept of the Single Market has been developed over the last seven years and is based on logic taken from the White Paper. In order to continue in business in the future, the exporters in the transformation countries of Central and Eastern Europe have but one choice: they must accept, by means of their behaviour and institutional legislative base, all the necessary elements of the Single Market. This includes the areas of law, technical norms, standards and health regulations. The transformation countries, along with the members of EFTA, will have to "Europeificate" the exports which they direct towards the EC. In reality, this implies that they will have to Europeificate their own production politics from the provisions of the Euroagreements. Naturally, a successful adoption of the Single Market is an ideal synergy process which can only contribute to the fulfilment of the Association Agreements.

*The basic framework of the Europe Agreements*
Political Dialogue
General Principles
Free Movement of Goods
- Industrial Products
- Agriculture
- Fisheries
- Common Provisions

Movement of Workers, Establishment, Supply of Services
- Movement of Workers
- Establishment
- Supply of Services

Payments, Capital, Competition and other Economic Provisions
- Approximation of Laws
- Current Payments and Movement of Capital
- Competition and other Provisions
- Approximation of Laws

Economic Cooperation
- Cultural Cooperation
- Financial Cooperation
- Institutional; general and final Provisions

This is based on the Europe Agreement signed between the EC and CFSR but in accordance with the principles of other European Agreements. Since the break–up of Czechoslovakia, there have been some new provisions added into the Association Agreements which the two independent republics of Czechland and Slovakia have signed with the EC. However, the final shape of their European Agreements will not become fully clear before the end of 1993. As a result, in order to understand the key role of these agreements in the Europeification of the transformation process, it is useful to analyse the last formal document signed between the Czechoslovakian Government and the EC.

The structure of the Association Agreement is based on a general scheme, prepared by the EC Commission for the Council and the European Parliament (Europe Agreements 1992). The framework includes political dialogue, free trade and freedom of movement, economic cooperation, cultural cooperation and institutions of association. It is important for the transformation countries to realize that the agreements do not provide an automatic assurance that they will be accepted into the EC. As stated in the preamble (all quotes are related to the Europe Agreements with the CFSR), the only thing which is acknowledged is "the fact that the CFSR's ultimate objective is to accede to the Community and that this association in the view of the parties will help the CFSR to achieve its objective". In the early 1990s, the "fathers" of the Association Agreements were under the influence of "Europephoria" which had gripped the public in their respective countries. It may, in fact, have been a good thing if they had been confronted with the realities of the Agreements at the time of meeting the EC Committee delegations. Indeed, perhaps the implementation of the Association Agreements and the complications of transformation, will result in other options being favoured above that of association.

Let us try to evaluate the different elements of the Association Agreements, based on their contribution to the Europeification of national level decision–making in the transformation countries.

*Preamble*

The link between national transformation and the educational role of the EC institutions is most strongly expressed in the Preamble. Here it is declared that the link should be made between full implementation of association on one hand, and the actual accomplishment of the political, economic and legal reforms on the other hand. The Preamble also speaks of the very strong commitment of the CFSR,

> recognising the political and economic freedoms which constitute the very basis of the association, the rule of law and human rights and to operate a multi–party system with free and democratic elections, and in recognition on the side of the CFSR, that the Community is one of the cornerstones of the system of stability in Europe, based on cooperation.

The Preamble also formulated another strong signal regarding the mutual relation between the transformation and the EC in this area. The conviction was expressed that the Association Agreements will create a new climate for development of the economic relations between the two sides, "and, in particular, for the development of trade and investment instruments which are indispensible for economic restructuring and technical modernization". The Preamble of the Europe Agreements creates the elements of political conditionality seen in the Association Agreements. In this sense, the "European context", with its norms and institutional structure, relates to the "global context" for the transformation countries. However, after ratification, this will spread through the EC level very quickly. In contrast to the members of the EC and the EEA, the EC level will not only play an important role for the association countries of Central and Eastern Europe, but also a "global" one. This does not just mean an Atlantic relation but also a relation directed towards the countries of the former Soviet Union. The parallel existence of the EC level and the "global" level has to be carefully watched, especially with the first steps of the transformation process; one would hope that the EC will create a self–sustaining dynamic structure.

*Political dialogue*

This dimension of the association process introduces a few important Europeification impulses directed towards the national institutions and it also creates an institutional base for them. This section is especially concerned with the, "rapprochement between the Community and the CFSR". Hope is expressed that the political and economic changes will strengthen "progressive rapprochement with the Community. The economic rapprochement provided for in this agreement will lead to greater political convergence" (Art.2). The conviction is expressed that the views of both parties on "security issues" will move closer together. A political dialogue creates a starting point for the broadest possible Europeification of the political values of the association countries.

In addition, it is important that one takes into account the institutions, procedures and mechanisms for political dialogue with the EC. Apart from the basic association institution, namely the Association Council, one must also consider:

(**a**) meetings with the Presidents of the Czech and Slovak Republics and the President of the Commission. One can expect that, following the division of the CFSR and the creation of the two independent republics, the contact between the Presidents of both republics and the EC will be formulated in a similar way in the new Association Agreements.

(**b**) meetings at the Senior Officer level (Political Directors). An association country is also part of the group of countries which receive regular information on the issues dealt with by the European Political Cooperation. In view of Europeification, it is also worth mentioning the development of political dialogue at parliamentary level within the framework of the Parliamentary Association Committee (Art. 5). Apart from the new institutions of the mutual European communication, there will also be impulses created in the existing national parliaments. This will be welcomed because they are only beginning to learn how the system of pluralistic, parliamentary democracy operates. A link with Europe is very important, especially in the complicated transition period from the post–communist societies to democratic ones.

*General principles*
This section is quite short but, from the point of view of the connection between the internal development of a transformation country and the mechanisms of the EC, it is very interesting. As well as shortening the transition period by ten years, it also gives the Association Council the possibility to evaluate the application of the Agreement and the accomplishment of the CFSR's economic reforms (on the basis of the principles established in the Preamble, Art. 6. This means that the evaluation of the reforms will not only be carried out on a national level, but also on an international and supranational level. This monitoring process may even lead to practical measures being carried out by the the Association Council, especially if the development of the reforms differs from the process outlined in the Preamble and expressed in the spirit of

the whole agreement. Since the association period is divided into two five–year segments, and the transition process in the second one is not automatic, Europe is connected into a national decision sphere. The exact meaning of these principles will be determined by the ability of the transformation country to consider the association process in a broader context than purely as a free trade zone.

*Free movement of goods*

This issue forms a very large segment of the Association Agreement (Art. 7–26). The economic movement of goods between the EC and the countries of Central Europe is a very important ingredient in the process of Europeification. A gradual establishment of a free trade area has been proposed, to be carried out over a transitional period of at least ten years. The core of this would be an asymmetrical abolition of all customs duties. Apart from the number of articles of a more technical–business nature (important for the opening up of export markets for both parties), some of the articles have important one–sided regulative potential. In particular, Articles 28–31 and Article 21 illustrate a number of examples of the connection between the internal export decisions and the conditions determined by the importer. These articles are formally and legislatively related to both parties, but the protective clauses cited by the economic "giant", may be the beginning of a process which could be called "negative Europeification". The basis of this is a cumulation of unfulfilled expectations which have affected the Central and Eastern European countries, and relate to promises made by the EC to open up their markets to the export activities of the newborn private companies and other Eastern exporters. Czechoslovakia has already been affected by this problem when, in the first half of 1992, her exporters exhausted her yearly quota of steel exports within a period of three months. The result of this was that importing by the EC states ceased and Czechoslovakia was accused of dumping. It is obvious that it was only due to these "symmetrical conditions of mutual protection" that it was possible to close this agreement. We have already said once that, unfortunately for the EC, it is in these "sensitive" products that the transformation countries are successful and it is in these that they valorize their cheap labour force in a legitimate manner. However, the transformation countries must develop a better understanding of the interests and limits of their EC partners, the social challenge of their structural changes and the political price of the possible concessions.

*The other provisions of the Association Agreement*

The Association Agreement includes various sectors of economic contact. As a result of this, it allows the association country to come closer to the standards of the EC, sometimes in a global way, sometimes in a more partial way. It is beyond the framework of this chapter to include all of the articles which deal with the movement of goods, people, capital and services but the sheer number of these is admirable. In spite of this, we would like to draw attention to some steps of a special character, which are of vital importance for the global Europeification process. We would like to do this because these steps determine the rules of behaviour and they reach beyond the framework of economics. In the first place, there is the "approximation of laws". At this point, it is clearly stated that both sides "recognize that an important condition for the CFSR's economic integration into the Community is the approximation of the CFSR's existing and future legislation to that of the Community" and "The CFSR shall endeavour to ensure that this legislation will gradually be made more compatible with that of the Community (Art. 68)." The process of approximating the laws is extremely complex. In fact, it can be regarded as one of the most important elements of the Europeification process in a transformation country and it includes these sectors: customs law, company law, banking law, company accounts and taxes, intellectual property, protection of workers in the workplace, financial services, rules regarding competition, protection of health and life of humans, animals and plants, consumer protection, indirect taxation, technical rules and standards, nuclear law and regulation, transport and the environment (Art. 69). The logic of approximation creates an important spill–over effect which will influence other activities within the framework of national institutions in an association country. The importance of this reaches over the delimited sectors.

This part of the Association Agreement, which also determines the nature of the economic cooperation (Art. 71–75), presents a broad spectrum of sectors. These sectors will be included in the Europeification process, even if this will probably happen gradually, and will be dependent on the success of the transformation process as a whole (the scheme of the Europe Agreements). While some of the articles are of a more general nature, there are others which clearly determine the obligation of an association country to take over certain segments "aquis communitaire". An example of this is the delimitation of industry branches. This area will also become a subject of special attention in the cooperation process between the CFSR and the EC. It is interesting to note the emphasis on the "social attention" which should be "devoted to measures capable of fostering cooperation between the countries of Central and Eastern Europe with a view to the harmonious development of the region" (Art. 72). There is also an example of Europeification which is not only aimed at the strengthening of the linkage between the EC and an association country, but which is also designed to strength the ties between association countries themselves. Therefore, it is not surprising that there were suggestions concerning the formation of a customs union between some of the states. The proposals were enthusiastically supported by the EC Commission. It was even suggested to the former Czechoslovakian authorities that a customs union between the Czech and Slovakian Republics, after their separation, could be a condition for the European Parliament's quick acceptance of the original Association Agreement, supplemented only by a political declaration.

The priorities present in the sector of industrial cooperation (Art. 72) are also detailed and it is quite remarkable that it is stated that "...the Association Council will examine, in particular, problems affecting the sectors of coal and steel and the conversion of the defence industry". Article 74 is also very specific. It concerns "full conformity with Community technical regulations and European standardisation and conformity assessment procedures". This article also promotes the use of Community technical regulations, European standards and conformity assessment procedures. What is also interesting is the mention in Article 78 of "the progressive integration of the energy markets of the CFSR and the Community". Article 84 deals with the linkage between the full convertibility of the crown and the European monetary system "gradual approximation of its [CFSR] policies to those of the European monetary system".

In the area of regional politics, there is the mention "of coordinated approaches for the development of border areas between the Community and the CFSR and other CFSR areas with severe regional disparities" (Art. 86). This development is stimulating from a Europeification point of view. Another point which is obligatory for the association country is contained in Article 91. This article concerns consumer protection and it states that, "the parties shall cooperate with the aim of achieving full compatibility of the CFSR with the Community's Consumer Protection scheme".

Yet another important element of Europeification relates to the sectors of banking, insurance, audit cooperation and other financial services. One example which is referred to here is the acceptance of a common accounting system which is compatible with European standards. The aim is also to develop efficient audit systems in the transformation country which follow standard Community methods and procedures (Art. 83). In a similar manner, cooperation in the customs sector is formulated (Art. 93). In this, a commitment is made to the "compliance with all the provisions scheduled for adoption in connection with trade and to achieve the approximation of the CFSR's customs system to that of the Community, thus helping to ease the steps towards liberalisation planned under this Agreement".

Article 101 is interesting from the material side of the Europeification process. In the spirit of the Preamble, this article confirms the conditions required for a successful transformation and takes into consideration, the financial help to be provided by the Community: "The need for Community financial assistance will be evaluated in the light of the needs which arise and the level of development of the CFSR, taking into account established priorities and the absorption capacity of the CFSR economy, the ability to repay loans and progress towards a market economy system and restructuring in the CFSR".

*Institutional safeguard of the association process*
The Association Agreement includes a huge amount of activities which will enter (in different intensities) into the decision–making process of the national subjects. At the same time, it creates new institutions which will become an interest representation between the EC level and the national level. This is an absolutely new situation in the contacts between Central and Eastern Europe and the Community. The functioning of these new institutions will, on one side, be a result of the Europeification process in post–Communist Europe. On the other hand, however, it is a catalyst and a point of regulation and monitoring in the development of the association process. It is the Association Council, in particular, which will supervise the implementation of the Euroagreement. This Council shall meet at ministerial level once a year or when circumstances require it to do so. What is important is the fact that the Council can not only deal with questions arising within the framework of the Agreement, but can also consider "any other bilateral or international issues of mutual interest".

Besides the Association Council, there will also be the Association Committee. This Committee will help the Council to perform its duties. In addition, there will be the possibility to set up any other special committee or body that can assist the Association Council in carrying out its duties. An Association Parliamentary Committee has also been established. This Committee is to act as a forum in which the members of the CSFR Parliament and the European Parliament can meet and exchange views. The Euroagreement only creates a legislative framework for Europeification of national policy–making in the Association Agreements. However, the spirit and text of the Agreement means that it is the core of the "Western" linkage to the transformation and association countries in Central and Eastern Europe. The real importance of the Agreement, in terms of its Europeification effects on the political, economic and social values of the country, will only be decided by the extent of the transformation process. However, a qualitatively new situation has already arisen through the process of preparation of the Association Agreement and of the transformation process itself. Already in 1992, evidence was produced which proved that the connection between the countries of Central and Eastern Europe and the EC (not underestimating contacts with EFTA) will differ from those which were expected. This is not caused by the institutions of the Community but is a result of the internal situation in the former CFSR. This situation was created by the fact that the elections held in June 1992 started the process of the formation of two states, motivated by the influence of the Slovak public and the victorious political elite. It is supposed that, after the division of Czechoslovakia in 1993, there will be a pragmatically effective contact established. Nevertheless, it was impossible for the Association Agreement to be ratified by the European Parliament and all discussions on the matter were stopped. On the contrary, on the 16 September 1992, Hungary and Poland successfully resolved the problem of ratification in the EP. This will certainly influence the practical dynamics which the Europeification process will have on the decision processes in all three countries in the near future because it means that Hungary and Poland will gain an important start. For the Czech and Slovak public, the priority at this stage was to come to a definitive solution regarding their mutual relationship and it is hoped that this can be obtained through a sense of support and understanding on the part of the EC. If a successful customs union can be created between the new states formed from the former Czechoslovakia, it is probable that this will create the necessary conditions for the acceptance of the existing Association Agreement, signed between the CFSR and the EC (with only a few modifications, especially in the sector of mutual trade).

The experiences taken from Western Europe, coupled with the lessons of 1989–1992, learned in overcoming Communist society, have provided (as far as Europeification is concerned), some important learning points for both sides.

First, it is already clear that, in spite of a common recent history, the post–communist countries of Central and Eastern Europe are very diverse, both among themselves and in relation to the EC. Moreover, this diversification in their economic and political situations will become stronger during the transformation period, despite the fact that their public and politicians will claim to share the same values as the EC.

The West would like to consider this area as a homogeneous unit since this would simplify mutual contact. This is, however, an illusion. In fact, the same situation already exists in democratic Western Europe which, despite sharing common values, still remains a largely heterogeneous complex of countries, with vast differences, not only in the cultural sector, but more especially in the economic and productive sectors. The transformation countries are on the verge of a similar differentiation. Naturally, this is based to a certain extent on the inherited material and social conditions and on spiritual ativisms. At the same time, the countries are beginning to react and see new possibilities opened up to them by the fall of Communism. In the differentiation process, internal economic and political situations will probably have a decisive role to play. Of particular importance in this will be: the level of social consensus and how prepared the public, government parties and opposition parties are to make sacrifices on the road to the type of state and economy for which, for many years, those in the East envied those in the West. The basic "technology" necessary for the economic transformation is beginning to appear but it will be neither the theorists nor the politicians who will ultimately determine the force of its implementation; this will depend on public feeling. The differences between Hungary, Poland, Bulgaria and the CFSR (not to mention the former GDR), will necessarily contribute to the conception of differentiated Europeification effects on national policy–making.

Secondly, the differentiation of the single transformation countries in relation to "Europe", the integration institutions and new visions, based on the transformation of the existing systems, will become stronger. There will also be a difference in the development of the members of the public in the various countries. Moreover, the political elites need to be part of the EC system, with all its obligations and important decision mechanisms. The end of the Cold War opened up a new space for development for the Central and Eastern European countries. It is still impossible to say with any certainty that the prospect of a democratic development means the same as the effort to become a full EC member in all of the regions, even though it is sometimes portrayed as such. The attractive impression created by the EC in the 1990s will be decisive in determining the degree of interest shown by the transformation countries, if indeed they decide to opt for this development option. The success of the past will not be decisive here. In this direction, however, the Maastricht Treaty and its conception of the European economic, monetary and political union, did not increase the prestige of the EC in the transformation countries, and did not offer much stimulation for becoming a member.

From this point of view, one arrives at an important question: what will be the internal developments which occur within the EC itself in the 1990s? This institution, which represents Europe "par excellence", also influences, through its "aquis communautaire", third countries. Will the EC continue along the paths outlined by the Rome Agreements, the Single European Act and the vision of the European Monetary and Political Union as detailed in the Maastricht Treaty? Since the Maastricht document won't have an immediate impact on Central and Eastern Europe, this line of development is only partially relevant. In fact, it leaves the historic post–Communist process on the margins of the Community's priority of interests and it may influence, in a negative way, the motivation of the Eastern political elites with regard to the European option. The accommodation of nationalism in the Eastern region may only be a pragmatic incorporation into the European processes of concentrical character with variable geometry. But, in the future, will the public of the "old" democratic Europe be prepared to undergo sacrifices in order to ensure the success of this alternative?

Finally, one should consider the strength of the destabilization potential which is an inherent part of the transformation process in Eastern Europe and which is increasingly finding its way into the West (as Germany well knows). The case of Yugoslavia is a painful but instructive example of the challenge which was brought before the EC; it was created by the volatile mixture of post–Communist reforms and revived nationalism. In their own interest, it seems that the EC and indeed, the whole of Western Europe, still have more to do, in order to bring the national decision–making structures of the transformation countries closer to the European standard. However, the greatest burden lies in the hands of the citizens of the Central and Eastern European countries and the political skills of their young and fragile political elites.

# 14
# POLICY–MAKING IN THE NEW EUROPE

*Svein S. Andersen and*
*Kjell A. Eliassen*

---

In this book we deal primarily with a selection of policy areas that seem to be moving towards a higher degree of Europeification. These sectors have different points of departure. Transport, for example, is an old EC core business, being one of the three sectors mentioned in the Treaty of Rome. On the other hand, EC immigration policy will, even after Maastricht, remain outside the EC decision–making structure. Policy areas also move on different tracks and at different speeds. In the telecommunications industry, national governments strongly support EC involvement and standardization, and on the other hand, in the area of police cooperation, nation states have only reluctantly and painfully started a process towards increased EC cooperation.

Three of the studies in this book looked at strategic sectors which are prerequisites for the effective functioning of the internal market, namely deregulation in the transport and energy sectors and standardization in the telecommunications industry. Three studies dealt with what we may call supporting sectors. Europeification in these sectors is necessary in order to deal with the effects of a Europe without frontiers in such issue areas as educational standardization and exchange programmes, minimum policy requirements in consumer policy and common rules of immigration. Finally, there was the area of EC police cooperation. Such cooperation is necessary in order to deal with open frontiers, but it also relates to the development of a common enforcement structure in the EC.

This book has emphasized the Europeification of the EC as a system of transnational authority and policy– making. Our approach to Europeification differs, however, from the foreign policy tradition and formal legal perspectives in emphasizing the totality of the EC–level institutions and the national political systems. Up until recently, there has been a tendency to view national political systems as being relatively closed. The transnational dimension has only partly been incorporated into studies involving actors operating across national boundaries. Studies of policy–making have continued to focus on national systems as the unit of analysis, even if national systems are frequently compared.

Even in a confederal model, the EC represents a new form of transnational system, and the link to the EC which stems from each of the member states is already much more than the mere extension of foreign policy. This creates new challenges and new solutions, in a situation where the logic of economic and social integration continuously demonstrates the need for increasingly tighter political unity in the EC system. There is a need for an open system approach which also takes into account the complexity embedded in national histories (Andersen and Eliassen 1991, Olsen 1992, van Schendelen 1993).

Our discussion of Europeification has dealt with two major aspects. First, we have introduced a conceptual model which describes the EC as a new type of political system. A fundamental aspect of this is the tension which exists between the member states and the emerging transnational authority at the EC level. A peculiar element of the new EC system is that institutional elaboration at the central level lacks the key dimensions which are normally found when studying the formation of a new state:

There exists more transnational authority at the central EC decision–making and legislative levels, than there does at the corresponding implementation and law enforcement stages. Formulations of legally binding intentions or objectives may follow procedures for transnational decision–making. However, there is almost no unified EC administrative structure or cohersive force which can reach into member countries. Consequently, national courts will, in the future, have to rule in accordance with the extensive body of EC law and also take on the bulk of law enforcement in EC countries. As a result, the growth of the EC as a transnational system is characterized, at least in the short run, by a certain degree of "statelessness" when compared to member countries.

Formal institutions and legislation provide a framework for policy–making, but there is considerable room for different outcomes. All formal systems have some degree of freedom in this sense. However, it seems that the loose structure combined with complexity and heterogeneity provides more room for process in determining outcomes than in national political systems. Actors bring to bear their own national styles, strategies and tactics. Consequently, we place emphasis on the different actor strategies, coalitions and dependencies; in short, on the complexity of policy–making and lobbying.

This kind of openness can sometimes lead to processes of a confusing nature. Definitions of issues, their relationship to formal procedures and the coalitions which stand behind them, are often complex and shifting. As a result, some of these processes may lend themselves to "garbage can" interpretations (Cohen et al. 1972, Olsen 1978). However, the fact that processes may seem to be of this nature, does not mean that outcomes are equally open. On the contrary, institutional features frame and limit the search for possible outcomes. In this sense, there are strong pressures stemming from the norms of rationality in the decision–points, as well as from the more general framework of EC legislation and cooperation (Andersen and Burns 1992).

When looking at specific policy–making areas, it is important to keep in mind the following questions:

What are the factors stimulating or blocking Europeification? At what level do we find the driving forces? Is it a down–up process driven by initiatives and alliances formed at the national level? Is it a top–down process reflecting central EC initiatives, perhaps supported by fundamental changes at the global level, as we have seen in the case of environmental policy? To what extent is policy development driven by the need to relate to other political areas?

The Europeification of EC policy–making has three aspects:

1. the policy–context
2. the policy–making processes
3. the policy output.

Let us briefly look at how the empirical studies vary with respect to these three aspects of Europeification.

If we look at the policy context, we can examine the degree to which policies are institutionalized at the EC level. Is the policy area based on the EC Treaty and, if so, when was it introduced? Has a strong EC policy actually been developed in this area and, if this is the case, what is the relationship to national policies?

Some areas are defined within the Treaty of Rome and so have been established for a long time. Transport was part of the original treaty but it is only recently that EC policy has succeeded in breaking down resistance to transnational intervention in national infrastructure development. Education, on the other hand, was only mentioned in the

Treaty of Rome with regards to vocational training. Other higher educational issues were gradually institutionalized at the EC level during the 1980s, but not before the Maastricht Treaty was signed was this policy area defined as an EC core policy sector.

Telecommunications and consumer policy were introduced in the Single Act as important aspects of internal market legislation. Within these areas, the member countries have increasingly supported the EC prerogative.

Some policy sectors like energy, immigration and policing are mainly based at the national level. Attempts to introduce EC level policies have been met with strong resistance from member states and affected industries. Europeification of energy policy has been attempted through links to internal market and environmental policy and legislation, but so far this has only met with limited success. Police cooperation, seen as an intergovernmental activity, has been included as part of the Maastricht Treaty. The long term goal is a gradual development of supranational authority, at least in certain areas. Immmigration policy is also weak at the EC level, and only a few aspects of it have been included in the Maastricht Treaty. Policies serve mainly as a source of norms and principles for national governments which are following quite restrictive national traditions.

These observations concerning the Europeification of the policy context indicate the ambiguity surrounding future developments in specific policy areas. It is important to see policy development in relation to EC institutional dynamics, but not in a neofunctionalistic sense. One should not rule out a spillover effect, but this should be regarded as something which requires special explanation and not as the driving force of the system. However, there is no doubt that there is a general interaction between economic development and belief in the need for the further progress of the EC on the one hand, and the success of specific policy initiatives on the other hand. Still, in the final analysis, such convictions must be based on a minimum of democratic support for these institutions. This involves not only the ability to deliver better solutions than those offered at the national level, but also the ability to respect the principles of democratic process and subsidiarity.

What characterizes the policy–making process in different sectors? To what extent can we identify the segmented and polarized conflicts which exist between the member countries, or between the member countries and the central EC institutions? To what extent are interests overlapping or complementary? What kinds of alliances are possible, and through which channels?

Telecommunications policy enjoys a high degree of agreement amongst member countries regarding such issues as standardization but suffers from stiff competition among the national industries with regard to key projects.

Police cooperation is the clearest example of an EC policy area which is not able to transcend the more traditional international cooperation agreements, despite the fact that it is linked to the general EC framework. This reflects the fact that the police service is at the core of national state sovereignty and there is widespread agreement that the development towards EC involvement should be very gradual in this area.

Education represents a policy area where, at the outset, a high degree of conflict existed between the EC Commission and the member countries over the extent of EC involvement. The Court of Justice decided in favour of the Commission's position and there are now few major conflicts between the member countries and the EC institutions in this area.

The consumer sector is a typical example of an alliance which has been formed between parliamentary groups and representative weak political interests, pitched against industry and market oriented forces. The Parliament is using the consumer interest to strengthen their weak position in the EC. Energy is perhaps the area where we find the strongest polarization between, on the one hand, national interests which are unwilling to accept transnational authority and, on the other hand, the Commission. To some extent, one can say that the transport sector represents the same mercantilistic tradition in the member countries against the free market ideology of the Commission.

With regard to immigration policy, the national states have retained control over the decision–making process. As a result, the conflicts between universalistic principles and more or less restrictive national practices have not yet been fully expressed. Part of this area doesn't lie within the EC decision–making structure, but has instead been left to other intergovernmental mechanisms.

What are the policy outputs; i.e. the kind of policies produced? To what extent do we find Europeification in different areas? This question is perhaps the one which is most comprehensively addressed in the various chapters on policy areas.

Telecommunications is a good example of how a well developed policy–making process is about to create a high degree of European standarization on products and procedures in that industry. On the other hand, transport demonstrates that well established transnational competence and decision mechanisms do not necessarily lead to a standardized output. Areas where there are difficulties in establishing a transnational policy mechanism will also have the most problems in creating European wide results.

A variation of this is also found in the energy sector where an attempt to link this issue area with a well established internal market procedure, got stuck in the quagmire of strong and well organized national interests. On the other hand, certain aspects of energy policy relating to increased efficiency and reduced imports of oil were carried out by all the member countries in a remarkably similar way during the 1970s and early 1980s, despite the lack of a common policy framework.

Within certain fields of education, one can also find examples of the latter, but here there is also a considerable amount of EC policy, particularly in relation to higher education matters. In consumer policy there are a lot of minimum standards for various products and services, but not a common policy. In the areas of immigration and police policy, there is very little common policy, but a gradual increase in the coordination of national administrative and operational activities is occurring.

Real implementation of Directives concerns the incorporation of EC law through national political–administrative systems by means of a top–down process. However, numerous studies show that successful implementation is also largely dependent on how the upstream process of legislation is handled (Siedentopf and Ziller 1988, Phillip 1987). As a result, we emphasize the interplay between legislation and implementation in order to develop an understanding of why the speed and quality of implementation in member states differ. Through the Treaty on a European Economic Area (EEA), some countries are in a special position. The EFTA countries will be partly outsiders and partly insiders in the Internal Market. Formally, they are only fully part of the downstream process. In the upstream legislative process, they are only allowed to air their views at the preparatory stage.

We have discussed how policy areas vary with respect to Europeification. However, this process does not only lead to new types of political institutions and the transfer of authority from the national to the transnational level, it also leads to increased complexity, and we may distinguish between three aspects of this.

One aspect of complexity concerns the linking of national traditions through a system of transnational policy–making. This widens the scope of the national policy–making process, and the number and types of actors to be taken into consideration. A key dimension is the relation between the national and transnational levels of authority. National traditions may vary a lot in terms of the order and predictability of the policy–making process, but at least they represent familiar settings for the actors.

The second aspect has to do with the fact that the EC is not only transnational, but also represents new and changing forms of transnational authority. It experiments with new kinds of political authority and new ways of regulating the economy and society. Harmonization and the principle of subsidiarity, for example, open up a number of possibilities which, to a large extent, have to be clarified through international market and political processes respectively.

The third aspect of complexity stems from the broadening of the EC. For a long time, EC policy was restricted to a few specific areas of economic and social life. The Single European Act and, in particular the Maastricht Treaty, broaden the scope and variety of policy issues which will come under the influence of the EC. In the future, almost all policy areas will have an EC dimension. This implies wider national differences and more intense conflicts which will have to be dealt with at the EC level.

The result is lobbyification at the central EC level while, at the same time, a higher degree of coordination is necessary at the national level if the national systems are to survive as key actors. The alternative is that various interests in the member countries will be articulated independently of, and even in conflict with, those of national authorities. It follows that the nature of EC policy–making processes may vary considerably, from a relatively high degree of order and rationality due to control by member states, to processes that may be quite disorderly.

Actors are most likely to pursue rational strategies in areas where there are only a few others with similar attitudes. This normally means that the subject matter limits which decisions can be made; from detailed questions of distribution to general technical rules. When the number of actors is high and the issue allows for complicated politics, the result may be a lack of an overall perspective and coordination. The latter may be described as organized anarchy or the garbage–can process (Cohen et al. 1974).

The focus of this book has been Europeification. In Part I we introduced conceptual frameworks for the study of EC institutions, policy–making and outputs. The empirical studies which were presented in Part II, demonstrated varying degrees of Europeification. When looking at specific policy areas, there is a considerable spread in terms of how far this process has gone and what should be expected for the future.

In order to analyse the future degree of Europeification in the different areas, we have to understand the nature of the EC's architecture.

The European village in Delors' terms and the corresponding institutions and decision–making structure of the European Union will be decided at the next intergovernmental conference in 1996/1997. The Maastricht Union was created for a previously divided Europe and the future European Union has to have both a more comprehensive and a more diversified structure.

From an optimistic point of view, the new European village will have strong supranational institutions in the economic area, the first pillar of the Maastricht Treaty. In his chapter of this book, Finn Laursen foresees that, if the European Union is realized and new countries are allowed to join, economic integration can be both deepened and widened. As we have described, however, there are many problems which need to be overcome.

There are strong possibilities of a Europe composed of two or more divisions in the economic field. There will be an inner core moving faster than the other members. Some members may not meet the requirements of the third stage until 1999 or later and some, like the UK and Denmark, have opted out with regard to the EMU. Others may not, in the foreseeable future, be able to join the EMU, including such countries as Greece and some of the Central and East European countries. This, not even multi speed, but "multi division" European Union will create problems regarding the appropriate decision–making structure to be employed and the relative influence of the various member countries.

There are also tremendous problems to be solved in even the most advanced Central and East European economies and major improvements will have to be made before they are able to fulfil the qualifications demanded for economic membership. On the other hand, they are, in political terms, willing to join immediately but the EU is not prepared to accept them as members before the year 2000.

In contrast to the economic architecture, it will be much more difficult to develop strong supranational institutions in other areas. We will experience a large range in the degree of supranational authority achieved.

The future European village will have both a varied and, at the same time, rapidly changing architectural structure. The main challenge, therefore, is to develop a framework which is capable of including all these variations and which has the power and legitimacy to run the village in an effective and efficient manner. These are the two old questions of democracy and governance, and their importance will increase with further EC integration.

# REFERENCES

Agence France Presse (1991) "French win 5.8 billion dollar contract for high speed train", May 29.

Alexander, E.R. (1989) "Improbable Implementation: The Pressman–Wildavsky Paradox Revisited", *Journal of Public Policy* 4:451–465.

Andersen, S.S. (1993) *The Struggle over North Sea Oil and Gas. Government Strategies in Denmark, Britain and Norway.* Oslo: Scandinavian University Press.

Andersen, S.S. and Burns, T.R. (1992) *Societal Decision–Making. Democratic Challenges to State Technocracy.* Aldershot: Dartmouth.

Andersen, S. S. and Eliassen, K. A. (1991) "European Community Lobbying", *European Journal of Political Research* 20: 173–187.

Andersen, S. S. and Eliassen, K. A. (1992) "EF lobbying etter Maastricht", *Sosiologi idag* no. 2.

Andersen, S. S., Eliassen, K. A., Kuvaas, B. and From, J. (1991) "Norsk implementering av EØS–regler – Hva kan vi lære av Danmark?", Handelshøyskolen BI. Arbeidsnotat 1991/46. (Rapport 1991–316–12) Senter for Europeiske studier.

Andersen S.S. and Midttun, A. (1989) *The Articulation of Capital–Interests in Norway: Embeddedness and the Organization of Capital.* Bærum: Norwegian School of Management.

Anderson, B. (1991) *Imagined Communities* (revised edition). London: Verso.

Anderson, M. (1989) *Policing the World: Interpol and the Politics of International Police Co–operation.* New York: Oxford University Press.

Archer, C. and Butler, F. (1992) *The European Community: Structure and Process.* New York: St. Martin's Press.

Austvik, O.G. (1991) "Norwegian Gas in the New Europe", in O.G. Austvik (ed.) *Norwegian Gas in the New Europe.* Sandvika: Vett og viten.

Azzi, G.C. (1988) "What is this New Researsh into the Implementation of Community Legislation Bringing Us?", in H. Siedentopf and J. Ziller (eds) *Making European Policies Work.* Volume I Comparative Syntheses. Brussel and London: EIPA/Sage.

Bartholomew, M. and Brooks, T. (1989) "Lobbying Brussels to Get What You Need for 1992", *The Wall Street Journal,* January 31:7.

Beer, P. de. (1991) "La visite de M. Michel Rocard en Corée du sud L'incontournable dossier du TGV", *Le Monde,* May 4.

Beltran, A. (Forthcoming) "The French National Railways (SNCF) and the Development of High Speed Trains, 1950–1981", in S. Hultèn and T. Flink (eds) *High Speed Trains: Entrepreneurship and Society.* London: Leading Edge.

Benyon, J. (1992) *Police Co–operation in Europe.* University of Leicester: Centre for the Study of Public Order.

Bergesen, H.O. (1991) *Symbol or Substance. The Climate Policy of the European Community.* Oslo: Fridtjof Nansen Institute.

Bigo, D. (1992) *The European Internal Security Field,* ECPR Joint Sessions, Limerick.

Birenbaum, P. (1985) "Political Strategies of Regulated Organizations as Functions of Context and Fear", *Strategic Management Journal.* (4):135–150.

Black, D. (1990) "European Rail Renaissance Could Leave Britain Isolated: Government reluctance to help finance a high–speed link to the Channel tunnel may undermine the benefits of the single market", *The Independent,* June 13:2.

Black, D. (1991) "High–speed Rail Plan for Europe Socially Divisive, *The Independent,* November 22: 8.

Black, D. (1991) "Tracks to Nowhere: The Government believes that privatisation is the cure for the ills of British Rail. The rest of the world disagrees", *The Independent,* October 6:19.

Boer, M. den (1991) Schengen: Intergovernmental Scenario for European Police Co–operation, Working Paper, University of Edinburgh, Department of Politics.

*Boston Globe* (1988) "Florida Unveils 4 Plans for a High–Speed Train", March 29:38.

Bradshaw, J. (1991) "Institutional Reform in the European Community beyond Maastricht", *EIU European Trends* 4.

Brickman, R., Jasanoff, S. and Ilgen, T. (1985) *Controlling Chemicals. The Politics of Regulation in Europe and the United States.* Ithaca: Cornell University Press.

Briggs, D. (1986) "Environmental Problems and Policies in the European Community", in C. Park (ed.) *Environmental Policies: An International Review.* London: Croom Helm.

Brodeur, J.P. (1983) "High Policing and Low Policing: Remarks about the policing of political activities", *Social Problems* 30:(5).

Bromberg, Elizabeth (1992) "European Community Environmental Policy: The Role of the European Parliament", Eighth Annual Conference of Europeanists, Chicago.

Budd, S. and Jones, A. (1989) *The European Community, A Guide to the Maze.* London: Kogan Page.

Buksti, J.A. and Johansen, L.N. (1979) "Variations in Organizational Participation in Government: The Case of Denmark", *Scandinavian Political Studies,* 197–220.

Buksti, J. A. and Martens. H. (1984) *Interesseorganisationer i EF.* Aarhus: Institut for Statskundskab.

Buzan, B., Kelstrup, M., Lemaitre, P., Tromer, E. and Wæver, O. (1990) *The European Security Order Recast. Scenarios for the Post–Cold War Era.* London and New York: Frances Pinter.

Cahen, A. (1989) *The Western European Union and NATO.* London: Brassey's (UK) Ltd.

Callovi, G. (1992) "Regulation of Immigration in 1993: Pieces of the European Community Jig–Saw Puzzle", *International Migration Review* 26:353–372.

Cameron, E. (1991) *The European Reformation.* Oxford: Clarendo Press.

Campbell, J. L., Hollingsworth, J.R. and Lindberg, L.N. (eds) (1991) *Governance of the American Economy.* New York: Cambridge University Press.

Capouet, Y. (1992) "Completion of the Internal Market for Electricity and Gas", *Energy in Europe* 19.

Cendrowicz, M. (1991) "The European Community's Relationship with Turkey: Looking Backwards, Looking Forwards", paper presented at Marmaris Conference, June.

Close, G. (1978) "Harmonization of Laws: Use or Abuse of the Powers Under the EEC Treaty", *European Law Review* 3:461–468.

Coffey, P. (1990) *Main Economic Policy Areas of the ECC toward 1992 : The Challenge to the Community''s Economic Policies when the "Real' Common Market is Created by the End of 1992.* Dordrecht : Kluwer Academic Press.

Cohen, M.D., March, J.G. and Olsen, J.P. (1972) "A Garbage–Can Model of Organizational Choice", *Administrative Science Quarterly,* 17:1–25.

Colchester, N. and Buchan, D. (1990) *Europe Relaunched: Truths and Illusions on the Way to 1992.* London: Hutchinson/Economist Books.

COM (88) 174: *Review of Member States' Energy Policies.*

COM (92) 226: *Proposed EC Directive on Taxation of $CO_2$ Emissions and Energy.*

The Commission (1990) *Environmental Policy in the European Community.* Bruxelles: The European Community.

Committee for the Study of Economic and Monetary Union (1989) *Report on Economic and Monetary Union in the European Community.* Luxembourg: Office for Official Publications of the EC.

Conférence Européenne des Ministres des Transports (CEMT) (1990) "Investissements Publics et Privés dans le Secteur des Transports: Table Ronde 81". Paris: OCDE.

Conférence Européenne des Ministres des Transports (CEMT) (1992) "Trains à Grande Vitesse: Table Ronde 87". Paris: OCDE.

Conference on Security and Co–operation in Europe (1991) "Charter of Paris for a New Europe and Supplementary Document to give effect to certain provisions of the Charter", *International Legal Materials* 30 (January):190–228.

Cordaro, G. (1990) "Towards 1992: The European Community Telecommunications Policy", *Telecommunications* (January):33–35.

Council of the European Communities (1990) *European Educational Policy Statements,* Supplement to the third edition (December 1989). Brussels, Luxembourg: General Secretariat.

Council of the European Communities (1988) *European Educational Policy Statements,* Third edition, June 1987. Brussels, Luxembourg: General Secretariat.

Damgaard, E. and Eliassen, K.A. (1978) "Corporate Pluralism in Danish Law–Making", *Scandinavian Political Studies*, 1(4):285–313.

Dang–Nguyen, G. (1986) "A European Telecommunications Policy. Which instruments for which prospects", unpublished manuscript. Brest: ENST.

De Witte, B. (ed.) (1989) *European Community Law of Education.* Baden–Baden: Nomos Verlagsgesellschaft.

De Witte, B. (1992) "The Influence of European Community Law on National Systems of Higher Education", in J. Pertek (ed.) *General Recognition of Diplomas and Free Movement of Professionals, Seminar Proceedings*, pp. 73–89. Maastricht: European Institute of Public Administration.

Dehousse, R. (1992) "Integration v. Regulation? On the Dynamics of Regulation in the European Community", *Journal of Common Market Studies*, XXX, (4):383–402.

Dehousse, R. and Weiler, J.H.H. (1990) "The Legal Dimension", in W. Wallace (ed.) *The Dynamics of European Integration,* 242–260. London and New York: Frances Pinter.

Delcourt, B. (1991) "EC Decisions and Directives on Information Technology and Telecommunications", *Telecommunications Policy* 15:15–21.

Delors, J. (1989) "The Broad Lines of Commission Policy", *Agence Europe*, Documents No 1542/1543 (26 January).

Diehl, J.(1988) "Choking on Their Own Development", *Washington Post National Weekly Edition,* June 4:9.

DiMaggio, P.J. and Powell, W.W. (1983) "The Iron Cage Revisited: Institutionalized Isomorphism and Collective Rationality in Organizational Fields", *American Sociological Review* 48:147–160.

Dobbin, F. (Forthcoming) "Public Policy and the Development of High Speed Trains in France and the United States", in S. Hultèn and T. Flink (eds) *High Speed Trains:*

*Entrepreneurship and Society*. London: Leading Edge.

Dobbin, F. (Forthcoming) *States and Industrial Cultures*. New York: Cambridge University Press.

Donnelly, J. (1986) "International Human Rights: A Regime Analysis", *International Organization* 40:559–642.

Douglas, M. (1986) *How Institutions Think*. Syracuse, New York: Syracuse University Press.

Drucker, P. F. (1989) *The New Realities. In Government and Politics/In Economics and Business/In Society and World View*. New York: Harper & Row.

Dunham, A.L. (1941) "How the First French Railways Were Planned", *Journal of Economic History* 14: 12–25.

Dyson, K. (1983) "The Cultural, Ideological and Structural Context", in K. Dyson and S. Wilks (eds) *Industrial Crisis: A Comparative Study of the State and Industry*, pp. 22–66. Oxford: Martin Robertson.

Economic and Social Committee (1980) *European Interest Groups and Their Relationships with the Economic and Social Committee*. Farnborough: Saxon House.

*Economist* (1983) "Faster Trains, Bigger Losses", November, 19 p. 76.

*Economist* (1984) "On a Rail and a Prayer", September, p. 49.

*Economist* (1985a) "Return Train", August, 24 p. 53–60.

*Economist* (1985b) "The World and its Railways: Redefining Their Role", August, 31 p. 25–32.

*Economist* (1985c) "The World and its Railways: Higher Speeds and Lower Costs", September, 7 p. 33–38.

*Economist* (1985d) "The World and its Railways: The Fast Track", September, 14 p. 25–28.

*Economist* (1988) "A Faster Route to Europe", July, 16 p. 53–54.

*Economist* (1989) "Faster and Still Faster", September, p. 52.

*Economist* (1989) "Freedom to be Cleaner than the Rest",, October, 14 p. 21–24.

*Economist* (1991) "A Wall of Waste", *Economist,* November, 30 p. 73.

*Economist* (1991) "Dirty Dozen", July, 20, p. 52.

*Economist* (1991) "Free Trade"s Green Hurdle", June 15, p. 61.

*Economist* (1991) "The Other Fortress Europe", June 1.

*Economist* (1992) "Europe"s Immigrants; Strangers Inside the Gates", February 15.

Eisenstadt, S.N. (1972) "Social Institutions", in D.L. Sills (ed.) *International Encyclopedia of the Social Sciences,* vol.13 p. 409–429.

Eliassen, K.A. and Mydske, K.K. (1991) "EF og Norsk Utdanning i 90–Årene", *Arbeidsnotat 1991/28*. Oslo: Senter for europeiske studier.

*Energy for Europe : Resources, Economy, Cooperation* (1991) Report From a Nordic Council Seminar at Holmenkollen, Oslo, Norway, 14–15 October 1991. København : Nordisk Ministerråd.

*Engineering News Record* (1985) "High Speed Rail Line Feasible", October, 31:14.

*Engineering News Record* (1986) "High–speed Rail Network Under Study in Europe", March.6:16.

*Environmental Policy in the European Community* (1990). 4 th edn. Luxembourg: Office of Official Publications on the European Communities.

Epstein, E. (1969) *The Corporation in American Poltics*. Englewood Cliffs, NJ: Prentice Hall.

Europe Agreements (1992) Establishing an Association between the European Communities and their Member States, of the one Part and Czech and Slovak Federal

Republic, of the other Part. Mimeo.

Europe Documents (1991) No. 1683, 15 January.

Europe Documents (1991) No. 1712, 22 May.

Europe Documents (1992) No. 1790, 3 July.

European Communities, Commission (1988) Energy in Europe: Energy Policies and Trends in the European Community. Brussels.

European Communities, Commission (1989) "Avis de la Commission sur la demande d'adhesion de la Turquie à la Communauté", SEC(89) 2290 final, Brussels, December 18.

European Communities, Commission (1990a) "Communication from the Commission to the Council and the Parliament. Association agreements with the countries of central and eastern Europe: a general outline", COM(90) 398 final, Brussels, August 27.

European Communities, Commission (1990b) Directorate–General Information, Communication, Culture, "The European Community and Cyprus", April.

European Communities, Commission (1991) Secretariat General, "A Strategy for Enlargement: Preliminary Report of the SG Study Group on Enlargement", Brussels, November 14.

European Communities, Council and Commission (1992) *Treaty on European Union* (Luxembourg: Office for Official Publications of the European Communities).

European Communities, Court of Justice (1991) "Opinion of the Court 14 December 1991", Opinion 1/91.

European Communities, Court of Justice (1992) "Opinion of the Court 10 April 1992", Opinion 1/92.

European Community Education Cooperation (1986) *The First Decade Eurydice: The education information network in the European Community.* Brussels.

European Conference of Ministers of Transport (1986) *European Dimension and Future Prospects of the Railways.* Paris: OECD.

European Council (1992) "European Council in Edinburgh – 11–12 December, 1992 – Conclusions of the Presidency", *Agence Europe*, 13 December.

*European Educational Policy Statements* (1988). 3rd. edn, June 1987. Brussels. Luxembourg: Council of the European Communities. General Secretariat.

*European Educational Policy Statements* (1990). Supplement to the 3rd edn, December 1989. Brussels, Luxembourg: Council of the European Communities. General Secretariat.

Fangmann, H. (1990) "Die Europäisierung des Fernmeldewesens. Ohne demokratische Legitimation", *Gewerkschaftliche Praxis* 35(1):22–28.

Fijnaut, C. (1991) "Police Co–operation in Europe", in F. Heidensohn and M. Farrell (eds) *Crime in Europe.* London:Routledge.

Fijnaut, C. (1992) "Policing Western Europe: Interpol, Trevi and Europol", *Police Studies*, 15:3, Fall.

*Financial Times* (1992) "Railway Finance", May, 1:14.

Finnemore, M. (1990) "International Organizations as Teachers of Norms: UNESCO and Science Policy", Department of Political Science, Stanford University.

Fligstein, N. and Brantley, P. (1992) "The 1992 Single Market Programme and the Interests of Business", Mimeo. Department of Sociology. University of California at Berkeley.

Flink, T. (1991) "The Economic and Technical Effects of an Extended Lead–time in R&D Projects – The Case of the Swedish High Speed Trains", Mimeo. Stockholm

School of Economics.

Flink, T. (1992) "On the Revitalisation of Mature Industries: The Case of High Speed Trains in Italy", Mimeo. Stockholm School of Economics.

Flynn, G. (1991) "The CSCE and the New European Order", in M. Wyatt (ed.) *CSCE and the New Blueprint for Europe,* pp. 23–33. Washington, DC: Institute for the Study of Diplomacy, Georgetown University.

Freeman, L. (1991) "Foreign Trains Could Run on BR Tracks", *Press Association Newsfile,* July 11.

Freestone, D. (1991) "European Community Environmental Policy and Law", *Journal of Law and Society,* 18:135–154.

Fünfter Gesamtbericht über die Tärigheit der Gemeinschaften 1971, (1972). Brussels.

Gable, R.W. (1953) "NAM: Influential Lobby or Kiss of Death", *Journal of Politics:*254–273.

Garrett, G. (1992a) "International Cooperation and Institutional Choice", *International Organization* 46:533–560.

Garrett, G. (1992b) "Intergovernmental Bargaining and European Integration", Paper presented at the International Conference of Europeanists, Chicago.

*General Report On The Activities Of The European Communities,* Brussels (Published yearly).

George, S. (1991) *Politics and Policy in the European Community.* Oxford: Oxford University Press.

Ghebali, V.Y. (1992) "La CSCE à la recherche de son rôle dans la nouvelle Europe", in M. Telò (ed.) *Vers une nouvelle Europe?,* pp. 49–79. Brussels: Editions de l'Université de Bruxelles.

Ginsberg, R.H. (1989) "US–EC relations", in J. Lodge (ed.) *The European Community And The Challenge of The Future,* pp.256–278. London: Frances Pinter.

Granovetter, M. (1985) "Economic Action and Social Structure: The Problem of Embeddedness", *American Journal of Sociology* 91:481–510.

Grant, W. (ed.) (1985) *The Political Economy of Corporatism.* London: Macmillan

Greenwood, J., Grote, J.R. and Ronit, K. (eds) (1992) *Organized Interests and the European Community.* London: Sage.

Gregory, F. and Collier, A. (1992) "Cross Frontier Crime and International Crime – Problems, Achievements and Prospects with reference to European Police Co-operation", in M. Anderson and M. den Boer (eds) *European Police Co–operation.* Proceedings of a Seminar, University of Edinburgh, Department of Politics, pp. 71–92.

Grote, J.R. (1990) "Steuerungsprobleme in transnationalen Beratungsgremien: Über soziale Kosten unkoordinierter Regulierung in der EG", in T. Ellwein, J.J. Hesse, R. Mayntz and F.W. Scharpf (eds), *Jahrbuch zur Staats–und Verwaltungswissenschaft.* Vol. 4 pp. 227–254. Baden–Baden: Nomos.

Haar, J.H. (1991) *European Integration and Interventionist Political Forces in Britain and Denmark.* Aarhus: Institut for Statskundskab.

Haas, E.B. (1958) *The Uniting of Europe: Political, Social, and Economic Forces, 1950–1957.* London: Stevens.

Haas, E.B. (1964) *Beyond the Nation state. Functionalism and International Organization.* Stanford, CA: Stanford University Press.

Haas, E.B. (1968) *The Uniting of Europe. Political, Social, And Economic Forces 1950–57.* Stanford, CA: Stanford University Press (first published 1958).

Haas, E.B. (1990) *When Knowledge Is Power. Three Models of Change in International*

*Organizations.* Berkeley: University of California Press.

Haigh, N. (1989) *EEC Environmental Policy and Britain, 2nd Ed.* Harlow: Longman.

Haigh, N. and Baldock, D. (1989) "Environmental Policy and 1992". London: Institute for European Environmental Policy.

Hall, P. (1986) *Governing the Economy: The Politics of State Intervention in Britain and France.* New York: Oxford University Press.

Hall, P. (Forthcoming) "The Movement From Keynesianism to Monetarism: Institutional Analysis and British Economic Policy in the 1970s", in S. Steinmo, K. Thelen and F. Longstreth (eds) *Historical Institutionalism in Comparative Politics: State, Society, and Economy.* New York: Cambridge University Press.

Hallstein, W., Goetz, H.H. and Narjes, K.H. (1969) *Der unvollendete Bundesstaat. Europäische Erfahrungen und Erkenntnisse.* Düsseldorf: Econ.

Harrison, M. (1991) "BR Train Delay Could Boost Tunnel Costs", *The Independent,* November 12, p. 23.

Hayes, M.T. (1981) *Lobbyists and Legislators.* New Brunswick: Rutgers University Press.

Hayward, J. (1974) *The One and Indivisible French Republic.* New York: Norton.

Heisler, M.O. (1979) "Corporate Pluralism Revisited: Where is Theory?", *Scandinavian Political Studies,* 2(3): 277–298.

Herman, Robin (1988) "An Ecological Epiphany", *Washington Post National Weekly Edition,* December 5–11 p.19.

Hoffmann, S. (1965) "The European Process at Atlantic Crosspurposes", *Journal of Common Market Studies,* 3(2), February:85–101.

Hoffmann, S. (1982) "Reflections on the Nation state in Western Europe Today", *Journal of Common Market Studies* 21:21–37.

Hoffmann, S. (1992) "Balance, Concert, Anarchy, or None of the Above", in G.F. Treverton (ed.) *The Shape of the New Europe* pp.194–220. New York: Council of Foreign Relations Press.

Hoop, J.J. van der (1991) "Europe: is Rail the Way; The Railroad Industry Situation", *Information Access,* October :80.

Hultén, S. and Flink. T. (Forthcoming) "The Swedish High Speed Train Project", in S. Hultén and T. Flink (eds) *High Speed Trains: Entrepreneurship and Society.* London: Leading Edge.

Hurwitz, L. and Lequesne, C. (eds) (1991) *The State Of The European Community.* Boulder, Colorado: Lynne Rienner Publishers.

Hyde–Price, A. (1991) *European Security beyond the Cold War: Four Scenarios for the Year 2010.* London: Sage.

*International Railway Journal* (1990) "SNCF Takes Initiative on HS Network", June, p. 10.

Iversen, A.W. (1992) "EFs miljøpolitikk", in S.S Andersen and K.A. Eliassen (eds). *Det nye Europa.* Oslo: Tano.

Jacobs, F., Corbett, R. and Shackleton, M. (1992) *The European Parliament.* 2nd edn. Harlow: Longman.

Jakobsen, M. (1992) Europe in the 1990s: the Stability in Sight. Occasional Paper no. 37. Geneva: EFTA.

Jaks, J. (1992) "Challenges and Paradoxes on the Way to a United Democratic Europe", in A. Cleese and R. Tokes (eds) *The Economic and Social Imperatives of the Future Europe.* Baden–Baden: Nomos Verlagsgesellschaft.

Johansen, L.N. and Kristensen, O.P. (1982) "Corporatist Traits in Denmark 1946–

1976", in Lembruch and Schmitter (eds) *Patterns of Corporatism in Policy–Making*. Beverly Hills: Sage.

Jordan, G. and McLaughlin, A. (1991) *The Rationality of Lobbying in Europe: Why are Euro Groups So Numerous and So Weak?* Oxford: Centre for European Studies Discussion.

Jublin, J. and Quatrepoint, J.–M. (1976) *French Ordinateurs. De l'affair bull à l'assassinat du Plan Calcul.* Paris: Moreau.

Kaiser, K. (1972) "Transnational Relations as a Threat to the Democratic Process", in R.O Keohane and J.S. Nye (eds) *Transnational Relations and World Politics*, pp. 356–370. Cambridge, MA: Harvard University Press.

Kenis, P. and Schneider, V. (1987) "The EC as an International Corporate Actor: Two Case Studies in Economic Diplomacy", *European Journal of Political Research* 15: 437–457.

Keohane, R.O. (1988) "International Institutions: Two Approaches", *International Studies Quarterly*, 32: 379–396.

Keohane, R.O. and Hoffmann, S. (1990) "Conclusions: Community politics and institutional change", in W. Wallace (ed.) *The Dynamics of European Integration.* pp. 276–300. London: Frances Pinter.

Keohane, R.O. and Nye, J.S. (1974) "Transgovernmental Relations and International Organizations", *World Politics* 27:39–62.

Keohane, R.O. and Nye J.S. (1977) *Power and interdependence: world politics in transition.* Boston: Little, Brown and Company.

Kirchner, E.J. (1981) *The Role of Interest Groups in the European Community.* Aldershot: Gower Publications.

Kirchner, E.J. (1992) *Decision Making in the European Community: The Council Presidency and European Integration.* Manchester: Manchester University Press.

Kirkland, R. (1988) "Environmental Anxiety Goes Global", *Fortune,* November 21 p.118.

Kohler–Koch, B. (1991) "Inselillusion und Interdependenz: Nationales Regieren unter den Bedingungen von "international governance"", in B. Blanke and H. Wollmann (eds) *Die alte Bundesrepublik. Kontinuität und Wandel,* pp. 45–67. Opladen: Westdeutscher Verlag, (Leviathan, Sonderheft 12/1991).

Kolte, L. (1989) "Beslutningsprocessen i EF 1985–89", *Politica* 4:376–395.

Koordinatorgruppen Fri Bevegelighet for Personer (1989) Rapport til Det Europæiske råd, Palma de Mallorca (CIRC 3624/89) 9 juni.

Kramer, L. (1987) "The Single European Act and Environmental Protection: Reflections on Several New Provisions in Community Law", *Common Market Law Review* 24:659–688.

Krasner, S.D. (1983) "Structural Causes and Regime Consequences: Regimes as intervening variables", in S.D. Krasner (ed.) *International Regimes.* Ithaca: Cornell University Press.

Kuvaas, B. (1992) "Maastrichtavtalen", in S.S. Andersen and K.A. Eliassen (eds) *Det nye Europa.* Oslo: Tano.

Labarrère, C. (1985) *L'Europe des postes et des télécommunications.* Paris: Masson.

Lange, P. (Forthcoming) "Maastricht and the Social Protocol: Why Did They do It?", *Politics and Society.*

Lasswell, H.D. (1956) *The Decision Process. Seven Categories of Functional Analysis.* University of Maryland.

Laursen, F. (1990a) "Explaining the EC''s New Momentum", in F. Laursen (ed.) *EFTA and the EC: Implications of 1992*, pp. 33–52. Maastricht: European Institute of Public Administration.

Laursen, F. (1990b) "The Community"s Policy Towards EFTA: Regime Formation in the European Economic Space (EES)", *Journal of Common Market Studies* 28 (June):303–325.

Laursen, F. (1991a) "Comparative Regional Economic Integration: the European and Other Processes", *International Review of Administrative Sciences* 57: 4 (December):515–526.

Laursen, F. (1991b) "EFTA Countries as Actors in European Integration: The Emergence of the European Economic Area (EEA)", *International Review of Administrative Sciences* 57 (December):543–555.

Laursen, F. (1991–92) "The EC and its European Neighbours: Special Partnerships or Widened Membership?", *International Journal* 47 (Winter):29–63.

Laursen, F. (1993) "The Maastricht Treaty: Implications for the Nordic Countries", *Cooperation and Conflict*, forthcoming.

Laursen, F. and Vanhoonacher, S. (eds) (1992) *The Intergovernmental Conference on Political Union: Institutional Reforms, New Policies and International Identity of the European Community*. Maastricht: European Institute of Public Administration.

Levy, R. (1990) "The Implementation of Budgetary Control in the European Community" in T. Younis (ed.) *Implementation in Public Policy*. Aldershot: Darthmount.

Liberatore, A. (1991) "Problems of Transnational Policymaking: Environmental Problems in the European Community", *European Journal of Political Research* 19:281–305.

Lindberg, L.N. (1971) "Political Integration as a Multidimensional Phenomenon Requiring Multivariate Measurement", in L.N. Lindberg and S.A. Scheingold (eds) *Regional Integration. Theory and Research*, pp. 45–127. Cambridge, MA: Harvard University Press.

Lindberg, L.N. and Scheingold, S.A. (eds) (1971) *Regional Integration. Theory and Research*. Cambridge, MA: Harvard University Press.

Lodge, J. (ed.) (1989) *The European Community and the Challenge of the Future*. London: Frances Pinter.

Lodge, J. (1992) "The European Community Foreign and Security Policy after Maastricht. New Problems and Dynamics", in M. Telò (ed.) *Vers une nouvelle Europe?*, pp. 111–132. Brussels: Editions de l'Université de Bruxelles.

Lonbay, J. (1989) "Education and Law: The Community context", *European Law Review*, 14 (6):363–387.

Louis, J.V. (1990) *The Community Legal Order*,.2nd. edn. Luxembourg: Office for Official Publications of the European Communities.

Lucron, C.P. (1992) "Contenu et portée des accords entre la Communauté et la Hongrie, la Pologne et la Tchécoslovaquie", *Revue du Marché commun* 357 (April):293–299.

Ludlow, P. (1991a) "Europe's Institutions: Europe's Politics", in G.F. Treverton (ed.) *The Shape of the New Europe*, pp. 59–91. New York: Council on Foreign Relations Press.

Ludlow, P. (1991b) "The European Commission", in R.O. Keohane and S. Hoffmann (eds) *The New European Community*. Boulder CO: Westview Press.

Lynn–Jones, S.M. (1991) *The Cold War and After: Prospects for Peace*. Cambridge, MA: The MIT Press.

Lyons, P. K. (1990) *The New Energy Markets of the Soviet Union and East Europe*. London: Financial Times Business Information.

Lyons, P. K. (1992) *EC Energy Policy. A detailed Guide to the Community's Impact on the Sector*. London: Financial Times Management Report.

Macdonald, A. (1991) "French Railway Courts Investors at High Speed", *The Reuter Library Report,* October 10.

Majone, G. (1991) "Cross–national Sources of Regulatory Policymaking in Europe and the United States", *Journal of Public Policy* 11:79–106.

Malta (1990) *Report by the EC Directorate to the Prime Minister and Minister of Foreign Affairs regarding Malta's membership of the European Community*. Valetta: Department of Information, March.

March, J.G. and Olsen, J.P. (1989) *Rediscovering Institutions. The Organizational Basis of Politics*. New York and London: The Free Press.

Maresceau, M. (1992) "The European Community and Eastern Europe and the USSR", in J. Redmond (ed.) *The External Relations of the EC: The International Response in 1992*. London: Macmillan.

Maresceau, M. (1993) ""Europe Agreements": a new form of cooperation between the European Community and Hungary, Poland and the Czech and Slovak Republic", in Prof. Müller–Graff (ed.) *Legal Adaptation to the Market Economy of the EC*. Baden–Baden: Nomos Verlag.

Marin, B. and Mayntz, R. (eds) (1991) *Policy Networks. Empirical Evidence and Theoretical Considerations*. Frankfurt a.M.: Campus.

Martin, P.L., Honekopp, E. and Ullmann, H. (1991) "Conference Report: Europe 1992, Effects on Labour Migration", *International Migration Review* 24:591–603.

Mathijsen, P.S.R.F. (1990) *A Guide to European Community Law*. 5th edn. London: Sweet & Maxwell.

Matlary, J.H. (1991) *From the Internal Energy Market to a Community Energy Policy?* Oslo: Fridtjof Nansen Institute.

May, K. (1992) "Politics Derailing High–Speed Train", *Ottowa Citizen,* March 26, p. D13.

Mayntz, R. (1983) "The Conditions of Effective Public Policy: A New Challenge for Policy Analysis", *Policy and Politics* 2:123–143.

Marks, G. (1992) "Structural Policy in the European Community", in A. Sbragia (ed.) *Euro–Politics.* Washington DC: The Brookings Institution.

Menanteau, J. (1991) "Les grands contrats du TGV. Avec les marchés à l'étranger, GEC–Alsthom découvre de nouveaux metiers", *Le Monde,* June 26.

Meyer, J.M. and Scott, R.W. (1983) *Organizational Environments. Ritual anmd Rationality*. London: Sage.

Meyer, J.W. (1980) "The World Polity and Authority of the Nation state System", in A. Bergesen (ed.) *Studies of the Modern World–System*. New York: Academic.

Miller, A.C. (1989) "Panel To Consider Ambitious Plan for Network of High–Speed Trains", *Los Angeles Times,* October 18, p. A24.

Miller, W.G. (1989) "Europe High–Speed Rail Network Closer as Three Nations Agree on a New Link", *Boston Globe,* August 14, p. 12.

Moe, A. (1988) *The Outlook for Soviet Gas Exports to Western Europe: A Country By Country Analysis*. Paper Presented at the 10th Annual Conference of the International Association of Energy Economists, Luxembourg, 4–7 July 1988.

Moravcsik, A. (1991) "Negotiating the Single European Act" in R.Keohane and S. Hoffmann (eds) *The New European Community*. Boulder, CO: Westview Press.

Morén, K. (1991) Den europeiske festning, – asylpolitikk og politisamarbeid mot 1992, avhandling kriminologi mellomfag h.91. Universitetet i Oslo: Institutt for kriminologi.

Morgenthau, H.J., Michelson, A.A. and Davis, Leonard (1973) *Politics among Nations: the Struggle for Power and Peace.* New York: Knopf

Morris, B., Boehm, K. and Vilcinskas, M. (1986) *The European Community: A Practical Directory and Guide for Business, Industry and Trade.* London: Macmillan.

Nadelmann, E.A. (1990) "Global Prohibition Regimes: The Evolution of Norms in International Society", *International Organization* 44:479–526.

Nash, C. (Forthcoming) "High Speed Rail Services: British Experience", in S. Hultèn and T. Flink (eds) *High Speed Trains: Entrepreneurship and Society.* London: Leading Edge.

Neave, G. (1984) *The EEC and Education.* Trentham Books: Stoke–on–Trent.

Neher, J. (1989) "French Hope U.S. Hears High–speed Train Whistle", *Chicago Tribune* September 25.

Newman, D. (1990) "Lobbying in the EC", *Business Journal*, February.

Nice, D.C. (1989) "Consideration of High–Speed Rail Service in the United States", *Transportation Research* 23A:359–65.

Nora, S. and Minc, A. (1978) *L'Informatisation de la société.* Paris: La Documentation française.

North, D. (1981) *Structure and Change in Economic History.* New York: Norton.

North, D. (1990) *Institutions, Institutional Change and Economic Performance.* New York: Cambridge University Press.

Nugent, N. (1991) *The Government and Politics of the European Community.* London:Macmillan

Nye, J.S. (1968) "Comparative Regional Integration: Concepts and Measurement", *International Organization* 22:855–80.

Nye, J.S. (1971) "Comparing Common Markets: A Revised neofunctionalist Model", in L.N. Lindberg and S.A. Scheingold (eds) *Regional Integration. Theory and Research*, pp.192–231. Cambridge, MA: Harvard University Press.

Nye, J.S. and Keohane, R.O. (1973) *Transnational Relations and World Politics.* Cambridge, MA: Harvard University Press (3rd printing).

Nye, J.S. and Keohane, R. (1975) "International Interdependence and Integration", in Grunskin and Polssy (eds) *Handbook of Political Science*, Vol. 8.

Nye, Jr., Biedenkopf, J.G. and Shiina (1992) *Globale Kooperation nach dem Ende des Kalten Krieges: eine Neueinschätzung des Trilateralismus. Ein Back–Force–Bericht an die Bilaterale Kommission.* Bonn: Forschungsinstitut der Deutschen Gesellschaft für Auswärtige Politik.

O'Riordan, Timothy (1979) "Role of Environmental Quality Objectives: The Politics of Pollution Control" in O'Riordan and D'Arge (eds) *Progress in Resource Management and Environmental Planning*, Vol. 1. New York: Wiley.

Olsen, J.P. (1978) *Politisk Organisering: Organisasjonsteoretiske synspunkt på folkestyre og politisk ulikhet.* Bergen: Universitetsforlaget.

Olsen, J.P. (1992) *Analysing Institutional Dynamics.* Bergen: LOS–sentret, notat 92/14.

Padgett, S. (1992) "The Single European Market: The Politics of Realization", *Journal of Common Market Studies*, XXX (1) (March).

Patel, P. and Pavitt, K. (1989) "European Technological Performance: Results and Prospects", *European Affairs.* 2:56–63.

Pedersen, T. (1992) "Political Change in the European Community. The Single European Act as a Case of System Transformation", *Cooperation and Conflict*, Vol. 27(1): 7–44.

Pelkmans, J. (1987) "The New Approach to Technical Harmonization and Standardization" *Journal of Common Markets Studies*. 25(3):249–269.

Perrin–Pelletier, F. (1985) "The European automobile industry in the context of 1992", *European Affairs* (1):85–95.

Pertek, J. (1992a) "L'Europe des universités", in J. Pertek and M. Soveroski (eds) *EC Competences and Programmes within the Field of Education*, pp.21–42. Maastricht: European Institute of Public Administration.

Pertek, J. (1992b) "TEMPUS: L'enseignement supérieur, point de rencontre priviliégié entre la Communauté et l'Europe centrale et orientale", in J. Pertek and M. Soveroski (eds) *EC Competences and Programmes within the Field of Education*, pp. 49–62. Maastricht: European Institute of Public Administration.

Pertek, J. (ed.) (1992) *General Recognition of Diplomas and Free Movement of Professionals, Seminar Proceedings*. Maastricht: European Institute of Public Administration.

Pertek, J. and Soveroski, M. (eds) (1992) *EC Competences and Programmes within the Field of Education*. Maastricht: European Institute of Public Administration.

Peters, G.B. (1992) "Bureaucratic Politics and the Institutions of the European Community", in A.M. Sbragia (ed.) *Europolitics: Institutions and Policymaking in the "New" European Community*, pp.75–123. Washington, DC: Brookings.

Petersen, J.H. and Nedergaard, P. (1992) *Det nye EF: traktaten om den europæiske union*. København: CO Metal, Industriens Arbejdsgivere; Den danske Europabevegelse.

Philip, A. B. (1983) *Pressure Groups in the European Community. In Institutions and Politics of the European Community*. London: Frances Pinter.

Philip, A. B. (1987) "Pressure Groups in the European Community and Informal Institutional Arrangements", in R. Beuter and P. Taskaloyannis (eds) *Experiences in Regional Co–operation*. Maastricht: European Institute of Public Administration.

Pinder, A. (1991) *The European Community and Eastern Europe*. London: Chatam House Papers.

Polino, M.N. (Forthcoming) "The French TGV Since 1976", in S. Hultèn and T. Flink (eds) *High Speed Trains: Entrepreneurship and Society*. London: Leading Edge.

Potter, S. (1989) "High–speed Rail Technology in the UK, France and Japan", *Technology Analysis and Strategic Management* 1: 99–121.

Potter, S. (Forthcoming) "Managing High Speed Train Projects", in S. Hultèn and T. Flink (eds) *High Speed Trains: Entrepreneurship and Society*. London: Leading Edge.

Pressman, J.L. and Wildavsky, A. (1984) *Implementation*, 3rd. edn. Berkeley, CA: University of California Press.

Puchala, D. J. (1972) "Of Blind Men, Elephants and International Integration", *Journal of Common Market Studies* 10:267–284.

Putnam, R.D. (1988) "Diplomacy and Domestic Politics: the Logic of Two–Level Games", *International Organization* 42:427–460.

*Railway Age* (1989) "Florida: One Contender Left", December, 42–43.

Rasmussen, H. (1988) "The Implementation of Directives" in H. Siedentopf and J. Ziller (eds) *Making European Policies Work* – Volume II National Reports.

Brussels and London: EIPA/Sage.

Reddy, W.M. (1984) *The Rise of Market Culture: The Textile Trade and French Society, 1750–1900*. Cambridge: Cambridge University Press.

*Register over gældende EF–retsforskrifter* (1992). 19. udgave. Bruxelles: De Europæiske Fællesskaber.

Republic of Cyprus (1991) *Cyprus: The Way to Full EC Membership*. Press and Information Office.

Rhodes, R.A.W (1986) "Euorpean Policy–Making, Implementation and Subcentral Governments: A Survey". Maastrich: European Institute of Public Administration.

Rhodes, R.A.W. and Marsh, D. (1992) "New Directions in the Study of Policy Networks", *European Journal of Political Research* 21:181–205.

Roche, M. (1991) "Retour au rail à Londres", *Le Monde,* May 30.

Rokkan, S. (1966) "Norway: Numerical Democracy and Corporate Pluralism", in R. A. Dahl (ed.) *Political Oppositions in Western Democracies*. New Haven: Yale University Press.

Rosecrance, R. (ed.) (1976) *America as an Ordinary Country*. Ithaca: Cornell University Press.

Rosenthal, G. (1991) "Education and Training Policy", in L. Hurwitz and C. Lequesne (eds) *The State Of The European Community,* pp. 273–283. Boulder, Colorado: Lynne Rienner Publishers.

Rotfeld, A.D. (1992) "European Security Structures in Transition", *SIPRI Yearbook 1992: World Armaments and Disarmament* pp. 563–582. Oxford: Oxford University Press.

Ruggie, G.R. (1975) "International Responses to Technology: Concepts and Trends", *International Organization* 29:557–583.

Sandholtz, W. and Zysman, J. (1989) "1992: Recasting the European Bargain", *World Politics* XLII (1) October: 95–128.

Sargent, J.A. (1985) "Corporatism and the European Community", in W. Grant (ed.) *The Political Economy of Corporatism,* pp. 229–253. London: Macmillan.

Sbragia, A. (1991) "Environmental Policy in the Political Economy of the European Community", prepared for Workshop of The Consortium for 1992. May 1992. Stanford, California.

Sbragia, A.M. (1992) "Thinking About the European Future: The Uses of Comparison", in A.M Sbragia (ed.) *Europolitics: Institutions and Policymaking in the "New" European Community,* pp. 257–292. Washington, DC: Brookings.

Scharpf, F.W. (1988) "The Joint–Decision Trap: Lessons from German Federalism and European Integration", *Public Administration* 66(3):239–278.

Schengen Convention on Border Controls (1990) *Commercial Laws of Europe,* Vol. 14, February 1991, Part 2.

Scherer, J. (1990) "Regulatory Instruments and EEC Powers to Regulate Telecommunications Services in Europe", in D. Elixmann and K.–H. Neumann (eds) *Communications in Europe* pp.235–256. Berlin: Springer.

Schmeltzer, J. (1992) "A Speeding Bullet Seeing Economic Benefits, Texas Takes Lead as High–speed Train Projects Gather Steam in U.S.", *Chicago Tribune,* January 12, p. 1.

Schmitter, P.C. (1974) "Still the Century of Corporatism", *Review of Politics* 1:85–131.

Schmitter, P.C. (1977) "Modes of Interest Intermediation and Modes of Societal Change in Western Europe", *Comparative Political Studies* 10:7–38.

Schmitter, P.C. (1992) *Interests, Powers, and Functions: Emergent Properties and*

*Unintended Consequences in the European Polity*. Department of Political Science, Stanford University.

Schmitter, P.C. and Streeck, W. (1992) "Organized Interests and the Europe of 1992", in N.J. Ornstein and M. Perlman (eds) *Political Power and Social Change. The United States Faces a United Europe*. Washington: American Enterprise Institute.

Schneider, V. and Werle, R. (1990) "International Regime or Corporate Actor? The European Community in Telecommunications Policy" in K. Dyson and P. Humphreys (eds) *The Political Economy of Communications. International and European Dimensions,* pp. 77–106. London, New York: Routledge.

Schneider, V. and Werle, R. (1991) "Policy Networks in the German Telecommunications Domain" in B. Marin and R. Mayntz (eds) *Policy Networks. Empirical Evidence and Theoretical Considerations,* pp. 97–136. Frankfurt a.M.: Campus.

Scholten, I. (1987) *Political Stability and Neo–Corporatism: Corporatist Integration and Societal Cleavages in Western Europe*. London: Sage.

Schutte, J. J.E. (1991) "Schengen: Its Meaning for the Free Movement of Persons in Europe", *Common Market Law Review* 28:855–875.

Schwarze, J. and Schermers, H.G. (eds) (1988) *Structure and Dimensions of European Community Policy*. Baden–Baden: Nomos Verlagsgesellschaft.

Shapiro, M. (1992) "The European Court of Justice", in A.M Sbragia (ed.) *Europolitics: Institutions and Policymaking in the "New" European Community,* pp. 123–156. Washington, DC: Brookings.

Shonfield, A. (1972) *Europe: Journey to an Unknown Destination*. London: Penguin Books.

Sidjanski, D. (1982) "Les groupes de pression dans la Communauté européenne", *Il politico* 3: 559–560.

Sidjanski, D. (1989) "Communauté Européenne 1992: Gouvernement de Comités?", *Pouvoirs* 48:71–80.

Siedentopf, H. and Ziller, J. (eds) (1988) *Making European Policies Work* – Volume I Comparative Syntheses. Brussels and London: EIPA/Sage.

Siedentopf, H. and Ziller, J. (eds) (1988) *Making European Policies Work* – Volume II National Reports. Brussels and London: EIPA/Sage.

Sills, D.L. (ed.) (1972) *International Encyclopedia of the Social Sciences*. Volume 13. New York: Macmillan.

Slot, T. and Vershuren, P. (1990) "Decision Making Speed in the European Community", *Journal of Common Market Studies* XXXIX (1):75–85.

SOPEMI (1992) *Continuous Reporting System on Migration*. Paris: OECD.

Soysal, N.Y. (Forthcoming) *Limits of Citizenship: Post–National Membership in the Contemporary Nation state System*. Chicago: University of Chicago Press.

Stein, A. A. (1982) "Coordination and Collaboration: Regimes in an Anarchic World", *International Organization* 36:299–324.

Streeck, W. and Schmitter, P.C. (1991) "From National Corporatism to Transnational Pluralism: Organized interests in the Single Market", *Politics and Society* 2.

Subcommittee on High–Speed Rail Systems (1985) "High–Speed Rail Systems in the United States", *Journal of Transportation Engineering* 2:79–94.

Suppl. 10/73 "For a Community Policy on Education", *Bulletin of the European Communities.* Report prepared by Henri Janne.

Suppl. 3/74 "Education in the European Community" (Communication from the Commission to the Council, presented on 11 March 1974), *Bulletin of the European Communities.*

Sweden, Utrikesdepartementets Handelsavdeling (1992) *Agreement on the European Economic Area.* 2 vols, Stockholm, February.

Teubner, G. (1992) "Die vielköpfige Hydra: Netzwerke als kollektive Akteure höherer Ordnung" in W. Krohn and G. Küppers (eds) *Emergenz und Selbstorganisation*, pp. 189–216. Frankfurt: Suhrkamp.

Thornhill, J. (1991) "Repackaged, Recycled, Restricted", *Financial Times,* December 6, p.17.

Toffler, A. (1990) *Power Shift. Knowledge, Wealth, and Violence at the Edge of the 21st Century.* New York: Bantam Books.

Tranholm–Mikkelsen, J. (1991) "Neofunctionalism: Obstinate or Obsolete? A Reappraisal in the Light of the New Dynamism of the EC", *Millennium* 20(1).

Treaty on European Union, Europe Documents, N 1759/60 7 February 1992.

Tulder, R. van, and Junne, G. (1988) *European Multinationals in Core Technologies.* Chichester: Wiley.

Ungerer, H. (1989) *Telecommunications in Europe.* Luxembourg: Office for Publications of the EC.

Ungerer, H., Berben, C. and Costello N.P. (eds) (1989) *Telecommunications for Europe 1992. The CEC Sources.* Amsterdam: IOS.

Ungerer, W. (1990) "The Development of the EC and its Relationship to Central and Eastern Europe", *Aussenpolitik* 41: (3):229–230.

Union Internationale des Chemins de Fer. (1989) *Proposal for a European High–speed Network.* Paris: UIC.

Van Craeyenest, F. (1989) "La Nature jurisdique des résolutions sur la ccopération en matière d'éducation", in B. De Witt (ed.) *European Community Law of Education,* pp. 127–133. Baden–Baden: Nomos Verlagsgesellschaft.

Van der Klugt, A. (1992) "EC Action in the Field of Education and Central and Eastern Europe", in J. Pertek (ed.) *General Recognition of Diplomas and Free Movement of Professionals, Seminar Proceedings,* pp. 93–102. Maastricht: European Institute of Public Administration.

Vandermeersch, D. (1987) "The Single European Act and the Environmental Policy of the European Community", *European Law Review* 12:407–429.

Van Dijck, J. (1989) "Towards Transnationalization of Economic and Social Life in Europe", *European Affairs,* 1.

Van Schendelen (1993) (ed.) *National Public and Private EC Lobbying.* Aldershot: Dartmouth Publishing Company.

Verheijen, T. (1992) "The PHARE Programme", in J. Pertek (ed.) *General Recognition of Diplomas and Free Movement of Professionals, Seminar Proceedings,* pp. 43–48. Maastricht: European Institute of Public Administration.

Vervaele, J.A.E (1992) *Fraud against the Community – The Need for European Fraud Legislation.* Deventer and Boston: Kluwer Law and Taxation Publisher.

Vogel, David (1986) *National Styles of Regulation.* Ithaca: Cornell University Press.

Von Molthe, G. (1992) "NATO takes up its new agenda", *NATO Review* 40 (1), February:3–7.

Wagerbaum, Rolf (1990) "The European Community's Policies on Implementation of Environmental Directives", *Fordham International Law Journal* 14:455–477.

Walker, N. (1991) The United Kingdom Police and European Co–operation, Working Paper, University of Edinburgh, Department of Politics.

Wallace, H. (1984) "Implementation across National Boundaries" in D. Lewis and H. Wallace (eds). *Policies into Practice: National and International Case Studies in*

*Implementation*. London: Heineman Educational Books.

Waltz, K.N. (1979) *Theory of International Politics*. New York: McGraw–Hill.

Weiler, J.H.H. (1991) "The Transformation of Europe", *The Yale Law Journal* 100:2403–2483.

Weitz, R. (1992a) "The CSCE and the Yugoslav Conflict", *RFE/RL Research Report* Vol. 1, No. 5 (31 January), pp. 24–26.

Weitz, R. (1992b) "The CSCE"s New Look", *RFE/RL Research Report* Vol. 1, No. 6 (7 February), pp. 27–31.

Werle, R. (1990) *Telekommunikation in der Bundesrepublik. Expansion, Differenzierung, Transformation*. Frankfurt a.M.: Campus.

Wessels, W. (1990) "Administrative Interaction", in W. Wallace (ed.) *The Dynamics of European Integration*, pp. 229–241. London: Frances Pinter.

Wessels, W. (1992) "The EC and the New European Architecture: The European Union as Trustee for a (Pan) European Weal", in M. Telò (ed.) *Vers une nouvelle Europe?*, pp.35–48. Brussels: Editions de l'Université de Bruxelles.

Weyman–Jones, T. G. (1986) *Energy in Europe: Issues and Policies*. London: Methuen.

White, H. (1988) "Varieties of Markets", in B. Wellman and S.D. Berkowitz (eds) *Social Structures: A Network Approach,* pp.226–260. New York: Cambridge University Press.

Williamson, P.J. (1989) *Corporatism in Perspective: An Introductory Guide to Corporatist Theory*. London: Sage.

Witte, E. (ed.) (1988) *Restructuring of the Telecommunications System. Report of the Government Commission for Telecommunications*. Heidelberg: R.v. Decker's.

Wyatt, D. and Dashwood, A. (1987) *The Substantive Law of the EEC,* 2nd. edn. London: Sweet & Maxwell.

Zagorin, R. (1989) "An Expanding Game", *Time Magazine* 29, May.

Zelizer, V.A. (1988) "Beyond the Polemics on the Market: Establishing a Theoretical and Empirical Agenda", *Sociological Forum* 4: 614–634.

Ørstrøm Møller, J. (1990) *Det Internationale Samfund*. Akademisk Forlag: København.

# INDEX